Dictionary of
Instructional Technology

AETT Occasional Publication Number 6

Dictionary of
Instructional Technology

compiled by

Henry Ellington
and
Duncan Harris

in consultation with

A J Trott, AETT General Editor, officers and members of the Association for Educational and Training Technology, and colleagues mainly at Robert Gordon's Institute of Technology and the University of Bath.

Illustrated by Stan Keir

Kogan Page, London/Nichols Publishing
Company, New York

First published in 1986 by Kogan Page Ltd,
120 Pentonville Road, London N1 9JN

British Library Cataloguing in Publication Data
Ellington, Henry
    Dictionary of instructional technology. –
    (AETT occasional publication; no. 6)
    1. Educational technology – Dictionaries
    I. Title   II. Harris, Duncan   III. Series
    371.3′07′8 LB1028.3

ISBN 1-85091-072-3

Published in the United States of America by Nichols
Publishing Company, PO Box 96, New York, NY 10024

Library of Congress Cataloging-in-Publication Data
Ellington, Henry.
    Dictionary of instructional technology.
    (AETT occasional publication; no. 6)
    1. Education – Dictionaries.   2. Educational
    technology – Dictionaries.   I. Harris, Norman Duncan
    Company. II. Title.   II. Series.
    LB15.E42   1986   370′.3′21   85-28530

ISBN 0-89397-243-6

Printed and bound in Great Britain by
The Garden City Press Ltd, Letchworth, Herts

Acknowledgements

The authors would like to thank the following officers and members of the Association for Educational and Training Technology and colleagues mainly at Robert Gordon's Institute of Technology and the University of Bath for the invaluable help that they have given during the production of this Dictionary: Eric Addinall, Stuart Allan, Bernard Alloway, Douglas Anderson, Chris Bell, Bill Black, Jim Duncan, Barry Murton, Nadia Mustafa, Nick Rushby, John Sinclair, Andrew Trott and Pat Weslake Hill.

They would also like to thank Stan Keir for producing the illustrations and Margaret Geddes for typing the manuscript.

Introduction

Instructional technology (which we shall consider to embrace both educational and training technology) is very much a cross-disciplinary field which practitioners enter from a wide variety of backgrounds. Such practitioners are, however, expected to master a vast and often bewildering vocabulary, covering not only what may be described as 'mainline' instructional technology (instructional design, audiovisual media, assessment, evaluation, etc) but also all the various fields and disciplines that overlap or interact with it – fields as diverse as educational psychology, statistics, film and television production, photography, reprography, computing and information technology.

In compiling this Dictionary, we and the various colleagues who have helped us have tried to produce a comprehensive glossary of the most important terms that educational and training technologists are liable to come across in the course of their work. No doubt we have included many terms that other compilers would have omitted, and, conversely, have missed out many terms that others would consider to be an essential part of such a Dictionary. If so, we would be glad to hear from them – particularly regarding important omissions that they feel should be included in future editions of the Dictionary. We and our colleagues hope that the Dictionary will prove to be a useful source of reference to educational and training technologists of all types and backgrounds – both established practitioners and people new to the field – as well as to other people who are involved in education and training.

The terms that we have included in the Dictionary, which total over 2800, come from two main areas.

As would be expected, the great majority are drawn from the various branches of 'mainline' instructional technology – instructional design and methodology, assessment and evaluation, audiovisual and other instructional media, and so on. Here, we have tried to strike a balance between the need to be as comprehensive as possible and the danger of overloading the Dictionary with terms that are – at one extreme – too well known to warrant inclusion (words like 'test' and 'television') or – at the other extreme – so specialized that they are only likely to be of interest to a tiny minority of readers. We hope that we have managed to get this balance – which is, in the end, a matter of subjective judgement – reasonably correct in most people's view.

The second group of terms is drawn from the main fields and disciplines that impinge upon or overlap with instructional technology, some of the more important of which are listed at the end of the opening paragraph. Here, we have again tried to strike a balance between the need to include the most important terms that educational and training technologists are liable to encounter and making the mistake of trying to compete with specialist dictionaries and glossaries in these various areas. Again, we hope that we have achieved a reasonable compromise.

The Dictionary includes both British and US terms, as well as terms used in other English-speaking countries. Thus, it should prove to be a useful source of reference on both sides of the Atlantic, as well as in other parts of the English-speaking world. US spellings have been indicated throughout by the use of brackets.

Finally, a word about the various methods of cross-referencing that are used in the Dictionary. As well as explicit cross-references such as 'see...', 'See also...' and 'cf...', some of the key words that are used in certain entries are printed in italic; this indicates that they themselves are defined elsewhere in the Dictionary.

Dr Henry Ellington,
Educational Technology Unit,
Robert Gordon's Institute of Technology

Professor Duncan Harris,
Faculty of Education and Design,
Brunel University
(formerly at the University of Bath)

A

AA See *audio-active, audio-active language laboratory*.

AAC See *audio-active comparative language laboratory*.

aberration An inherent flaw in an optical system that results in the formation of an *image* that is imperfect or distorted (see, for example, *barrel distortion, chromatic aberration, spherical aberration*).

ability grouping Dividing learners into groups, classes or streams according to some aspect or aspects of their ability, so that learners of comparable ability can be taught together. See also *setting, streaming*.

ability profile A chart or diagram which provides a graphical representation of an individual's *scores* in respect of a number of separately-assessed aptitudes and abilities, and which thus gives a balanced picture of his/her overall ability.

ability test A *psychological test* that is designed to assess a person's overall mental ability without necessarily measuring skills in specific subjects or areas; most *intelligence tests* are of this type.

of trainee pharmacists to mix medicines, where no departure from the standard procedure can be allowed).

absolute evaluation A US term for *absolute assessment*.

absurdities test A form of *psychological test* in which the person being assessed has to indicate whatever is absurd, wrong or anomalous in a statement, story, picture, etc.

AC Alternating current.

accelerated motion A technique used in film making whereby movement takes place at a greater rate than in real life; the opposite of *slow motion*. See also *undercranking*.

accelerated speech Another name for *compressed speech*.

accent light A *spotlight* used to accentuate or highlight an object in a scene.

acceptance angle The angular width of vision of a camera, usually measured in a horizontal plane (see figure 1). Should not be confused with *angle of view*.

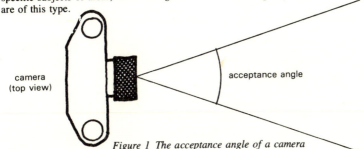

camera
(top view)

acceptance angle

Figure 1 The acceptance angle of a camera

absolute assessment *Assessment* where a precise specification of what must be achieved in order to pass is laid down, usually in behavio(u)ral terms (eg in assessing the ability

access and survey skills Skills which enable a student to find and choose *resource materials* pertinent to a topic or area being studied, eg in a library or *resource(s) centre (center)*.

access point 1. In indexing, any unique or qualified heading whereby a user can gain entry to an *index*. 2. In a *computer* system, any *terminal* whereby a user can gain access to the facilities of the computer. 3. In a *network*, a *terminal* or location via which a user can gain entry to the system.

accessory materials A US term for any teaching materials that are used to supplement basic textbooks, eg *audiotapes, tape-slide program(me)s, video* materials; cf *accompanying documents*.

accompanying documents Any *printed materials* or *audiovisual materials* that are designed to be used in conjunction with a *film*, educational broadcast, *textbook* or other instructional item; cf *accessory materials*.

acetate (film) Cellulose acetate, also known as *cel(l)* — a transparent plastic material used in the manufacture of *photographic film*, for *OHP transparencies*, and in *animation* work etc. See also *frosted acetate*.

achievement Satisfactory completion or accomplishment of a task, etc. Should not be confused with *performance*, for which it is often (incorrectly) used as a synonym. See also *achievement test*.

achievement test A test that is designed or administered in order to assess a person's *achievement* in a particular area, ie to determine what he or she has succeeded in accomplishing rather than his or her potential; cf *prognostic test*.

achromatic A term applied to a lens or lens system that has been designed so as to minimize *chromatic aberration*.

acoustic coupler A device that enables a *remote terminal* to be connected to a *computer* via an ordinary telephone link. It uses a *modem* to convert the *digital* signal into an *analog* signal, and a similar device is used to convert the signal back into digital form after transmission. It can be also be used to link one computer with another.

acoustic feedback A howl, rumble or other unwanted sound from a *loudspeaker* system caused by sound from the loudspeaker finding its way back into an earlier stage of the public address or reproduction system of which the loudspeaker is a part, usually via a *microphone* or the *pick-up* of a *record player*. Microphone-induced acoustic feedback is also known as *howl round*.

acoustic screen A panel or barrier of acoustically reflective and/or absorbent material that is used to alter the acoustic properties of a room such as a television *studio*, sound recording studio or *resources centre*.

action In film or television production: 1. The performance of a scene in front of the camera, 2. The main activity that is being depicted at any given time, 3. The *film* that records the pictures as distinct from the sound, 4. A command given by the director for performance of a scene to begin.

action frame Another name for a *response frame* in an *interactive videotex(t)* system.

action learning *Learning* that takes place by the learner actually taking on a particular role, either in real life or in a contrived or simulated situation.

active, activity learning *Learning* which involves active participation on the part of the learner; cf *passive learning*. See also *action learning*.

actual sound In film and television production, sound recorded at the actual time of filming as opposed to sound recorded or added later.

adaptability test A test of particular or general abilities that is used to forecast how a person is likely to perform in real-life job situations; used in personnel selection and placement.

adaptation 1. A work or exercise that is derived from or based on another work or exercise; it is usually developed for some special purpose, and often has a different *format* from that of the original. 2. A *psychomotor* process in which motor activities are altered to meet the demands of new problematic situations that require a physical response; this is Level 6 of Harrow's *psychomotor domain*.

adaptive program 1. A *computer program* that incorporates *branching*, ie points at which alternative courses of action are possible. 2. A *computer program* that has an in-built facility for modifying its own structure in order to accommodate changing circumstances, new input data, etc; such programs are used in fields such as robotics and *artificial intelligence*.

adaptive program(me) A flexible form of self-instructional program(me) in which the sequence of *frames* presented is varied according to the ability and performance of the learner. The term is used in the context of both *programmed learning* and *computer-based learning*.

adaptive teaching machine A *teaching machine* that is designed to handle *adaptive program(me)s*, and thus possesses more sophisticated facilities than one simply designed to handle *linear program(me)s*.

adaptive test Another name for a *response-contingent test*.

adaptor, adapter A device for interconnecting components of a system that have different terminations or couplings.

additive colo(u)r Colo(u)r that is produced by mixing light of the three *primary colo(u)rs* (red, green and blue) in certain proportions. This is the system used in colo(u)r television.

address When a specified piece of information is recorded in a *computer program* or on a *disk, digital optical disk* etc, its location is given a code to facilitate its retrieval, this is called its address.

adjunct, adjunctive program(me) A type of instructional *program(me)* which incorporates a set of questions that are presented to the learner at the end of a text (or a section of a text) in order to determine what has been learned. Such program(me)s can be built round text of any type, including *textbooks*, and can also relate to practical tasks in a laboratory, workshop, training classroom, etc. See also *mathmagenic information*.

adjustable curve A flexible ruler that can be bent to any desired shape in order to draw curved lines. Also called a *flexible curve, flexicurve* or *French curve*.

advance cue, signal Another name for a *synchronizing signal*.

advance, advanced organizer An overview of new material which is presented before teaching (or exposing a learner to) the material in order to prepare the learner's *cognitive* structure and counteract the effects of *proactive inhibition*. A term suggested by Ausubel. See also *expository organizer, meaningful learning, meta-analysis*.

aerial An input or output termination system

for the reception or transmission of radio, television or other electromagnetic *carrier waves*. The corresponding US term is *antenna*.

AFC See *automatic frequency control*.

affective Relating to attitudes, feelings and values. See also *affective domain*.

affective domain One of three broad sets into which *educational objectives* are conventionally divided as a result of the work of Bloom and his co-workers, containing all those connected with attitudes, feelings and values. The definitive *taxonomy* of the affective domain of educational objectives was published by Krathwohl et al. in 1964.

after-image A visual illusion which remains after the removal of a visual *stimulus*. See also *persistence*.

AGC See *automatic gain control*.

agricultural/botanical approach (to evaluation) A 'scientific' approach to *evaluation* that involves measuring the extent to which specific *objectives* are achieved by an instructional system under controlled conditions; cf *social/anthropological approach (to evaluation)*. See also *objective evaluation*.

AI See *artificial intelligence*.

aims The desired outcomes of an exercise, program(me), etc often expressed in general terms; cf *objectives*.

air brush 1. A small compressed-air-driven spray used to add soft, even areas of tone or shading to *artwork* or to remove flaws or unwanted features from *photographs*; the term is also applied to similar effects achieved in *computer graphics* work by electronic means. 2. A compressed-air cleaner used to blow the dust off photographic lenses, *transparencies, slides*, etc.

algorithm A series of instructions or procedural steps that can be used to solve problems of a given type, reach decisions in a given area, etc. Algorithms are often presented in the form of *flow charts* like the one shown in figure 2.

aliasing The unwanted visual effects that occur in a *computer graphics* or *video* display when the detail of the *image* is greater than the available *resolution*, eg the 'staircase' effect that occurs with diagonal or curved lines (see

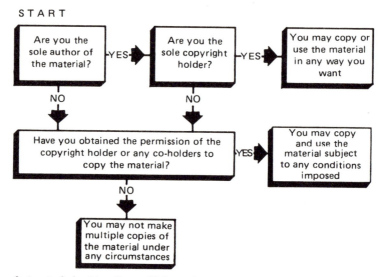

START

| Are you the sole author of the material? | —YES→ | Are you the sole copyright holder? | —YES→ | You may copy or use the material in any way you want |

NO ↓ (from first box)

NO ↓ (from second box)

| Have you obtained the permission of the copyright holder or any co-holders to copy the material? | —YES→ | You may copy and use the material subject to any conditions imposed |

NO ↓

| You may not make multiple copies of the material under any circumstances |

Figure 2 A typical algorithm (for establishing whether a person has the right to make multiple copies of material)

figure 38 on page 129). See also *pixel*.

alignment The process of adjusting a system (such as a *videorecorder* or optical system) for optimum performance.

alphanumeric, alphanumerical A term applied to a *character set* that includes the complete alphabet, numerals from 0 to 9, and certain special *characters* such as punctuation marks. The term is also applied to devices (such as *computer terminals*) that handle such character sets, and to materials composed solely of alphanumerical characters.

alpha wrap A tape configuration in a *helical scanning* videorecorder shaped like the Greek letter *α*. Such a configuration gives a full 360° contact between the tape and the *head-drum* (see figure 3); cf *omega wrap, u-wrap*.

aluminium screen A projection screen which uses an aluminium coating to give high forward reflectivity. It is often used as a *daylight screen*.

AM See *amplitude modulation*.

ambient light 1. The existing light in a room, *studio* etc before light is specially provided for a particular purpose. 2. Illumination from natural or other sources that may interfere with planned lighting in a *studio*, etc.

ambient noise The *background noise* in a room, *studio*, etc. Should not be confused with *ambient sound*.

ambient sound In film or audiovisual presentations that use multi-channel sound, the sound that is fed to the loudspeakers in the actual auditorium as opposed to that which comes from behind the screen(s). Should not be confused with *ambient noise*.

ambiophony Creation of artificial *reverberation* effects in an auditorium by means of multiple *loudspeaker* systems and time delays.

amplifier An electronic device which increases the strength of an electrical signal fed into it while minimizing any distortion of the signal. See also *audio amplifier, power amplifier, pre-amplifier, video amplifier*.

amplitude modulation (AM) A method whereby information (eg an *audio signal* or *video signal*) is added to a high-frequency *carrier wave/signal* by causing the amplitude of the latter to vary in correspondence with the signal that is being added; cf *frequency modulation*.

anaglyph A technique used to reproduce *stereoscopic* pictures in books and other publications. It involves double-image printing and the use of special colo(u)r-filter spectacles for viewing. See also *stereograph*.

analog computer A *computer* that is designed to handle signals supplied in *analog* form, ie signals that have not been converted into *digital*

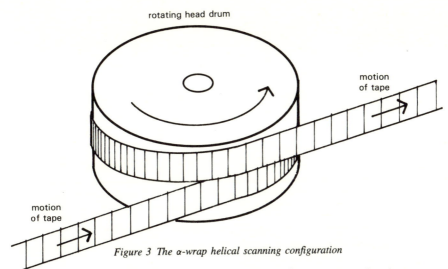

rotating head drum

motion of tape

motion of tape

Figure 3 The α-wrap helical scanning configuration

form. Such computers are mainly used in scientific research and similar fields; cf *digital computer*.

analog-to-digital (A to D) converter An electronic or electro-mechanical device for converting an *analog* signal or movement into a *digital* signal, eg for feeding into a *digital computer*.

analog(ue) A term applied to something that is continuously proportional to some *variable* (eg a signal that is continuously proportional to some physical quantity) or to a device or system that handles or processes material in analog(ue) form (eg an *analog computer*); cf *digital*.

analogy test A widely-used type of *completion test* in which *items* take the form: 'A is to B as X is to . . .?'.

analysis A *cognitive* process that involves breaking down an idea, system, process, etc into its constituent parts and examining the relationship between these parts. Level 4 of Bloom's *cognitive domain*.

analysis of variance The use of statistical procedures and tests to determine whether an observed difference between *samples* can reasonably be inferred to be due to a significant difference between the samples, or can be explained in terms of the random variations that occur within the *population(s)* from which the samples are drawn.

analytical method of marking A method of

marking essays, *projects*, etc based on a separate assessment of specified aspects or features; cf *impression method of marking*.

analyzing, analysis projector A projection system that enables a *motion picture* film to be run at variable speeds and studied *frame* by frame. Also known as a *stop motion projector*.

anamorphic A term applied to optical systems (such as the lenses used in cinemascope filming and projection) that produce different horizontal and vertical magnifications, and thus either compress or expand the image laterally.

anastigmatic A term applied to a lens or lens system that has been designed so as to minimise distortion due to *astigmatism*.

andragogy The science and art of teaching adults; cf *pedagogy*.

angle of view 1. In photographic, film and television work, the angle subtended by the scene at the lens of the camera (see figure 4 (a)); should not be confused with *acceptance angle*. 2. In projection, the angle subtended by the projection screen as seen by the viewer (see figure 4 (b)).

angle shot In film and television production, a *shot* which continues the action of a preceding shot, but from a different camera angle. See also *high-angle shot, low-angle shot*.

animation Creation of an illusion of movement in a visual display by use of special effects. Examples include animated *motion pictures*

13

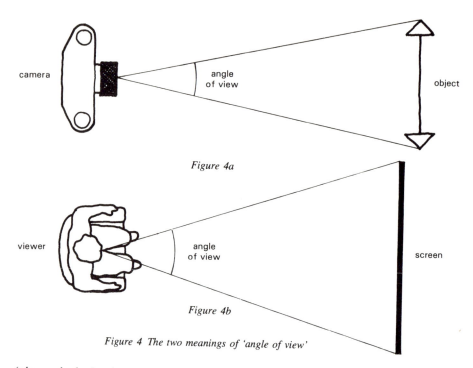

Figure 4a

Figure 4b

Figure 4 The two meanings of 'angle of view'

(where a slowly-changing sequence of drawings is produced and shot one frame at a time), animated *computer graphics* (where the display on the screen is made to change in the required manner), and animated *OHP transparencies* (where an impression of movement is produced by the use of polarized light or *moirée fringes*). See also *animation camera, moirée patterns, fringes, polarized animation.*

animation camera A *motion picture camera* specially designed for *animation* work. It is usually mounted on an *animation stand.*

animation stand An adjustable stand for an *animation camera*, incorporating a moveable bed designed to carry the sequence of drawings being photographed.

ANSI American National Standards Institute. A US body that has established many internationally accepted standards in the fields of computing and information handling.

answer print The first combined picture-and-sound print of a finished *motion picture* in release form. It is usually studied carefully to see whether any changes are needed prior to the mass production of *release prints.*

antenna The US term for an *aerial.*

anti-Newton A term applied to glass *slide mounts* where the glass surfaces are specially treated to prevent the formation of *Newton's rings* during projection or viewing.

AP See *audio-passive.*

aperture 1. In an optical system such as a camera, the opening that controls the amount of light admitted or transmitted; the size of the aperture can usually be varied by means of an *iris diaphragm* or similar device, and is usually expressed in terms of the *f-number*; see also *stop*. 2. In a *motion picture camera* or projector, the opening at which the film is exposed or projected. 3. The gap in the middle of a *slide mount* through which light is transmitted.

application A *cognitive* process in which a learner, given a new problem, will be able to make use of appropriate theories, principles, facts, etc needed to tackle it. Level 3 of Bloom's *cognitive domain.*

applications program, package A *computer program* (or set of programs) designed to carry out a particular task, eg word processing, data analysis, or information storage/retrieval. The term is often applied to off-the-shelf programs or *suites* of programs where the user only has

14

to supply his own parameters and data in order to use them. See also *package*.

applications software *Computer programs* or *suites* of programs that are designed to carry out specific jobs for the user of the computer, as opposed to *system software*, the programs that control the operation of the computer system itself. See also *applications program*, *package*.

appraisal The collection and analysis of information about the *performance* of something or somebody. It is often regarded as one aspect of *evaluation*; cf *assessment*.

approach term In information retrieval, a term that is used as a preliminary to the formulation of a precise search question or for providing entry into a classification or indexing system.

aptitude test A test designed to assess the aptitude or potential of an individual in a particular field or area. Such tests often involve the assessment of *spatial ability* and/or *psychomotor skills*; cf *attainment test*.

arithmetic age A measure of a child's basic *numerical ability*. It is equal to the mean *chronological age* of the children who attain the same score in a standardized test (or *battery* of tests) of such ability.

arithmetic mean See *mean*.

arithmetic unit The part of the *central processing unit* of a *digital computer* where arithmetical, logical and shift operations are carried out.

arm-hand steadiness test A test of *psychomotor skill* involving assessment of the ability to make accurate and steady movements of the arm and hand; used in personnel selection.

arrow diagram A diagram that represents a chain of events, each of which depends entirely on the occurrence of the previous event for its own occurrence; a type of *flow chart*.

art-aid camera A specially-designed camera that is used for enlarging or reducing original *artwork*.

art-aid projector A special *opaque projector*, often mounted on a vertical pillar to facilitate positional adjustment, that is used to project suitably-sized images of graphic material on to a drawing board surface so that they can be copied manually. Also known as a *visualizer*.

artificial intelligence (AI) Simulation of the characteristics and *cognitive* functions of the human brain using 'intelligent' computer systems such as the *fifth-generation computers* currently being developed.

artificial intelligence program A *computer program* that is designed to simulate one or more of the *cognitive* functions of the human brain when used in conjunction with appropriate *hardware*. See also *artificial intelligence*.

artwork A term applied to graphic or other material prepared for copying, printing, etc. See also *camera-ready artwork*.

ASA American Standards Association. A US body, one of whose responsibilities is the internationally used system of rating *film speeds*. In the ASA system, the film speed doubles as the ASA rating doubles. See also *DIN, ISO*.

ascenders The upper parts of *lower-case* letters like 'b' and 'd' that rise above the *x-height* of a *typeface*; cf *descenders*.

ASCII American Standard Code for Information Interchange. The internationally accepted standard system used to code alphanumerical and other symbols into the binary form used in computing and communications.

aspect ratio The numerical ratio of the horizontal length of a picture, screen, etc to its height, eg a television screen (aspect ratio 4:3) and a 35 mm photographic *frame* (aspect ratio 3:2). See also *landscape (format)*, *portrait (format)*.

aspheric A term applied to a lens or mirror which is not spherical in shape, eg the cylindrical condenser lenses and mirrors used in some projectors and *anamorphic* lenses such as the ones used in cinemascope photography and projection. Aspheric lenses are used to correct *aberrations* in optical systems.

assertion-reason item, question An *item* or question, either of the true-false or *matching item* format, in which a series of assertions are associated with a series of reasons.

assessment An attempt to measure the *performance* of something or somebody; cf *appraisal, evaluation*.

assessment grid A table or grid used in the *analytical method of marking* in order to help the marker assess specific aspects of an essay, *project*, etc independently.

assignment A piece of work which a learner is required to carry out either to enable him/her to learn or to provide evidence of studying. The work is usually carried out without formal supervision, either in a fixed time or to be completed by a particular date.

association test 1. A *psychological test* which measures different mental abilities and the inter-connections between them. 2. A *psychological test* which measures the nature and/or speed of verbal *responses* to verbal *stimuli*.

associative discussion A form of *free group discussion* in which the participants are encouraged to express perceived relationships between their experiences within the group and similar experiences in the outside world.

assumed behavio(u)r The prerequisite skills and attitudes that a learner must (or should) have in order to embark on a particular course or learning sequence; cf *entry behavio(u)r*. See also *entry level performance*.

astigmatism A type of lens *aberration* that causes points away from the *optical axis* to be focused as pairs of lines in different planes, thus producing blurring of the resulting image. See also *anastigmatic*.

asynchronous A term applied to two signals (eg an *audio signal* and a *video signal* or two *television signals*) that are not properly synchronized, ie locked in the correct phase with one another.

AT See *audio tutorial*.

A to D converter See *analog-to-digital converter*.

atomist A person whose preferred learning style is *atomistic learning*; cf *holist*.

atomistic learning A *learning style* in which ideas are developed piece by piece, with the result that sequences of pieces can be repeated without the learner necessarily having a clear understanding of the whole. See also *serial(ist) learning*.

attainment test A test that measures what a person has actually achieved in a particular area, skill, etc at the time of testing; often used

as a *pre-test* or *post-test*; cf *aptitude test*.

attention span The length of time over which a learner can give his full attention to a topic, activity, program(me), etc. See also *microsleep*.

attitude scale A diagnostic instrument designed to assess a person's attitude to a specific issue, phenomenon, etc by determining his position on some form of *scale* (see, for example, *Likert scale*, *semantic differential scale*).

attitude test A test administered for the purpose of assessing a person's attitude to a specific set of issues, phenomena, etc. It generally consists of a series of *attitude scales*.

audible advance A term applied to a synchronized sound/vision presentation with an audible synchronizing signal (such as a high-frequency 'bleep') which indicates when the next *frame* should be shown; cf *inaudible advance*.

audio Relating to sound, or to the sound aspects of a system, signal, program(me), etc (see the various entries given below).

audio-active (AA) A term used to describe listening-speaking practice in which the learner is required to give oral *responses*; cf *audio-passive*.

audio-active comparative (AAC) language laboratory A *language laboratory* that has all the facilities of an *audio-active language laboratory* plus individual tape recorders for the learners to record their own material. Also called a *listen-respond-compare laboratory*.

audio-active (AA) language laboratory A *language laboratory* in which learners can listen to and respond to material, but cannot record their responses for comparative purposes; cf *audio-active comparative language laboratory*.

audio aids Instructional aids such as *audio discs* and *audiotapes* which rely solely on sound for their effects, as opposed to *audiovisual aids* (in the strict meaning of the term) and *visual aids*.

audio amplifier An *amplifier* that is designed to handle signals of *audio frequency* (ie in the range 20Hz–20kHz); cf *video amplifier*.

audiocard A thin card carrying a magnetic oxide strip capable of carrying a short *audio signal* (usually not more than 30 seconds in length) and also having space for words and/or pictures. Such cards are studied using special playback machines; cf *audiopage*.

audioconference A *teleconference* in which only sound channels are used.

audio disc An *audio recording* stored on the surface of a flat circular rotating medium, either in *analog* form (see *black disc*) or in *digital* form (see *compact disc*). Also known as a *sound disc*.

audio frequency A term used to describe a signal or oscillation with a frequency that falls somewhere in the *audio spectrum*, ie between 20Hz and 20kHz; cf *radio frequency*.

audio induction loop See *audio induction system*.

audio induction system A low-power sound broadcasting system in which an *audio signal* is transmitted to a restricted area (usually a single room or small group of rooms) by means of a loop of wire (an *audio induction loop* or *wireless loop*) fitted round the perimeter of the area. The signal is usually picked up using special *headphones* that incorporate small radio *receivers*.

audiolingual method An approach to teaching foreign languages that is based on the use of *drill* and speaking the language rather than on reading and writing the language.

audiopage A specially-prepared page or sheet coated on the back with magnetic oxide capable of carrying an *audio signal* of up to several minutes duration. Such pages are studied using special playback machines; cf *audiocard*. Also known as an *audiosheet*, *sound page*, *sound sheet* or *talking page*.

audio-passive (AP) A term used to describe listening practice in which no oral *response* is expected; cf *audio-active*.

audio recording 1. Any recording of sound on *disc*, *tape*, etc. 2. The process by which such a recording is produced.

audiosheet Another name for an *audiopage*.

audio signal An electronic signal, either in *analog* or *digital form*, representing sound and capable of being used to reproduce that sound.

audioslide A photographic *slide* whose mount incorporates a storage medium for carrying a short recorded *audio signal* (generally up to 30

seconds in length). Such slides are used in conjunction with special projectors or viewers incorporating suitable playback facilities. Also known as *sound-on-slide*.

audio spectrum The range of sound frequencies to which the normal human ear is sensitive. The lower limit is usually taken to be 20 Hz and the upper limit 20 kHz.

audiotape A length of *magnetic tape* on which *audio signals* are (or can be) recorded. Also known as a *phonotape* or *sound tape*.

audiotape duplicator A special *tape recorder* used for producing copies of *audiotapes* at high speed, often more than one at a time.

audiotape player A device which can play back *audio signals* recorded on *audiotape* but has no recording facilities.

audiotape recorder A device for recording and playing back *audio signals* recorded on *magnetic tape*; often simply referred to as a *tape recorder*; cf *videotape recorder*, *audiotape player*.

audio-tutorial (AT) An *individualized learning* system based on the use of *audiotapes*, generally in conjunction with other types of learning materials to which the learner is directed by the recorded commentary.

audio-video mixer An electronic device that combines the *video signal* from a television camera or *vision mixer* and the *audio signal* from a *microphone* or *sound mixer* and impresses them on a *carrier signal* for transmission in a *closed-circuit television* system.

audiovisual aids, materials, media Strictly speaking, instructional materials or *media* that rely on both hearing and vision for their effects, but loosely used to describe virtually all instructional materials and media other than conventional *printed materials*; cf *audio aids*, *visual aids*.

audiovisual resources centre (center) See *resource(s) centre (center)*.

author entry An entry in a catalog(ue), bibliography or *index* under the name of the author (or one of the authors) of a work.

author index, catalog(ue) An *index* or catalog(ue) of *author entries*.

B

back coating A thin layer of conductive material that is applied to the non-magnetic side of *magnetic tape* in order to improve its winding qualities, especially at high speed.

back focus The distance from the rearmost element of a lens to the plane in which the image is formed; cf *focal length*.

background lighting Lighting the background of a scene in order to give it depth and separate the subject from the background. Should not be confused with *back lighting*.

background noise 1. The audible *noise* that is naturally present in a particular environment. 2. The *noise* that is inevitably present in an *audio signal* or *video signal* because of the limitations of the equipment handling the signal (see *signal-to-noise ratio*).

background projection. A presentation technique involving the use of live actors in front of a *translucent screen* on to which a background scene is projected from the rear.

backing store An addition to the *main store* of a *computer*, generally physically distinct from it (eg an external *tape store* or *disk store*).

backing track 1. Pre-recorded audio accompaniment. 2. An audio recording of material designed to support a main performance or presentation.

back lighting Studio lighting, directed partly towards the camera from behind the subject, that is introduced in order to emphasize the subject's outline. Should not be confused with *background lighting*. See also *model(l)ing* (3.).

back projection Projection of an *image* on to the back of a *translucent screen* for viewing from the opposite side; also known as *rear projection*; cf *front projection*.

backward branching A type of *branching* in *programmed instruction* in which the learner is sent back to repeat items which he/she has not yet mastered. Also known as *washback*.

backward chaining In learning theory, a type of *chaining* in which a learner performs the last step first, then the last two steps, then the last three, and so on until he/she can perform the whole chain.

back wind A facility on some *motion picture cameras* that allows the film to be wound backwards in order to expose the same piece of film twice. It is used for *dissolves* and *special effects*.

baffle A panel in which a *loudspeaker* is mounted in order to improve its performance at low frequencies by preventing the sound waves from the front and back surfaces of the loudspeaker cone from cancelling one another out.

balance 1. The correct intensity relationship between the various frequencies of an *audio signal* or the various colo(u)rs of a *video signal*. 2. The correct intensity relation between the various components of a multi-channel signal, eg between the right and left signals of *stereophonic* sound.

balanced line A standard twin-conductor 600 ohm cable used in sound distribution systems.

Banda A widely-used term for a hectographic duplicator, ie a machine that can be used to run off multiple copies of a document from a specially-prepared reverse-image master (see *hectographic duplication*). Banda is the name of one of the leading manufacturers of such machines.

band curve graph, chart A graph (chart) in which the area below the line or curve is shaded in order to give a visual impression of the quantity represented by the shaded portion (see figure 5); cf *zone curve graph, chart*.

barney A soft padded cover used to reduce the noise output of a *motion picture camera* during operation; cf *blimp*.

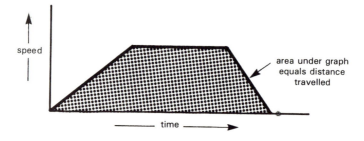

Figure 5 A band curve graph

bandwidth The range of frequencies over which a communications channel, piece of equipment or system is capable of operating. The greater the bandwidth of a communications channel, etc, the greater is its capacity for carrying or handling information. Also known as *frequency range*.

bank See *data bank, item bank*.

bar chart A graphical representation of data in which values are shown as discrete vertical or horizontal bars of different lengths (see figure 6). See also *histogram*.

barrel distortion Distortion of a projected *image* in such a way that straight lines parallel to the edges of the field bulge outwards at their centres (centers) (see figure 8); cf *pincushion distortion*.

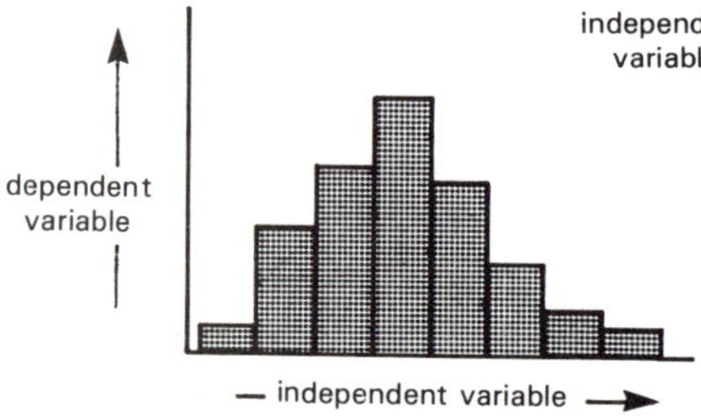

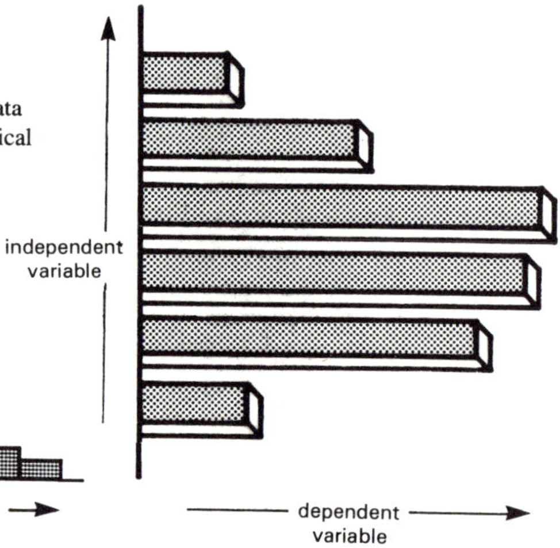

Figure 6 Two different forms of bar chart

bar code A type of code used on *labels* (eg on documents in a library) consisting of a series of parallel lines of different widths and spacings that can be read using a *bar code scanner* such as *light pen* (see figure 7).

bar code scanner See *bar code*.

barn doors Adjustable hinged metal plates attached to a *luminaire* in order to control the amount of light emerging from it.

base 1. In film or tape, the flexible support medium on which the *emulsion* or magnetic coating is carried. 2. See *data base*. 3. See *base lighting*.

base lighting The main overall lighting system in a *studio* or *set*, adjusted so as to give as near a shadowless effect as possible, and to provide a sufficient light level to permit effective pick-up of images. Supplementary light sources may be added in order to produce special effects.

Figure 7 A bar code label

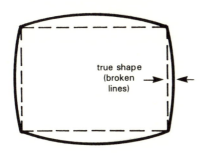

true shape
(broken
lines) →

← image shape
(solid lines)

Figure 8 Barrel distortion

baseline data Data available at the start of an experiment, study, research program(me), etc, as opposed to new data obtained in the course thereof.

bass A term used to denote the lowest frequencies of the *audio spectrum*; cf *treble*.

bass (tone) control A *tone control* for enhancing or suppressing the lowest frequencies of an *audio signal*; cf *treble (tone) control*.

batch mode, processing, system A method of using a *digital computer* in which all the data relating to a given job (or set of jobs) is fed into the computer at one time and processed to give a specific output (or set of outputs) based on this; cf *interactive mode*.

battery 1. Any group of tests, *scales*, etc, that are normally administered consecutively over a short period, the results being used to give an overall picture of performance, ability, attitude, etc in the area of interest; see also *multi-factor battery*. 2. A cluster of inter-connected electric cells.

baud In communications and computing a measure of the speed at which signals are transmitted, one baud being equal to one signal event (eg a 'morse code' pulse) per second.

bayonet mount, socket A push-and-twist type of mounting for a camera lens, lamp, etc. It uses pins which engage L-shaped grooves to locate and hold the item.

BCU See *big close up*.

beaded screen A projection screen with a surface which consists of a very large number of tiny glass beads, thus giving high forward reflection. It is often used as a *daylight screen*.

bearding A defect in video reproduction where the edges of dark areas overflow into adjacent light ones, generally due to *overload*.

beginning spurt A (generally short) period of abnormally fast work or high concentration displayed by an individual at the start of a lesson, activity, shift etc. See also *end spurt*.

behavio(u)ral instruction A term that is usually applied to *learning* where the desired outcomes are specified as *behavio(u)ral objectives*, and where the learner is required (through a *post-test*) to demonstrate mastery of each unit of instruction before being allowed to proceed to the next. See also *Keller plan, mastery learning, monitor, pre-test*.

behavio(u)ral objective A precise statement indicating the *performance* that is expected of a learner after undertaking a particular instructional program(me) or section thereof. See also *Magerian objective*.

behavio(u)ral (-ist) psychology The school of psychology (based on the work of B.F. Skinner) which holds that all behavio(u)r of an organism can be explained in terms of *stimulus-response bonds*. Also known as *behavio(u)rism*.

behavio(u)rism See *behavio(u)ral psychology*.

bel The basic unit used to compare sound intensities or signal strengths. Two sounds or signals of respective intensities I_1 and I_2 differ by $\log_{10} I_1/I_2$ bels. See also *decibel*.

bellow lens (system) A special lens system with a continuously-adjustable *back focus* that is used in close-up photography. It enables objects to be photographed from much closer distances than is possible using an ordinary camera lens.

Betacam A broadcast-quality *videocassette recorder* system developed by Sony. It uses the same format of tape cassettes as the domestic-quality *Betamax* system but a completely different signal coding system, so that the two systems are not compatible.

beta-format The tape configuration used in the *Betamax* and *Betacam* videocassette systems.

Betamax A widely-used domestic quality *videocassette recorder* system developed by Sony. It uses ½ inch tape, held in cassettes that are slightly smaller than those used in the *VHS* system, to which it is similar in many respects, both, for example, use a *U-wrap* helical scanning system, and both use the whole width of the tape to carry a single *video signal*, so that the tape cannot be reversed in order to record on the 'other side'; cf *Betacam*.

B-format A broadcast-quality *videotape recorder* system that uses 1 inch tape.

bias 1. In research, *evaluation* or *assessment*, an effect that systematically distorts the outcome of an experiment or study so that the results are not truly representative of the phenomenon or system under investigation. 2. In tape recording, a high-frequency signal that is fed into the system during the recording process in order to linearise the magnetization process and thus minimise distortion. 3. A fixed DC voltage or current that is used to set a *valve* or *transistor* at its optimum operating point. 4. An outward-acting moment that is applied to the *tone arm* of a record player in order to reduce distortion produced by inward-acting dynamic forces on the *stylus*.

biased sample A statistical *sample* which does not typically reflect the characteristics of the *population* that it is supposed to represent.

bibliographic data base A *data base* that contains information relating to documents, including (in some cases) abstracts of the material that they contain; cf *non-bibliographic data base*.

bi-directional microphone A *microphone* that is sensitive in two opposite directions but not in directions at right angles to these. It is also called a *figure-of-eight microphone* because of the shape of its *polar diagram* (see figure 9). (Note that the arrows in the figure are vectors representing the sensitivity of the microphone in different directions.)

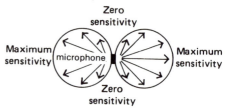

Figure 9 The polar diagram of a figure-of-eight microphone

bi-directional printing A method of speeding up the operation of a *line printer* by printing successive *lines* in opposite directions, thus avoiding the need for back-tracking between lines.

big close up (BCU) In film or television production, a *shot* taken with the camera even closer to the subject than for a *close-up*, eg showing only part of the subject's face.

bimodal distribution A statistical term for a distribution in which two *modes* are present (see, for example, figure 10).

binary code A code based on the digits 0 and 1, which are combined in different sequences to represent different letters, numbers, etc. See also *digital*.

binary notation, number system A number system based on the radix 2 rather than the radix 10 used in the conventional *denary number system*. The only digits in the binary system are 0 and 1, with successive digits representing multiples of successive powers of 2; thus, the binary number 1010 represents $(1 \times 2^3 + 0 \times 2^2 + 1 \times 2^1 + 0 \times 2^0)$, ie the denary number 10. The binary equivalents of the denary numbers from 0–10 are given in figure 11.

binaural recording, reproduction Audio recording (reproduction) that employs separate sound channels for the signals heard by the left and right ears. It is used synonymously with *stereophonic* recording or reproduction.

biserial correlation A statistical term for a relationship between two *variables* where one is measured in marks or *scores* and the other has only two categories (eg male/female).

bit An abbreviation for binary digit. One bit

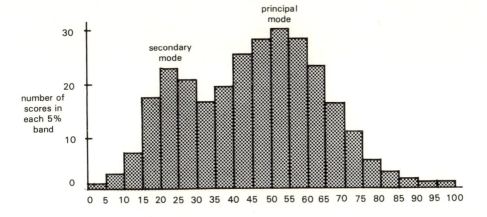

Figure 10 A histogram of test scores displaying a bimodal distribution

denary notation	binary notation	denary notation	binary notation
0	0000	6	0110
1	0001	7	0111
2	0010	8	1000
3	0011	9	1001
4	0100	10	1010
5	0101		

Figure 11 The binary equivalents of the denary numbers from 0–10

represents the smallest amount of information that can be held in a *computer store* or carried by a communication channel, the two binary digits '0' and '1' representing 'off' and 'on', or 'no signal' and 'signal', and being used to build up more complicated units of information. See also *binary notation, byte.*

BITE An acronym for built-in test equipment, ie electronic equipment that is incorporated in a *computer* or other system in order to monitor its operation. Should not be confused with *byte*.

bivariate analysis A simple form of statistical *analysis* in which only one *independent variable* and one *dependent variable* are considered at any one time.

bivariate distribution A statistical term for a graphical plot of one *variable* against another, eg a *histogram* or *scattergram*.

blackboard See *chalkboard.*

blackboard ink Special white ink designed for use on *chalkboards*. It resists erasing or washing, but can be removed with a special solvent.

Black box An electronic device or other system whose internal mechanism is hidden from (or irrelevant to) the user, only the input and output being significant. The term originates from the name of an early worker in the field of systems theory. See also *systems approach (to instruction)*, and figure 47 on page 163.

black disc A name sometimes given to conventional vinyl *audio discs* to distinguish them from *compact discs*.

black level A television term for the level of a *video signal* corresponding to zero illumination in the scene being recorded or transmitted.

blank An opaque photographic *slide*. Such slides can be incorporated in *slide sequences* in order to produce a blank screen without the dazzle that occurs if a gap is simply left in the sequence.

blanking The process by which the scanning electron beam that produces a television picture produces no effect on the screen as it moves between successive *fields* or as it back-tracks between successive *lines* in a given field.

23

blimp A sound-proof housing that is fitted over a *motion picture camera* in order to prevent camera noise from being picked up by an external *microphone*; cf *barney*.

blind keyboard A *keyboard* which does not produce a *soft copy* or *hard copy* display of information entered through it.

blinking Alternately displaying and not displaying a *title, caption* etc in order to draw attention to it, eg in a film or video presentation.

block design A type of *non-verbal intelligence test* in which the subject is asked to arrange colo(u)red blocks in a given pattern.

block diagram, schematic A schematic representation of a system or process in terms of interconnected blocks, each representing part of the system or process.

block release A UK term for the release of an employee from his/her normal occupation for one or more extended periods of time for educational or training purposes; cf *day release*.

blond A 2kW *spotlight*. This is a standard size used in *studios*, on *sets*, etc.

blooming An optical coating on the surface of a lens designed to reduce reflection losses by producing destructive interference between the light reflected from the surface of the coating and the light reflected from the interface between the coating and glass. Should not be confused with *blooping*.

bloop See *blooping*.

blooping A technique whereby special opaque ink, paint or tape is applied to an *optical sound track* or similar system in order to eliminate the clicks (*bloops*) caused by joins. Should not be confused with *blooming*.

blow-up 1. To enlarge a photographic or other *image*. 2. The resulting enlarged image.

blueprint process A type of *diazo process* used to produce copies of large *line drawings*, usually in the form of blue lines on a white background (hence the name).

body language *Non-verbal communication* (either deliberate or unconscious) involving signs, gestures, etc made by parts of (or the entire) body.

bold face In printing, a heavier or stronger version of a particular typeface, frequently used in contrast to types of ordinary weight (as in **bold face**).

boom A mounting arm for a *microphone*, camera, light source, etc that enables it to be held in position over a *set* while being supported from outside the set.

booster training Training given to a worker to improve performance in his/her present job, as opposed to training given to prepare him/her to take on another job or position.

booth an acoustically-treated individual study cubicle in an audio or audiovisual learning area, *language laboratory*, etc. See also *carrel*.

booting 1. A computer term for transferring a *computer program* from a *disk* to a computer's *working memory* and running the program. 2. Also used in computing to denote the use of an extremely simple process to initiate a more complex one, eg pressing one or two *keys* on a *keyboard* in order to run a simple *program* which in turn runs a more complex one.

bounce 1. Vertical unsteadiness in a projected *motion picture* image; cf *weave*. 2. Short-term periodic variation in the brightness of a television picture.

BPI Bits per inch. A unit used for measuring the density of data held on a linear storage medium such as a *magnetic tape*.

brainstorming A technique for generating ideas, solving problems, etc by encouraging members of a group to originate ideas, no matter how wild or apparently unrelated to the topic under discussion, and then to consider their potential.

branch, branching See *branching program, branching program(me)*.

branching program A *computer program* that incorporates *branches*, ie points at which alternative courses of action are possible.

branching program(me) A *programmed learning* sequence that incorporates *branches*, ie points at which the learner is directed to alternative *items* depending on his/her *response* to the item just tackled; cf *linear program(me)*.

bridge course A program(me) of instruction which is deliberately designed to start in one institution and continue or terminate in another.

Should not be confused with a *bridging course*.

bridging course A program(me) of instruction which is designed to equip students to embark on a new subject or course. Should not be confused with a *bridge course*.

briefing An introductory session for the participants' in a *game, simulation* or other exercise that is used to describe the background to the exercise, assign roles, etc; cf *debriefing*.

brightness range, ratio The ratio of the brightness of the lightest or brightest parts of an object, scene, image, etc to that of the darkest parts.

broad A *luminaire* designed to give wide general illumination.

broadcast videotex(t) *Videotex(t)* in which a limited number of *pages* of information are incorporated into ordinary television transmissions and can be 'called up' by owners of *receivers* that incorporate the necessary decoding facilities using a special *keypad*. The British CEEFAX and ORACLE systems are typical examples; cf *interactive videotex(t)*. Also known as *teletext*.

broad-fields curriculum A *curriculum* in which an attempt is made to integrate a number of related subjects.

brush pen A type of fibre- (fiber-)tipped pen with a brush-like tip used in preparing *artwork*. It has a softer, more versatile point than a conventional fibre- (fiber-)tipped pen.

brute A large *spotlight* of high power — usually an arc lamp.

bubble memory In computing, a solid-state device for storing data. It uses microscopic magnetic domains (regions magnetized in a particular direction) held within a metallic substrate.

bubble screen A screen that uses magnetic bubbles to produce a *video* image.

bubble sort In computing, a method of sorting data into a particular order. It involves inter-changing pairs of data items until the required order is achieved.

buddy system 1. A technique whereby a person acquires practical experience of a job by working closely with an experienced person; see also *sitting next to Nellie*. 2. A system

whereby trainees or other learners work in pairs, each responsible in some way for monitoring the other; often used as a safety measure.

buffer 1. Any device or system which acts as a temporary store for information or signals passing between two systems, pieces of equipment, etc with different data handling rates; in computing, for example, data is often transferred from the *main store* of a *computer* to a (slower) *backing store* via a suitable *buffer store*, and is also often transferred to such a store prior to being printed. 2. In electronics, a system which is used to connect two parts of a circuit that cannot be directly inter-connected.

buffer store See *buffer*.

bug A mechanical, electrical, syntactical or other fault in a piece of equipment, system, *computer program*, etc that causes it to malfunction or fail to perform in the desired way. See also *glitch*.

bulk eraser A device (incorporating a powerful electromagnet) that can erase the signals recorded on an entire *reel* or *cassette* of *magnetic tape* at one time, without the need to unwind the tape.

bulletin board 1. A panel of cork, wood or other soft material to which pictures, notices or other display material may be pinned; also called a *pinboard*. 2. A computer-based message and information system often accessed from remote computers via the public telephone network.

bulletin typewriter A special typewriter which produces extra-large print suitable for use on notices and *OHP transparencies*. Also called a *primary typewriter*.

burned-in image An *image* which persists in a fixed position in the output signal of a television camera tube for a short time after the camera has been turned to a different scene.

burnisher A small bone, wood or plastic tool used for pressing down *transfer film, transfer letters*, etc.

bus An electrical connection between different components or sub-systems of a system.

business game An educational or training *game* based on one or more of the financial or management disciplines. Also called a *management game*.

butt splice, weld A join in a tape or film in which the two cut ends touch, but do not overlap.

buzz board Another name for an *electric board*.

buzz group See *buzz session*.

buzz session A short period in a larger session or exercise in which small groups of people (*buzz groups*) intensively discuss a given issue, topic, problem, etc. Such sessions are often followed by a plenary feedback session in which the conclusions of the groups are reported and discussed.

by-passing Missing out part of an instructional program(me) because of successful performance of earlier parts, successful performance in a diagnostic test, etc. See also *forward branching, skip branching*.

byte In computing and data processing, a group of adjacent *bits* (usually eight) that together form a larger unit, such as the code for one of the members of a *character set*, an instruction or an *address*. It is normally shorter than a *word*, which generally consists of two or more bytes. Should not be confused with *BITE*. See also *kilobyte, megabyte, gigabyte*.

C

CA See *chronological age*.

cablecasting A name sometimes given to *cable television*, to distinguish it from conventional broadcast television (broadcasting).

cable television A television system in which the signal is distributed to users or subscribers via coaxial or optical cable links rather than by broadcasting. Cable systems can carry a much larger number of channels than broadcast systems, and (in some cases) allow two-way communication to take place between the user and the distribution centre. See also *fibrevision (fibervision), switched-star system, tree-and-branch system*.

CAD See *computer-aided (-assisted) design*.

cafeteria plan See *course unit plan*.

CAI Computer-aided (-assisted) instruction (see *computer-aided (-assisted) instruction, learning, training*).

CAL Computer-aided (-assisted) learning (see *computer-aided (-assisted) instruction, learning, training*).

calibration tape A pre-recorded *magnetic tape* containing *tones* of different frequencies recorded at standardized intensity levels; used in calibrating and setting up equipment.

calligraphic plotter A plotter (used in *computer graphics*) which produces *line drawings* in *soft-copy* form on the screen of a *visual display unit*.

camera chain, channel A television camera connected to a *camera control unit* and *monitor*, either on its own or one of several forming a multi-camera system in a television *studio*, *mobile unit*, etc.

camera control unit (CCU) The equipment in

a *camera chain* which provides the television camera with operating signals and processes the signals from the camera prior to recording or mixing. Use of such an external control unit enables the amount of electronic equipment in the actual camera to be kept to a minimum.

camera mount The support for a television, motion picture or still camera, generally incorporating a *pan-tilt head* or ball-and-socket joint fixed to the top of the *pedestal* or *tripod* that carries the camera.

camera-ready artwork Finished *artwork* ready for photographing prior to reproduction or use.

camera speed Another term for *filming speed*.

can Film and television jargon for a *reel* of film or videotape. The term 'in the can' is commonly used to describe a shot, film or program(me) that has been satisfactorily taken or completed.

candela (cd) The S1 unit of *luminous intensity* (the amount of light emitted by a body), one candela being defined as the luminous intensity of 1/6000,000 of a square metre (meter) of a black body at a temperature of 2042 degrees Kelvin.

canned paragraphs Pre-recorded paragraphs that are stored in a *word processor* as complete units because of their frequent use; they can be combined in various ways or adapted as required.

capacitance, capacitive videodisc A *videodisc* which depends on the variation of the electrical capacitance between the disc and the sensor to read the information stored. Current systems use a sensor which does not actually touch the disc surface, thus preventing wear; cf *contact videodisc, optical videodisc*.

capacitor microphone Another term for a *condenser microphone*.

capstan A device in a *tape recorder* or similar device for pulling the tape through the *head* systems at constant speed.

caption 1. Printed or spoken information that identifies or explains the content or significance of graphical material such as a photograph or diagram. 2. In television and film work, a general term for still *artwork, titles,* etc incorporated in a program(me) or film.

caption camera A fixed television camera used exclusively for *caption* work, generally in conjunction with a *caption stand* (see entry).

caption generator An electronic device for creating alphanumerical *captions* using a *keyboard* and feeding them directly into a *video signal*; use of such a device avoids the need to produce separate *artwork* for each caption. Also known as a *video typewriter*.

caption stand A device for holding caption cards in a convenient position for shooting (see *caption camera*).

carbon microphone A low-fidelity *microphone* in which sound-induced vibrations of a diaphragm are transmitted to carbon granules, thus causing their electrical resistance (and hence the current in a DC circuit) to vary in accordance with the sound.

cardinal scale Another name for an *interval scale*.

cardioid microphone A *microphone* whose sensitivity is at a maximum in one particular direction, falling off steadily as the angle from that direction increases. Such a microphone has a heart-shaped *polar response curve* (see figure 12) — hence the name. (Note that the arrows in the figure are vectors representing the sensitivity of the microphone in different directions.)

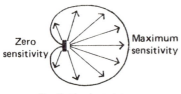

Zero sensitivity / Maximum sensitivity

Cardioid microphone

Figure 12 The polar response curve for a cardioid microphone

card punch, punching unit A device that encodes data on special cards in the form of patterns of rectangular holes. The data can be entered manually via a *keyboard* or fed in direct from a *computer* or data storage device.

card reader, reading unit A device that decodes the data contained in the patterns of holes on *punched cards*.

card-stacking method A method of rating or ranking a group of employees, trainees or students. It involves stacking sets of cards bearing the names of individuals according to various factors (productivity, job knowledge, quality of work, etc).

carousel A general term for an automatic slide projector with a circular gravity-fed *magazine*, or for the magazines used with such projectors.

carrel A small, enclosed space in a library, *resources centre (center), language laboratory* etc designed for individual or private study; such carrels are often equipped with *hardware* suitable for the study of *audiovisual materials* such as *tape-slide program(me)s* or *videotapes*. See also *dry carrel, wet carrel, booth*.

carrier wave, signal A high-frequency electromagnetic wave or signal used to carry a signal of lower frequency, generally incorporated in it by *amplitude modulation* or *frequency modulation*.

cartogram Literally, a 'map-graph' — a map that has one or more *variables* (eg average rainfall or population density) plotted on its surface, with different values of the variable(s) being indicated by different colo(u)rs, symbols, etc.

cartoon 1. An interpretative still drawing which satirizes or exaggerates in order to stress a point. 2. An animated *motion picture* made by photographing a succession of gradually-changing drawings.

cartridge 1. A container for a single *reel* of film or tape, feeding into a separate reel. 2. A type of *cassette* carrying a closed loop of *audiotape, videotape* or *film* that does not require re-winding. 3. The device in the *pick-up* of a *record player* that contains the *stylus* holder and *transducer*. 4. A unit of solid-state *software* (such as a *ROM, PROM* or *EPROM*) that can be plugged into a *microcomputer*.

case book method A method of instruction (based on the *case study* approach) that is used particularly in US law schools. It involves students writing up specific law cases for subsequent critical discussion in class.

case study An in-depth examination of a real-life or simulated situation carried out in order to illustrate particular characteristics — either characteristics specific to the case being studied or more general characteristics of the wider set to which it belongs. See also *case book method, simulated case study*.

cassette A container for film or tape that contains both the *feed reel* and *take-up reel*, and which is loaded into a camera, projector, recorder, etc as a single unit, without the need for *lacing*. See also *cartridge*.

CAT Computer-aided (-assisted) training (see *computer-aided (-assisted) instruction, learning, training*).

catchword 1. A word at the foot of a page in a document that anticipates the first word of the next page. 2. In catalog(u)ing, a significant or easily-remembered word (other than the first) selected from the title of a document for use as an *approach term* in a *catchword index* (an *index* composed of such catchwords).

catchword index See *catchword*.

causal relationship A relationship between two *variables* such that a change in one automatically gives rise to a non-random change in the other; cf *functional relationship*.

CAV *Constant angular velocity* (see entry).

CBE 1. Competency-based education (see *competency-based education, learning, teaching, training*). 2. See *computer-based education*.

CBI See *computer-based instruction*.

CBL 1. Competency-based learning (see *competency-based education, learning, teaching, training*). 2. See *computer-based learning*.

CBT 1. Competency-based teaching, training (see *competency-based education, learning, teaching, training*). 2. See *computer-based training*.

CCTV See *closed-circuit television*.

CCU See *camera control unit*.

cd See *candela*.

CD See *compact disc*.

ceiling and floor effects Reduction of the usefulness or effectiveness of a test or other form of *assessment* due to the upper and lower limits of performance (the ceiling and floor) being too close together.

cel, cell Short for cellulose acetate, the transparent plastic sheeting used for making

OHP transparencies, in *animation* work, etc.

centile A statistical term for the point in a distribution below which a specific percentage of the measures in the distribution fall. The *median*, for example, is the 50th centile.

central processor, processing unit (CPU) The main part of a *computer* system, comprising the *main store, arithmetic unit* and *control unit*, or (in the case of some modern computers) simply the arithmetic and control units.

central service unit A name given to an organizational unit (such as a library, educational technology unit or computer services unit) that houses, under one structure, a service that is available to all departments in an educational, training or other institution.

central sound system An inter-communication system which permits messages, program(me)s, music, etc to be distributed throughout a building or complex of buildings.

central tendency A statistical concept referring to the tendency for *scores* in a distribution to cluster around a typical or average score. See also *mean, median, mode*.

ceramic cartridge A type of *cartridge* (used mainly in the *pick-up* systems of inexpensive *record players*) that uses a piezo-electric ceramic *transducer* to convert the *stylus* movements into an electrical signal. Such cartridges produce a high-level output signal compared with other types of cartridge, but their frequency response and fidelity are generally poor.

C-format A broadcast-quality *videotape recorder* system that uses one inch tape.

chained list A list of data where each item contains a pointer to the next item in the list, thus making it unnecessary for logically consecutive items to be physically adjacent when stored in, for example, a *computer store*.

chaining A mode of *learning* in which the learner connects two or more previously-learned *stimulus-response bonds* into a linked sequence; one of Gagné's eight types of learning (Level 3). See also *backward chaining, conversational chaining*.

chalk-and-talk A traditional expository method of teaching that involves talking to a class and illustrating what is said by writing and/or drawing on a *chalkboard* or similar aid.

chalkboard A panel with a dark surface of wood, fabric, glass etc on which display material can be written or drawn with chalk. It is commonly referred to as a *blackboard*, although many chalkboards are now of different colo(u)rs (eg green or blue). See also *magnetic chalkboard*.

changeable display letters Plastic letters designed for use on *display boards* fitted with suitable grooves or holes.

changeover In multi-reel film projection, change from one projector to another without interrupting the continuity of presentation. It is accomplished by starting up the second projector before the reel in the first projector has finished, and synchronizing the two projectors before the change from one to the other takes place. See also *cue marks*.

channel 1. An allocated frequency band for transmission of a radio-frequency signal. 2. A discrete chain for carrying a specific signal, eg one of the two channels used in *stereophonic* sound recording and reproduction. 3. See *perception channel*.

channel loading A method of loading film or tape into a camera, projector, recorder, etc by sliding it in sideways rather than by *lacing* it through the device. Also known as *slot loading*.

character 1. A special letter, number of other symbol available for use in printing, typing etc or for display on a *visual display unit*; see also *character set*. 2. A computing term for the pattern of *bits* that represents such a symbol in *binary code*.

character generator 1. That part of a *visual display unit* or similar device that generates the signals which correspond to the various *characters* displayed. 2. Another name for a *caption generator*.

characterization An *affective* process that involves the organization of values into a total and consistent philosophy. The highest level (Level 5) of Krathwohl's *affective domain*.

character set The sum total of all the *characters* available within a system, eg the characters on a particular *golf ball (printer)* or *daisy wheel (printer)*, or available for use in a *visual display unit* or *word processor*.

check list A predetermined list of items to be looked for or asked about. Such a list can form the basis of an *observation schedule, interview schedule* or *questionnaire*.

chi-square (x^2) test A statistical test that is used to determine whether a set of observed frequency values can be said to conform to a specified pattern, eg to see whether a set of such values conforms to a standard distribution pattern such as the *normal distribution*. It is sometimes called the x^2 goodness-of-fit test.

chromatic aberration A type of *aberration* that occurs with single-element lenses, causing colo(u)red *fringing* of the *images* that they produce. It is generally corrected by designing lenses with two or more components made of different types of glass, so that the aberrations produced by the different components cancel out. See also *achromatic*.

chronological age (CA) A person's actual physical age (ie the time that has elapsed since his/her birth) as opposed to his/her *mental age, reading age*, etc.

chunking A technique used in remembering which involves gathering items into related groups or 'chunks', each containing up to a maximum of seven items, and then remembering them as groups.

cinching 1. Uneven winding of *magnetic tape* on a *reel*, possibly affecting the quality of the signal produced on playback. 2. Tightening the winding of a loosely-wound *reel* of *motion picture* film, *magnetic tape* or *paper tape* manually.

cinch marks Longitudinal abrasions on *motion picture* film or *videotape* produced by one turn rubbing against another during *cinching*.

cine camera A *motion picture camera*, particularly one used with 8 mm or 16 mm film.

cinematograph An early (now largely

obsolete) term for a *motion picture* projector. Also spelt *kinematograph*.

cinemicrography Creation of a *motion picture* of microscopic processes by using a *cine camera* mounted so as to shoot down a microscope barrel. Also known as *cinemicroscopy*.

cinemicroscopy Another name for *cinemicrography*.

circle chart Another name for a *pie chart*.

circuit time A term used in *distance learning* to denote the 'turn-around' time needed to process students' assignments, queries, etc.

circulation space Those parts of an educational or training establishment which are accessible to learners but which are not actually used for instructional purposes, eg corridors, entrance halls, etc.

citation index A bibliography of documents, usually arranged alphabetically by author, in which each entry is followed by a list of other documents which have cited the entry document in their references.

clapper board In *motion picture* production, a 'take' board with a hinged flap that is banged down to make a synchronizing 'mark' on both the picture sequence and the sound track of the film at the start of a *shot*. The clapper board has now been partly superseded by electronic systems built into the cameras and recording equipment, although many directors and editors still prefer to use it.

class analysis chart A chart on which the relative performances of the members of a class of pupils, students or trainees are displayed in graphical form.

classical conditioning Another term for *respondent conditioning*.

class interval The *range* of *scores* between the upper and lower boundaries of a class of scores in a test of other form of *assessment*, eg the range of scores over which a 'B' grade or an upper second class honours degree is awarded.

classroom climate The authority pattern and pattern of social and emotional relationships within a teaching group (instructors *and* learners). It can vary from highly authoritarian to 'laissez-faire'.

classroom ecology The branch of educational research which studies teaching problems and situations in the real settings of the classroom environment rather than in simulated or contrived settings.

classroom observation The use of systematic *observation* to record learner behavio(u)r in actual classroom situations. See also *participant classroom observation, systematic classroom observation*.

clean A term used to describe an *audio signal, video signal*, recording, etc that is free from noticeable distortion or *noise*.

clip A term used to describe a short excerpt from a *motion picture* or *video* presentation, especially when it is used in a different context (eg in a lesson, or as part of a larger presentation).

clip art Ready-to-use illustrations that can be transferred on to *artwork* from plastic sheets.

clip-on microphone An extremely small *microphone* which can be clipped on to the clothing of a speaker (eg on to a tie or lapel) so that it is positioned near his/her mouth. Also known as a *lapel microphone* or *tie microphone*.

clipping Distortion of an *audio signal* or *video signal* brought about by the peak signal amplitude exceeding the capacity of the system.

closed access A practice whereby users are not normally given direct access to the stock of a library or *resources centre (center)* or to parts thereof, such access being restricted to the staff of the library or centre (center); cf *open access*.

closed-circuit television (CCTV) A television system which limits distribution of the signal to those *monitors* or *receivers* which are directly connected to the origination point by cable or microwave link, as opposed to broadcast television, which can be picked up by anyone with suitable receiving equipment.

closed loop A *system* or *sub-system* in which there is *feedback* between the output and the input, so that the former affects the latter.

closed question A question in a test, *programmed learning* sequence, etc in which a unique answer is required, and where there is no scope for divergent thinking, qualification, etc; cf *open-ended*.

closed system Strictly speaking, a *system* that has no interaction with its environment or with external systems. In practice, the term is used to describe any organization that is largely self-contained and self-sufficient, and has little or no contact with outside bodies.

closed test 1. A test designed for use in public examinations and available only to the official administrators of these examinations. 2. A test that is available only to suitably-trained users or qualified psychologists. 3. A test that can only be taken by someone who has undergone a particular course; cf *open test*. Should not be confused with *cloze test*.

close-up (CU or CS) In photography, film production or television production, a *shot* that is taken from such a distance that only part of the subject is seen, eg the head and shoulders or face of a human subject; cf *medium shot, long shot*. See also figure 29 on page 106.

Cloze procedure A language development technique that is widely used in primary schools. It involves learners in trying to understand passages from which words have been deleted at regular intervals (typically every sixth or seventh word) or from which certain parts of speech have been deleted. See also *Cloze test*.

Cloze test A standard test for assessing the *readability* of textual material. It involves determining whether typical members of the group for which the material is written are capable of understanding passages from which certain words have been deleted, eg every sixth or seventh word or certain parts of speech. Should not be confused with a *closed test*. See also *Cloze procedure, Flesch formula, fog index*.

cluster analysis A statistical data-processing technique that involves reducing a large amount of data to manageable groups having related characteristics before carrying out further, more detailed *analysis* of each group.

cluster organizational concept An approach to *vocational training* in which the trainees are taught a number of related skills at one centre (center), then pass on to other centres (centers) to learn other groups of skills.

cluster sampling Random selection of intact groups within a *population* for research or other purposes, rather than selecting individual members of the population, eg selection of entire classes or schools of pupils to take part in a study.

CLV *Constant linear velocity* (see entry).

CMI Computer-managed instruction (see *computer-managed instruction, learning, training*).

CML Computer-managed learning (see *computer-managed instruction, learning, training*).

C-mount A standard screw-in *lens mount* system used on 16 mm *cine cameras* and small television cameras of the type used in *CCTV* work.

CMT Computer-managed training (see *computer-managed instruction, learning, training*).

coach-and-pupil method An instructional technique in which pairs of learners take turns in teaching each other a procedure which has been explained or introduced by the instructor. See also *peer teaching, Keller plan*.

coaxial cable Electrical cable consisting of a central signal-carrying conductor surrounded by a cylindrical conducting screen separated from it by a layer of insulating material. Used to carry electrical signals of all types, particularly high-frequency signals such as *television signals*.

cognition A generic term for the various rational processes (memorizing, reasoning, evaluating, etc) through which an individual obtains *knowledge* and conceptual understanding, as opposed to the various *affective* processes, which are related to attitudes, feelings and values.

cognitive Relating to *cognition*. See also *cognitive domain, lower cognitive, higher cognitive*.

cognitive channel One or other of the physical senses (vision, hearing, etc) or mental processes (remembering, reasoning, etc) whereby information relevant to some aspect of *cognition* is obtained; cf *perception channel*.

cognitive domain One of the three broad sets into which *educational objectives* are conventionally divided as a result of the work of Bloom and his co-workers, containing all those associated with the development of *cognitive skills*. The definitive *taxonomy* of the cognitive domain of educational objectives was published by Bloom et al. in 1956. See also *lower cognitive, higher cognitive*.

cognitive map A mental picture or schema built up by an individual as a result of experience or instruction.

cognitive psychology, learning theories In contrast with proponents of *behavio(u)ral psychology*, cognitive psychologists maintain that *learning* comes about as a result of the restructuring of perceptions and thoughts *within* the individual, enabling him/her to perceive new relationships and solve new problems.

cognitive skill A skill associated with the acquisition, application or manipulation of *knowledge*, ie relating to *cognition* or the *cognitive domain*. See also *lower cognitive, higher cognitive*.

cognitive strategies The capabilities that govern the way in which an individual learns, remembers, reasons, etc. Internally-organized skills that come into play in selecting and operating the internal mental processes involved in defining and solving novel problems; one of the five types of capabilities identified by Gagné and Briggs.

cognitive style Another name for *learning style*.

cognitive time The time that elapses between the initial presentation of instructional material and the desired acquisition of knowledge, understanding, skill, etc by the learner.

cohort A group (or set of groups) of individuals chosen for investigation, analysis, etc on the grounds of a particular criterion, eg the year in which they entered a course.

coincident pair A microphone arrangement for *stereophonic* sound recording in which two *directional microphones* are placed adjacent to and at right angles to each other.

cold type A term applied to any typesetting system that does not involve the formation of *characters* from hot metal as and when they are required.

collage An art form or picture produced by sticking various materials (cloth, wood, plastic, metal, paper etc) on to a paper, board or other flat base.

collator A machine (or section of a machine) which uses a series of boxes or shelves to sort or order sheets, cards, etc automatically, eg in *reprography*, data processing or the preparation of books for binding.

colophon In publishing, details of author, title, publisher, date of publication, etc given at the beginning or end of a document (see, for example, the page following the main title page of this book).

colo(u)r addition, subtraction See *primary colo(u)rs*.

colo(u)r balance The appearance of a colo(u)r *image* (eg on a television screen) considered in terms of the proportions of its three *primary colo(u)r* components.

colo(u)r filter A type of filter used in photographic and similar work. It consists of a sheet of transparent material that stops all or part of the light in a particular band of wavelengths.

colo(u)r standards Colo(u)r television pictures are composed and transmitted using agreed standards. Three incompatible standards are used, they are: *PAL, NTSC, SECAM* (see entries).

colo(u)r temperature A measure of the colo(u)r quality of light, being equal to the absolute temperature at which a black body (full radiator) produces a similar spectrum. To simulate natural daylight, a light source would require to have a colo(u)r temperature of 6000K (6000 degrees Kelvin) — the temperature of the surface of the sun.

column (speaker) An enclosure containing a vertical array of *loudspeaker* units.

COM See *computer output microform*.

coma A type of lens *aberration* in which a point away from the *optical axis* is focused as an asymmetrical patch of light with a comet-like tail, thus producing blurring of the resulting *image*.

comb binding A method of binding documents that involves using a special machine to punch a line of rectangular holes along the left-hand edge of each sheet and then fastening the sheets together using a cylindrical 'comb' whose teeth pass through the holes; cf *spiral binding*.

combined print Another term for a *married print*.

COMMAG Combined magnetic — a term applied to a *motion picture* that carries a *magnetic sound track* on the actual picture film; cf *SEPMAG*.

command-driven program A *computer program* where events are controlled by commands (instructions) keyed in or otherwise entered by the user; cf *menu-driven program*.

command mode See *command-driven program*.

commentary track A *track* on an *audiotape*, etc on which a commentary, narrative or other form of *voice over* is recorded.

commercial materials A term applied to instructional materials that are produced and/or distributed by a commercial firm and which have to be paid for, as opposed to materials that are produced in-house or are available free of charge.

communicating word processors Two or more *word processors* that are interconnected via some form of communication system, so that a user of any word processor in the system can gain access to material stored in all the other word processors in the *network*.

communication skills Skills associated with the transfer of information in oral, written, non-verbal or pictorial form.

communications satellite An Earth satellite (usually geostationary) that is used to relay telephone messages, television program(me)s, etc from one part of the world to another.

community-based learning A *learning* situation that does not involve the use of specialized classrooms, *resources centres (centers)*, etc. Instead, it makes use of all the various cultural, industrial and other resources of the community as the motivation for, site of, and tools for learning. See also *community resource*.

community resource A resource available within a community which, while not specifically designed as a learning resource, can nevertheless be used by the members of the community to meet specific learning needs. Typical examples are libraries, museums, parks, playgrounds and cultural events.

COMOPT Combined optical — a term applied to a *motion picture* that carries an *optical sound track* on the actual picture film; cf *SEPOPT*.

compact 1. An alternative term for *compress*. 2. See *compact cassette*, etc.

compact cassette The most common type of *cassette* used to hold *audiotape*, containing tape 4 mm wide wound on separate supply and take-up *reels*; such cassettes normally have playing times ranging from 15 minutes a side (C30) to 60 minutes a side (C120).

compact disc (CD) A recently-developed ultra-high-fidelity *audio disc* on which the *audio signal* is recorded in *digital* form. Such discs are only 12 cm in diameter (hence the name) and are played in a similar way to an *optical videodisc*, using a *laser* to read the signal.

compact disc player A *record player* designed for use with *compact discs* rather than conventional *black discs*.

compact slide A 2″ × 2″ photographic *slide*; cf *jumbo slide, lantern slide*.

company game A *game* (usually some form of *business game*) that is specially developed by (or for) a commercial or industrial organization for use in the in-service development of its staff.

comparative assessment *Assessment* which is designed to compare the *performances* of the individuals to whom the assessment is being applied (eg O level and degree examinations). Also known as *discriminative assessment*.

compatibility The extent to which one learning resource can be used in conjunction with another learning resource, eg a computer *software package* and a particular type of *computer* or two items of *video* equipment such as a camera and a *videorecorder*.

competencies See *competency-based education, learning, teaching, training*.

competency-based education, learning, teaching, training Education, learning, teaching or training in which the desired outcomes (usually referred to as *competencies*) are specified in advance, in written form. The three essential characteristics are: (i) selection of appropriate competencies; (ii) specification of appropriate methods of *assessment* to determine success; (iii) development of a functional instructional *delivery system* (this often involves *individualized learning*).

competency testing, assessment Testing or *assessment* carried out within the context of *competency-based education, learning, teaching, training*.

compiler A special *computer program* that enables user programs written in a particular *high-level (programming) language* to be handled by a particular make or model of *computer*. The compiler translates the high-level program into the appropriate *machine code*.

complementary colo(u)rs Colo(u)rs produced by subtracting a particular colo(u)r from white light, the complementary colo(u)rs of red, blue and green being cyan (blue-green), yellow and magenta respectively. See also *primary colo(u)rs*.

completion item See *completion test*.

completion test A test in which incomplete statements, series, diagrams, matrices etc have to be completed by the person taking the test, usually by supplying missing words, symbols, numbers, sections, etc. A typical *item* in such a test (known as a *completion item*) might be: 'Cow is to calf as horse is to ___?'.

complex overt response A *psychomotor* process in which a skill or set of skills has been attained to such an extent that a desired activity can be carried out smoothly and efficiently; Level 5 of Harrow's *psychomotor domain*.

component bar chart A *bar chart* in which the individual bars are divided into parts whose sizes represent the magnitudes of the various components of which they are composed (see figure 13). Also known as a *compound bar chart* or *multiple bar chart*.

expected to master in a program(me) of instruction or learning situation.

component resources *Learning resources* that are versatile, user-acceptable and generally available, so that they can be used as components of a wide range of instructional program(me)s.

composite 1. A *montage* of photographic or projected images. 2. More than one *image* incorporated in a single photographic *slide*.

composite print Another term for a *married print*.

composite video A *video signal* containing both the pictures and the associated synchronizing information.

compound bar chart Another name for a *component bar chart*.

comprehension A *cognitive* process which involves understanding a particular idea, set of *knowledge*, etc without necessarily being able to relate it to other material or appreciate its wider implications; Level 2 of Bloom's *cognitive domain*.

compress An instruction given to a *microcomputer* to re-assemble the material

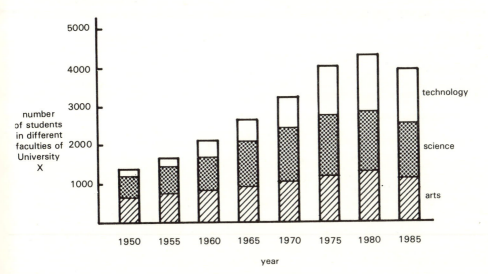

Figure 13 A component bar chart

component behavio(u)r A specific component of the *criterion behavio(u)r* which a learner is

stored on a *disk* in such a way as to take up the least storage space. See also *data compression*.

compressed speech Recorded speech that is processed in such a way as to produce a greater number of words per minute without the increase in pitch and distortion (the *Donald Duck effect*) that results if the speech is simply played back at a greater speed than that at which it was recorded. Also known as *accelerated speech*. Should not be confused with *compression*.

compression 1. A technique used in *audio recording* whereby the *dynamic range* of the original sound is reduced electronically prior to recording it on disc or tape. The original dynamic range is restored electronically during the playback process; see also *Dolby system*. 2. See *data compression*.

computer Any device, usually electronic, which is able to accept data, apply some *processing* procedure to it, and supply the resulting new data in a form suitable to the user. See also *analog computer*, *digital computer*.

computer-aided (-assisted) assessment, examination, test An *assessment*, examination or test that is constructed and/or administered and/or marked with the aid of a *digital computer*.

computer-aided (-assisted) design (CAD) Use of a *computer* as a vehicle whereby a design process is carried out, eg by exploiting its facility to generate and manipulate sophisticated graphic displays.

computer-aided (-assisted) instruction, learning, training Use of a *computer* as an integral part of an instructional system, with the learner generally engaging in *real-time* interaction with the computer via a *terminal*; cf *computer-managed instruction, learning, training*.

computer audio Recognition and/or generation of sounds by a *computer*.

computer-based education (CBE) Education involving *computer-aided instruction, computer-managed instruction*, or both.

computer-based instruction (CBI) A term which encompasses both *computer-aided instruction* and *computer-managed instruction*.

computer-based learning (CBL) A term which encompasses both *computer-aided learning* and *computer-managed learning*.

computer-based training (CBT) A term which encompasses both *computer-aided training* and *computer-managed training*.

computer graphics The generation and/or display of *graphic materials* using a *computer*, either in *soft copy* form on a *visual display unit* or in *hard copy* form produced by an electronic, optical or mechanical *plotter* or *printer*.

computerized item bank 1. A bank of *test items* that is held in a *digital computer* and can be accessed via a *computer terminal*. 2. Another term for a *data bank* or *data base*.

computer literacy Basic familiarity with *computers* and their applications to the extent of knowing when and how to use them to good effect.

computer-managed instruction, learning, training Use of a *computer* in a supervisory or managerial rather than a teaching role, the computer prescribing work schedules, carrying out diagnostic *assessment*, maintaining student records, etc; cf *computer-aided instruction, learning, training*.

computer-marked assignment A technique whereby a *computer* is used to mark *assignments* completed by students. The student fills in his/her *responses* on special sheets which can be read by the computer.

computer output microform (COM) A *microform* that is produced by transferring data directly from a *computer* on to the required storage medium (*microfiche, microfilm*, etc) using a special output *peripheral*.

computer peripheral See *peripheral*.

computer program The coded instructions that are given to a *computer* in order to make it, or enable it to, carry out a specific set of actions. Such programs are written in special *programming languages*.

computer simulation A *simulation* of a real or hypothetical situation, process, etc presented or experienced through a *model* programmed into a *computer*.

computer store Any *computer* subsystem or *peripheral* in which data can be stored in a form in which it can be read by the computer. See also *backing store, main store*.

computer terminal An electronic device which

permits two-way communication between a user and a *computer*, eg a *keyboard terminal*.

concentric method, curriculum 1. An instructional technique that involves covering the same basic ground in successive stages of a course, but in increasing depth and detail at each stage; see also *spiral curriculum*. 2. Continuous review, discussion and instruction in any one part of a particular subject.

concept cards Instructional cards that carry key pieces of information relating to a particular topic or subject.

concept film, loop, tape A short sequence, recorded on film or tape, that gives an illustration or demonstration of a particular topic or subject.

concept keyboard A system of touch-sensitive pads set into a matrix, the pads being connected to a *microcomputer*. Such a system can be programmed by a teacher to provide different learning experiences, the learner only having to touch the appropriate picture, word or symbol in order to make a response. Concept keyboards are most commonly used with very young or handicapped learners.

conceptual learning A highly-developed form of *learning* in which meanings take on generalized understanding; one of the steps in Gagné's *learning hierarchy*.

concomitant variation A statistical term for parallel changes in two or more *variables* which are not necessarily the result of a direct *causal relationship* between the variables. See also *functional relationship*.

concrete concept A concept that involves identifying a novel *stimulus* as a member of a class whose members have some concrete characteristic in common, even though such stimuli may otherwise differ from one another markedly. The ability to form such concepts is one of the types of intellectual skill identified by Gagné and Briggs.

concrete materials Physical objects (eg *models* or *realia*) used as aids to instruction or learning.

concrete-operational stage The stage in the *learning* process where the learner begins to deal with concepts that are not directly associated with concrete experiences.

condenser lens A lens, lens system or

lens/mirror combination used to concentrate light into a confined beam, as in a projector.

condenser microphone A high-quality *microphone* that uses a variable-separation capacitor system to convert incident sound waves into an electrical signal. Also known as a *capacitor microphone*.

conditioned reflex In *behavio(u)ral psychology* or learning theory, a *response* that is produced by a *stimulus* with which it is not normally or naturally associated, eg the salivation that Pavlov's dogs were conditioned to produce on hearing a bell rung. Also known as a *conditioned response*. See also *respondent conditioning*.

conditioned response Another name for a *conditioned reflex*.

conditioning In *behavio(u)ral psychology*, deliberate manipulation of an individual's behavio(u)r in order to produce a desired *response* to a given *stimulus*. See also *operant conditioning, respondent conditioning*.

cone of experience A graphical representation of a theory proposed by Dale in which all general categories of experience are arranged in a continuum at different levels of a gradually-narrowing cone, with concrete, sensory experiences at the base and highly-abstract, symbolic experiences at the top (see figure 14). The cone thus constitutes 'a visual analogy to show the progression of learning experiences from direct, first-hand participation to fictional representation and on to purely abstract symbolic expression'.

confidence interval, limit A statistical measure of confidence in the range of values within which a particular quantity (usually the *mean* of a set of *scores*) is believed to lie.

confidence testing A method for discriminating between levels of partial knowledge relating to the content of a *test item* in which the testee indicates his/her degree of confidence in the answer chosen.

conflation Integration of two separate sets of *scores* to produce a single overall set, eg combining the *continuous assessment* scores obtained by the members of a class with the scores obtained in *terminal assessment*.

congruence evaluation *Evaluation* that is carried out in order to bring to light any discrepancies between the *design objectives* of a

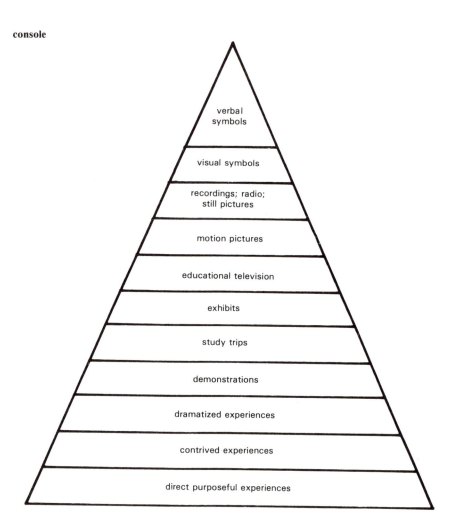

verbal
symbols

visual symbols

recordings; radio;
still pictures

motion pictures

educational television

exhibits

study trips

demonstrations

dramatized experiences

contrived experiences

direct purposeful experiences

Figure 14 Dale's cone of experience

system and its actual performance.

console A generic term for a piece of equipment (often desk-like and non-moveable) carrying the control boards, monitoring systems and other equipment needed to control a large piece of machinery or plant, a *computer*, a television or sound recording *studio*, an *electronic classroom*, etc.

constant angular velocity (CAV) A *videodisc* or *digital optical disk* replay mode in which the disc(k) spins at a constant number of revolutions per second. In the case of a constant angular velocity videodisc, each *frame* of the video content occupies a complete circular track. Such a system enables only up to 54,000 frames (36 minutes of video) to be stored on each side of a 12 inch *laser disc*, but

allows any of these frames to be held rock steady, thus making the mode suitable for *interactive video* use; cf *constant linear velocity (CLV)*.

constant linear velocity (CLV) A *videodisc, compact disc* and *digital optical disk* replay mode in which information is read at constant linear speed along a continuous spiral track stretching from the outside of the disc(k) to near the centre (center). In the case of a *constant angular velocity* videodisc, such a system enables up to 60 minutes of video content to be stored on each side of a 12 inch *laser disc*, but only allows linear playback; thus, the system is ideal for showing continuous material like feature films but is not suited for use in *interactive video*; cf *constant angular velocity (CAV)*.

constant spacing A term applied to *text* that is set, typed or printed with equal spaces between the *characters*; cf *proportional spacing*.

construct See *construct validity*.

constructed response A *response* to a *test item* or *frame* in an instructional program(me) that actually has to be supplied by the testee or learner rather than merely selected from a list of alternatives; cf *fixed-response item*.

construct validity The extent to which a test of a particular psychological *construct* (an index such as *general intelligence* or a quality such as introversion/extroversion) actually provides a reliable measure of that index or quality.

consumable materials Another name for *expendable materials*.

contact printing Still photograph or motion picture printing in which the processed film being copied is held in contact with the raw film or paper during copying, thus producing 1:1 reproduction.

contact videodisc A type of *videodisc* from which the signal is read using a *stylus* that is in actual contact with the surface, generally by capacitive (ie charge-storing) methods; cf *optical videodisc, capicitance, capacitive videodisc*.

content analysis A detailed study of the contents of a course carried out in order to check that the course covers all the prescribed subject matter content. The results are often presented in diagrammatic or quantitative (eg tabular) form.

content-centred (centered) A term applied to a *game, simulation* or other exercise whose *educational objectives* relate mainly to the subject matter on which the exercise is based rather than on the activities that the exercise involves; cf *process-centred (centered)*.

content validity The extent to which the content of a test or examination reflects the content of the course or instructional program(me) in respect of which the test or examination is being administered.

context-free response A *response* to a *test item* or *frame* in an instructional program(me) that is not influenced by the immediately preceding or following material in the test or program(me), ie is not influenced by the context in which it is placed; cf *context-sensitive response*.

context-sensitive response A *response* to a *test item* or *frame* in an instructional program(me) that may be influenced by the immediately preceding or following material in the program(me), ie may be influenced by the context in which it is placed; cf *context-free response*.

contiguous teaching Face-to-face teaching, with the instructor and learners in direct contact; cf *distance learning*.

contingency 1. A statistical term for the degree to which one *variable* depends on another variable (or other variables). 2. In instructional design, *rewards* and *punishments* that are built into a program(me) in order to reinforce wanted and discourage unwanted responses or behavio(u)r.

contingency contracting A form of *contract-based learning* in which it is recognised that the learner may exceed or fall below expectations. The contract therefore includes a clause to enable re-negotiation to take place as learning progresses. *Project* work, for example, is an area where contingency contracting would often be particularly appropriate because of the possibility of unexpected difficulties or outcomes.

continuity 1. In film and television production, the correct sequence and matching of all aspects of *action* and setting between successive *scenes*. 2. Linking announcements or information presented between sequences of a *program(me)* or between different program(me)s.

continuity still In film or television production, a still photograph of a *scene* taken to record details to ensure correct matching in subsequent *shots* or scenes.

continuous assessment On-going *assessment* of a learner throughout an extended course or instructional program(me); cf *terminal assessment*.

continuous cassette A *cassette* that contains a closed loop of *audiotape*, and can therefore be played continuously, without rewinding.

continuous tone A term applied to an *image* with continuously-varying grey *tones*, eg a *monochrome* photograph or television picture.

continuous variable A *variable* that can have any value within a given range; cf *discrete variable*.

contract-based learning, teaching, training Learning, teaching or training in which an agreed contract of learning expectation or objectives is drawn up between the learner and his/her tutor; the learner is expected to fulfil the terms of the contract for *assessment* purposes. See also *contingency contracting, contract plan, negotiated learning*.

contract plan An instructional system in which a course is divided into a sequence of *assignments*, each covered by a separate contract between the individual learner and the course organizers. Under such a system, a learner must fulfil the terms of each successive contract before being allowed to take on the next one. See also *contract-based learning, teaching, training*.

contrast The intensity relationship between the light and dark areas of a photograph, video picture, etc.

contrived experiences Learning experiences that are designed to simulate real-life situations in so far as this is possible, often employing real objects, tools, systems, etc (or effective substitutes) in order to add verisimilitude.

control group A *sample* of objects in a research study which resembles the *experimental group* in all important respects except the one being studied or varied, and with which meaningful comparisons can be made.

controlled discussion A discussion in which learners may raise questions or make relevant comments, but whose general direction is under the strict control of the teacher, tutor or instructor; cf *free group discussion*.

controlled experiment An experiment in which all the *variables* apart from those under actual investigation are kept as constant as circumstances allow.

control track 1. On an *audiotape*, a *track* carrying instructions on operations to be carried out during running. 2. On a *videotape*, a *track* used to carry synchronization and similar information.

control unit 1. The part of the *central processing unit* that controls a *computer's* internal operations. 2. An electronic system used to control TV cameras and video systems.

convergence In colo(u)r television work, adjustment of the electron or light beams in order to produce exact *registration* of the red, blue and green images.

convergent thinking A rational, systematic approach to problem solving normally leading to the single correct, most conventional or most logical solution; cf *divergent thinking*.

converger A learner who is more proficient at *convergent thinking* than at *divergent thinking*; cf *diverger*.

conversational chaining A *programmed instruction* technique in which the correct *response* to each item is not presented on its own but is built into the text of the following item; thus, the *response* to one item becomes part of the *stimulus* of the next.

conversational language Natural language used to communicate *on-line* with a *digital computer*, as opposed to an artificial *programming language*.

conversational mode *On-line* dialog(ue) between a user and a *digital computer* via a suitable *terminal*.

conversion course, training Instruction given to a learner or trainee whose previous experience and/or qualifications are not directly relevant to the course, job, profession, etc that he/she now wishes to enter.

cookbook laboratory experiment An experiment (carried out by students as part of a laboratory program(me)) that consists simply of following detailed instructions, without any element of *discovery learning, problem solving* or *divergent thinking*.

copy camera In printing or *reprography*, a special camera used to transfer finished copy, artwork, etc on to a *photographic film* or *photographic plate*, together with its ancillary equipment (lighting system, stand, timer, etc).

copying stand, copystand An adjustable stand, generally fitted with a system of lights, using which an ordinary *still camera* can photograph flat material (*artwork*, existing photographs, etc).

copyright The right to reproduce or to authorize reproduction or performance of a literary, dramatic, musical or artistic work. See also *copyright holder, easement*.

copyright holder The person, group of persons, or corporate body that owns the *copyright* of a given work at a particular time, and from whom permission must be obtained before the work may legally be reproduced or performed. See also *easement*.

core course 1. A teaching course in which a skeleton framework of ideas and teaching activities is provided and in which the individual teacher is able to add his/her own methods, ideas, etc. 2. A course that has to be taken as part of the *core curriculum* of a school, college, etc. See also *core module, subject*.

core curriculum 1. Key elements or subjects in the *curriculum* operated by a school, college, etc that are taken by all students. 2. Basic elements in a course that have to be taken by all students, regardless of their selection of optional modules, materials, etc.

core memory See *main store*.

core module, subject A *module* or subject that forms part of the *core curriculum* of a course.

correction for chance, guessing Reduction of the total in a test *score* according to a standard correction formula that is designed to allow for correct answers made by the candidate purely as a result of guessing.

correlation A statistical term for the degree to which two *variables* vary together, ie the degree to which changes in one are automatically accompanied by changes in the other. Such correlation is expressed in terms of the *correlation coefficient* for the two variables, a number which can range from -1.0 (perfect *negative correlation*, where one variable decreases as the other increases), through 0.0 (no correlation) to $+1.0$ (perfect *positive correlation*, where the two variables increase or decrease in lockstep).

correlation coefficient See *correlation*.

correspondence course A form of *distance learning* course that relies mainly on the postal service to provide a link between individual learners and the course organizer(s).

corrupt In computing or data processing, to introduce irrelevant material or errors into a *computer program, file*, etc.

Cosford cube A classroom *feedback* device developed at the RAF Training Centre at Cosford (UK). It uses cubes with different colo(u)red faces as the vehicle for feedback, the learners holding up their cubes so that the instructor sees one particular face.

cost analysis A formalized *analysis* of the costs (which may include costs associated with staff time and use of accommodation and/or equipment as well as directly-incurred costs) of a particular course or component thereof; cf *cost benefit analysis*.

cost benefit analysis Determination of the economic effectiveness of a program(me) by calculating, in monetary terms, both the cost associated with and the benefits accruing from the program(me); cf *cost analysis*.

course unit plan A type of *modular course* run in the USA. It allows a student to build up credits by taking a series of optional courses, courses that often have different credit values depending on their relative importance and difficulty and (in some cases) their length. Also known as the *cafeteria plan* and, in the UK, as the *pathway scheme*.

courseware 1. The actual instructional material, including both the content and the instructional technique, that is incorporated in a *computer-based instruction* system. When used in this sense, courseware is different from *software*, which is taken to refer to the *computer program* that controls the computer's operation. 2. A term that is becoming increasingly widely used as a synonym for instructional *software*, in the broadest sense of the word.

covert response An internalized *response* which a learner is assumed to make, but which is neither recorded by, nor otherwise apparent to, an observer; cf *overt response*.

covert stimulus An internalized *stimulus* (such as recollection) which cannot be directly observed; cf *overt stimulus*.

CPM See *critical path method*.

CPU See *central processing unit*.

crab In film or television production, to move a *microphone* or camera sideways across a *set*; cf *dolly* (2.). Should not be confused with *pan*.

crash The complete shutdown of a *computer* system because of a serious *hardware* or *software* malfunction; cf *glitch, hang-up*.

crash course, program(me) An intensive course or instructional program(me) designed to provide specified instruction or training in a much shorter period than would normally be required. See also *minicourse*.

crash editing Videotape *editing* carried out by switching a *videotape recorder* straight from the *playback* to the *record* mode. In such editing, the new recording may not be synchronized with the earlier one; cf *electronic editing*.

crawling titles A line of *titles* or *captions* that moves horizontally across a film picture or television screen; cf *creeping titles*.

creativity test A *psychological test* of *divergent thinking* in which the questions are *open-ended*, unlike the *closed questions* that make up most standard *intelligence tests*.

creeping titles A line of *titles* or *captions* that moves vertically across a film picture or television screen; cf *crawling titles*.

crisis game A type of *business game* in which the participants are confronted with crisis situations which they have to attempt to resolve.

criterion behavio(u)r In *program(m)ed instruction*, the detailed behavio(u)r that is expected of an individual at the end of the program(me) or after a specified part thereof. See also *component behavio(u)r*.

criterion frame In *program(m)ed instruction*, another name for a *test frame*.

criterion-referenced assessment *Assessment* designed to determine an individual's *performance* with reference to pre-determined standards, such as *behavio(u)ral objectives*); cf *norm-referenced assessment*.

criterion test A quantitative or qualitative measure of *performance* used as a basis for checking the *validity* of another measuring or testing process.

critical incident method, technique 1. A technique used in *work study* that involves identifying incidents which are critical in the sense that they make the difference between success and failure in a given job situation. 2. A *group training* method which starts with the participants describing incidents which presented them with difficulties.

critical path See *critical path method*.

critical path method (CPM) A method of

analyzing a *project* or process that involves determining the *critical path*, ie the sequence of interconnected events between the start and finish of the project or process that requires the longest time to complete. This then gives the shortest time in which the project or process can be completed, and can be used as a planning and monitoring aid.

cross-age teaching A technique in which some or all of the teaching in a course or program(me) is carried out by other pupils, usually older, who have already mastered the material being taught. See also *peer teaching*.

cross-fade To change from one *video signal* or *audio signal* to another, or from one slide projector to another focused on the same screen, by a *dissolve* effect.

cross lighting In photographic, film or television work, lighting from a direction nearly perpendicular to the direction of view introduced in order to emphasize texture and produce *model(l)ing* of the subject.

cross-media approach An instructional methodology based on the principle that the use of a variety of correlated instructional materials and experiences of different types can produce highly effective *reinforcement* of what is being taught.

cross-over groups A group discussion technique in which the groups exchange members in a pre-determined way after each cycle of discussion, thus producing variety and cross-fertilization of ideas.

crossover network, unit A system of electronic *filters* that divides an *audio signal* between different *loudspeakers* covering different parts of the *audio spectrum*, eg between separate bass, mid-range and treble speakers.

crosstalk Unwanted breakthrough between different *channels* of a multi-channel system, eg between the two channels of a *stereophonic* sound system.

cross-validation Measuring the *validity* of a research study by applying statistical tests to sets of data obtained from different *samples* drawn from the same *population* to see if there is satisfactory *correlation* between them.

CRT Cathode ray tube.

crystal microphone A low-fidelity *microphone*

that uses a *piezoelectric crystal* to produce an electrical signal from the sound that impinges on it.

crystal sync A method of synchronizing an *audiotape recorder* with a *motion picture camera*. It involves generating *frame* signals using an electronic system incorporated in the camera, recording these on a *control track* on the tape, and subsequently using the signals to make sure that the film's *sound track* is properly synchronized with the pictures.

CS, CU See *close-up*.

cue 1. A command or signal for a previously-specified event to take place, eg the start of a particular piece of action or a change to another *frame* of a *program(me)*. 2. Another name for a *prompt*.

cueing 1. In *programmed instruction*, adding a *prompt* or *stimulus* in order to make it more likely that the learner will make a required *response*. 2. Giving warning to a presenter that he/she should now start talking.

cue marks Small marks that appear on *frames* near the end of each *reel* of a multi-reel *motion picture* in order to warn the projectionist that the end of the reel is approaching and give the cue to start the next reel during *changeover*.

cue numbers A decreasing series of numbers on the *leader* frames of a *motion picture* film which indicate how soon the film proper is due to start.

cue track A separate *track* on an *audiotape* or *videotape* used for carrying *cues* and similar information.

cuisenaire rods Sets of colo(u)r-coded square rods of different lengths (1cm–10cm) that are used as aids to the formation of number concepts in young children.

culture-free test A test which does not rely upon the understanding of any particular language or culture, and is therefore suitable for use with subjects with different cultural backgrounds. A number of widely-used tests of *general intelligence* fall into this category, eg the *draw-a-man test*, *dominoes test*, and *progressive matrices test*.

cumulative-part method A training technique in which the operation to be learned is divided into separate parts or elements which are mastered in a cumulative fashion, starting with

the first element only, then the first and second, and eventually building up to the entire operation; cf *part method, whole method*.

cumulative rating scale An *attitude scale* in which an attempt is made to measure an individual's intensity of attitude in respect of one particular factor (eg tolerance of noise or dislike of foreigners) by using a series of linked *items* whose cumulative *score* gives a meaningful quantitative measure of the testee's overall attitude.

curriculum 1. A term which encompasses all the *learning* that goes on in a school or other learning environment and expresses the aims, assumptions and values of the learning environment and of the educational system that supports it. 2. An attempt to communicate the essential principles and features of an educational or training proposal in such a form that it is open to critical scrutiny and capable of translation into practice. See also *hidden curriculum*.

curriculum guide A written guide to a particular *curriculum*, specifying what is to be covered and how it is to be taught.

cursor A *character* on a *visual display unit* screen indicating the currently-active position.

customized instruction Instruction that is designed to meet the specific needs of individual learners, as in *programmed instruction*.

cut 1. In film or television *editing*, an instantaneous change from one *scene* or *shot* to another. 2. In a dual-projector slide display, a rapid change from one *image* to the next. 3. In film or television production, a command given by the director for the performance and the recording thereof to stop.

cut-away In film or television production, a *shot* which shows an activity which is taking place at the same time as, but not as part of, the main *action*.

cut-in In film or television production, a non-critical *shot* used to break up or link sections of the principal *action*.

cut-off point A point in a ranking or mark list that is used as a criterion to determine whether a person passes or fails, is accepted or rejected etc. Also known as *cutting score*.

cutting *Editing* a *motion picture* by cutting up

lengths of exposed and processed film and joining them into a new continuity.

cutting copy Another name for a *work point*.

cutting score Another name for a *cut-off point*.

cybernetic model A *model* associated with the concept of *artificial intelligence*. The most basic cybernetic model would include the following four elements: input, process, output and *feedback*.

cybernetics The entire field of control and communication theory applied across a wide range of studies from neurosurgery to mathematics. It is often associated with *artificial intelligence* when used in an educational context.

cyclorama (cyc) A continuous curtain or back cloth suspended around the periphery of a film or television *studio* or stage. It is usually grey in colo(u)r.

D

D See *discrimination index*.

daisy wheel (printer) A *printer* system (used in typewriters, computer printers, etc) that employs interchangeable circular *heads* each of which carries a different *character set*, the individual characters being attached to a central disc by flexible stalks.

Dalton Plan An *individualized teaching* plan that originated at Dalton High School, Massachusetts (USA) around 1920. It requires pupils to carry out monthly *assignments*, their progress being recorded on job cards, and involves a combination of individual and group work supported by regular pupil-teacher conferences. See also *Winnetka plan*.

darkroom An area specially equipped for the processing and printing of photographic materials. Illumination is generally provided by a red *safelight* so that unexposed and undeveloped materials can be handled without being spoiled.

data bank, databank 1. A term that is sometimes used as an alternative name for a *data base*, but is usually taken to refer exclusively to a *non-bibliographic data base*;. also known as an *item bank* or *item base*. 2. In computing, a *file* (or set of files) of data that is held in a *backing store* and is common to several different *programs* or users.

data base (database) A collection of data which is systematically organized so as to make retrieval, manipulation and editing easy. Data bases can be manual (eg a card index or filing cabinet) or electronic, the latter being accessed via a computer terminal, either locally or at a distance. Also known as an *item bank* or *item base*. See also *bibliographic data base, non-bibliographic data base*.

data capture A general term for techniques by which data are converted into *machine-readable* format.

data carrier Any medium (*punched cards, paper, tape, magnetic tape*, etc) that is used to store data.

data compression Reducing the size of data elements by altering the way in which they are coded, thus increasing the rate at which information can be transmitted or the amount which can be stored in a medium of a given capacity. Should not be confused with *data reduction*.

data degradation Loss of some of the information contained in a set of data as a result of a processing procedure that is not reversible, eg when a series of *raw scores* are converted to a *rank order*.

data link A communication line along which data can be transmitted, eg between a *remote terminal* and the *central processing unit* of a *computer*.

data network A system of inter-connected *terminals* via which data can be communicated between users. See also *network*.

data reduction Converting large collections of data into useful, ordered or simplified information, eg during a research or *evaluation* programme. Should not be confused with *data compression*.

data set Another name for a *modem*.

data set adaptor A device that acts as an interface between a *modem* and a *digital computer*.

data tablet A device by which *graphical material* can be input into a *digital computer* by 'writing' or 'drawing' on its (electromagnetically-sensitive) surface using a device such as a *light pen* or *mouse*; also known as a *graphics tablet*.

daylight Lighting from a natural source or from an artificial source that produces light of a similar *colo(u)r temperature*, generally between 5000 and 6000 degrees Kelvin.

daylight projection A projection system (such as an *overhead projector*) that produces an *image* bright enough to be seen without *room darkening*. See also *daylight screen*.

daylight screen A projection *screen* so constructed that clear *images* from a slide or other *projector* can be seen in an undarkened room; examples of daylight screens are the *beaded screen, lenticular screen* and *silvered screen*.

day release A UK term for the release of an employee from his/her place of employment (usually on a one-day-per-week basis) in order to attend a further education course relating to his/her training; cf *block release*.

debriefing Review and discussion of the processes and outcomes of an exercise, particularly one that involves interaction, role-playing etc; cf *briefing*.

debug To remove errors from a system, particularly a *computer program*.

decade counter A counter that registers from 0 to 9, thereafter resetting at zero and starting again. Such counters are used as the basis of a wide range of counting devices, eg the rev. counters in *tape recorders*.

decay A term used in *memory* research to denote the disappearance from the brain, over time, of memory traces that are not strengthened by *reinforcement*.

decentring (decentering) A term used in Piaget's theory of *learning* to denote the stage in the process of concept acquisition when it is realised that the same number, volume, height etc exists no matter how the apparent dimensions of the perceived object are changed.

decibel A logarithmic measure of the intensity of a sound or the power of a signal. It is equal to one tenth of a *bel*.

decimal notation A type of notation (used in classifying library stock) that is based on decimal numbers, the various subclasses within a given class being distinguished by using as many decimal places as are necessary. The *Dewey Decimal Classification* is one of the best known examples. See also *denary notation, number system*.

decision dynamics training A management training technique (originally developed at Strathclyde University, Scotland) that uses *videorecordings* of interactive *simulations* to study *group dynamics*.

decision tree A type of *flow chart* which summarizes the various alternatives and options available in a complex decision-making process, together with their likely consequences. It is used as an aid to decision making and systems analysis.

deck 1. The *turntable* and drive systems in a *record player*. 2. The tape transport system, *heads* and associated electronics of an *audiotape recorder*, generally without *power amplifiers* or *loudspeakers*. 3. In computing or data processing, a set of *punched cards* prepared for use in a specific program run. 4. A pack of cards, eg of conventional playing cards or cards designed for use in a particular *game* or other exercise.

decomposition method 1. A method of solving complex planning or other problems by breaking them down into soluble sub-problems. 2. A method of teaching subtraction that involves 'borrowing' from an adjacent decimal.

decoy Another name for a *distractor* in multiple-choice testing.

dedicated A term that is applied to a *computer*, machine, system etc that is set apart for special use, eg a *microcomputer* that is permanently incorporated in an experiment in a teaching laboratory or is specifically designed for use as a *word processor*.

deductive method A method of teaching, study or argument which proceeds from general or universally-applicable principles to particular applications of same and shows the validity of the conclusions, eg the *ruleg* system used in *program(m)ed instruction*; cf *inductive method*. See also *hypothetico-deductive method*.

deep processing A type of study method in which a learner reads material in order to gain deep understanding of the material being studied; cf *surface processing*.

deferred imitation The ability of a child to imitate the behavio(u)r of a person when the person being imitated is not actually present; an important stage in concept formation.

defined concept A concept that is acquired indirectly by means of verbal information rather than by direct reference to actual objects or systems. The ability to acquire such concepts is one of the types of intellectual skill identified by Gagné and Briggs.

definition Another term for *resolution*.

degausser A device for reducing the residual magnetism in a system such as a *head* in a *tape recorder* by subjecting it to an alternating magnetic field of gradually diminishing intensity. Also known as a *demagnetizer*.

delayed feedback A *feedback* system that is sometimes used in *audio-active comparative language laboratories* whereby the student's performance of a set of *drill* items is played back at the end of the set of items rather than after each individual item.

delivery reel, spool The *reel* (*spool*) from which the tape or film is fed into a *tape recorder*, film projector, etc. Also known as a *feed reel, spool*.

delivery system 1. In teaching, training, *individualized learning, distance learning*, etc a combination of medium and method of usage that is employed to present instructional information to a learner. 2. In *distance learning*, the method by which distribution of instructional materials to learners is organized.

demodulation The recovery of an original signal from a *carrier wave* or *carrier signal* into which it has been incorporated by *modulation*, eg in a radio or television *receiver*.

demonstrate A term used in *mathetics*, where the stage of an instructional process in which the learner is shown how to carry out a particular procedure (eg a calculation) is known as the *demonstrate phase*. See also *release*.

demonstrate phase See *demonstrate*.

demonstration board Another name for a *display board*.

denary notation, number system The conventional 'decimal' number system based on the radix 10; cf *binary notation, number system*.

density 1. A measure of the darkness or opacity of a photographic or other *image*. 2. In *information technology*, a measure of the capacity per unit length, area or volume of a data storage medium, eg the number of *bits* per mm that can be stored on a *magnetic tape*.

dependent variable A *variable* whose behavio(u)r is studied or measured in an experimental procedure, as opposed to one that is under the direct control of the experimenter (an *independent variable*).

depth of field The range of object distances from a camera within which objects will

range within which
objects are in focus

Figure 15 The depth of field of a camera

Delphi approach, technique A technique used in problem solving and technological forecasting whereby a multi-disciplinary team produce a set of possible solutions or forecasts by *brainstorming* or some similar method, after which the solutions are ranked in order of preference and importance, discussed in depth, and used to produce a consensus solution or prediction.

demagnetizer Another name for a *degausser*.

produce reasonably sharp *images* at a given *aperture* setting (see figure 15). Should not be confused with *depth of focus*.

depth of focus The (comparatively short) range over which the distance of the *image plane* from the lens of a camera can be varied while still keeping the image in *focus* (see figure 16). Should not be confused with *depth of field*.

descenders The lower parts of lower-case

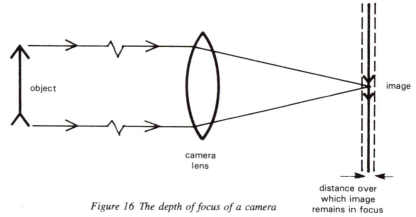

object

camera
lens

image

distance over
which image
remains in focus

Figure 16 The depth of focus of a camera

letters like 'g' and 'y' that fall below the *x-height* of a *typeface*; cf *ascenders*.

descriptor 1. In documentation, a term that is used loosely as a synonym for a *keyword*. 2. In data storage, a broad subject heading that stands for a particular idea or concept and is used to facilitate retrieval of information on same.

design criteria, objectives, specifications The criteria, *objectives* or specifications that it is intended a course, program(me), exercise, system, etc should satisfy or achieve once its development has been satisfactorily completed.

de-skilling Changing the method by which a task of some sort is performed in order to reduce the level of skill that it requires and thus make it easier to carry out.

desk-top computer Another name for a *microcomputer*.

destructive readout *Readout* data from a *computer store* that causes the record of the data in the store to be lost; cf *non-destructive readout*.

developing The chemical *processing* by which the *latent image* in an exposed *photographic film*, *photographic plate* or *photographic paper* is made permanently visible.

developmental testing Testing of a course, *program(me)*, exercise, *system* etc carried out while it is actually being developed in order to identify and eliminate weaknesses.

development method A method of instruction

in which a learner is taken step by step through the various stages of a task or piece of work in increasing order of difficulty, until he or she can eventually carry out the entire process.

deviation IQ A measure of the extent to which an individual's *intelligence quotient* (IQ) differs from the *norm* for his or her age group.

deviation score A statistical term for the amount by which an individual *score* differs from the *mean* for the *population* under study (see also *average deviation, standard deviation*).

Dewey Decimal Classification A *decimal notation* system that is widely used in libraries for classifying stock. It was originally developed by M. Dewey in 1876.

D-group training A type of *T-group training* (see in management training) in which the instructor or course leader attempts to relate the behavio(u)r of the group to the participants' own work experience.

diagnosis The process of determining the existing capabilities of a learner in a given area by testing and analyzing his/her performance of a carefully-planned *hierarchy* of tasks, usually for the purpose of assigning appropriate remedial and/or more advanced learning tasks.

diagnostic ability 1. A measure of the extent to which a test or other form of *assessment* is able to identify strengths or weaknesses of the person being tested in the area of interest. 2. The skill with which a teacher, instructor or trainer can identify strengths and weaknesses in learners.

diagnostic teaching Teaching that is based on *diagnosis*, with individual learners being assigned tasks appropriate to the stage of development that they have shown they have reached.

diaporama A general term (of French origin) for an audiovisual presentation that involves the use of one or more slide projectors in conjunction with (and controlled by) an *audiotape recorder*.

diapositive A *positive* photographic *image* on a transparent base intended for viewing or showing by transmitted light, eg as a *slide* or *OHP transparency*.

diascope A (now largely obsolete) term for a projector designed to display on an external screen *images* held on still *transparencies* such as photographic *slides*.

diazo process A process for producing coloured *images* or backgrounds on *transparencies, slides, prints*, etc (eg white line images on a bright blue background). The process is based on the use of chemicals containing diazonium compounds — hence the name.

dichotomous variable A *variable* which can only have two values or states, eg male/female or pass/fail.

didactic method A method of instruction, predominantly based on verbal face-to-face instruction, that emphasizes rules, principles, standards of conduct and authoritative guidelines.

didactogram A diagram that shows how students perform in the different parts of a *programmed instruction* scheme; such diagrams are used in program(me) analysis, eg during program(me) development.

didule The basic instructional unit in a *programmed instruction* sequence. It constitutes one of the two components of a *frame*, which consists of an instructional element (the didule) and the method by which this is presented.

differential-aptitude test A standardized *objective test* that is designed to measure several aspects of *mental ability* separately. Such tests are based on the assumption that *intelligence* is a combination of several identifiable abilities or *factors*.

differential sensitivity The ability of a test or measuring instrument to identify small variations in the particular *factor*, attribute etc being studied.

differential weighting Assigning different weights (marks) to different questions or options in a *multiple-choice item* in order to give some reward for partly-correct answers.

difficulty index Another name for *facility index*.

difficulty score A *score* that indicates the highest level of difficulty achieved by an individual in the *assessment* of a particular skill, quality etc.

diffuser A translucent *filter* that is placed in front of a light source in order to soften the resultant shadows, or in front of a camera lens to reduce the sharpness of the *image* produced.

diffusion 1. Informal, unsystematic spreading of information about a development by casual word of mouth, meeting others by accident, etc; cf *dissemination*. 2. See *diffusion transfer process*.

diffusion transfer process A photographic or reprographic process that produces a permanent *positive* image of the scene or document being photographed or copied without the need for *wet processing*, the chemicals needed to bring about the development of the image being contained in the actual film or copy paper. The process used in *Polaroid* cameras is one of the best known examples.

digital A term applied to an information processing, storage or transfer system in which the signal is translated into *binary code* before processing, storage or transmission, or to the signal handled by such a system.

digital camera A camera which records textual or graphical images in *digital* form.

digital computer A *computer* in which the information being processed is handled in *digital* form, ie as strings of electronic pulses representing the binary digits 1 and 0; cf *analog computer*.

digital optical disk (DOD) A disk designed for the recording, storage and retrieval of *digital* information, using *laser* optics. There are three basic types of digital optical disks — optical read only memory disks (*OROM*s), write once optical disks (*WOOD*s) and erasable digital optical disks (*EDOD*s).

digital recording Recording of information in *digital* as opposed to *analog(ue)* form.

digitized A term applied to information that has been converted into *digital* form for storage, transmission or processing.

digitizer A device for converting a graphical *image* into a *digital* signal capable of being handled by a *digital computer*. It consists of a flat drawing board-like surface on which the original graphical material is placed, the required signal then being produced by tracing over the image using a *light pen* or *mouse*. See also *data tablet*.

dimmer An electronic or electrical device for varying the intensity of a light source.

DIN Deutsche Industrie Normen — the West German standards association. DIN standards apply to a wide range of products, including electrical plugs, sockets, etc, and the association also operates a system for rating *film speeds* (the DIN system). See also *ASA* and *ISO*.

dioptre (diopter) The unit of magnifying power of a lens, the power in dioptres being the reciprocal of the *focal length* of the lens in metres (meters); thus, a converging lens of focal length 1 metre has a power of +1 dioptre and a diverging lens of the same focal length a power of −1 dioptres.

diorama A three-dimensional representation of a scene in front of a (generally curved) two-dimensional background.

direct access 1. In computing, another term for *random access*. 2. A situation where users of a library, *resources centre (center)*, *computer* system, etc have unrestricted access to all (or part) of the stock, or to the system.

directed learning *Learning* in which there is a strong element of direction and guidance from the teacher or instructor; cf *autonomous learner, independent learning, negotiated learning*.

directed private study, reading A form of *directed learning*, normally done outside formal class time, that takes the form of study of specified sections of books or other learning materials. It is often used as a supplement to *direct teaching*. Directed reading is also known as *guided reading*.

direct experience A *learning* process based on actual experience in a real-life (as opposed to a simulated or artificial) situation.

directional microphone A *microphone* whose sensitivity is different in different horizontal directions, thus giving it an asymmetrical polar diagram (see, for example, *cardioid microphone, gun microphone*).

direct method A method of teaching foreign languages which stresses complete (or nearly complete) reliance on the spoken use of the foreign tongue rather than the learner's native tongue or the written form of the foreign tongue.

directory 1. A bibliographic term for a compilation of systematically-organized information, primarily intended for the identification or location of persons, places, institutions, etc. 2. In computing, the facilities given to a particular user of a large *computer* of the *multi-access* type.

direct teaching Conventional face-to-face instruction of students by a teacher; cf *resource-based learning*.

disc 1. See *audio disc*. 2. See *videodisc*. 3. An alternative spelling of *disk*.

discovery area A section of an *open classroom* which is provided with *printed materials, audiovisual materials* and *manipulative materials* that pupils can study or use independently. Also known as an *interest area* or *interest/discovery area*.

discovery learning, method An instructional method that attempts to teach principles or general concepts by providing the learner with a set of relevant experiences from which it is hoped he/she will arrive at the principle or concept by the process of *induction*. See also *inductive method, problem method*.

Discovision A widely-used *optical videodisc* system that was developed in the USA.

discrete variable 1. A *variable* in which the possible values change by discrete steps (eg by unity) with no intermediate values being possible; cf *continuous variable*. 2. Any clearly-identifiable changeable quantity in a experiment or study.

discriminating power Another name for *discrimination index*.

discrimination index A measure of the ability of a *multiple-choice item* to discriminate between good and bad students. It is equal to the difference between the *facility value* for the top third of the candidates in the test as a whole and that for the bottom third of the candidates. Also known as *discriminating power*.

discrimination learning One of the types of intellectual skill identified by Gagné. It involves the ability to make appropriate (different) *responses* to a series of *stimuli* that differ in a systematic way, eg in terms of a particular mental *factor*.

discriminative assessment Another term for *comparative assessment*.

disk 1. A magnetically-coated disk (or stacked system of disks) used for storage of *digital* data, eg in computer *backing stores*; see also *hard disk, floppy disk*. 2. See *digital optical disk*. (Note that the alternative spelling, *disc*, is also widely used.)

disk drive A *computer peripheral* using which data can be read into or out of a *hard disk* or *floppy disk*.

diskette A term that is usually reserved for a 5¼ inch *floppy disk*, although it is sometimes also applied to other disk sizes below 8″.

disk store A data storage system in which the data is held on a *hard disk* or *floppy disk*.

disk unit Another name for a *disk drive*.

dispersion 1. A statistical term for a quantitative measure of the spread of values in a distribution, eg the *standard deviation* or *range*. 2. Separation of light into its constituent wavelengths, eg on passing through a prism, or through a lens that has not been corrected for *chromatic aberration*.

display board, panel A flat vertical surface on to which opaque materials such as tables, graphs or charts can be pinned or stuck for display purposes. Also known as a *demonstration board*.

disputation A teaching or *assessment* technique (derived from medieval university practice) in which a student defends, in oral argument with instructors or examiners, an original piece of work (such as a *thesis*) that he/she has prepared.

dissemination Deliberately and systematically making others aware of a development by circulating information, running conferences or workshops, etc; cf *diffusion*.

dissertation See *thesis*.

dissolve A gradual transition between two visual *images* in which one fades out as the other fades in; cf *cut*.

distance education, learning, teaching An instructional system in which the learner is geographically remote from the body or person organizing the instruction, as, for example, in a *correspondence course*; cf *contiguous teaching*.

distractor A wrong answer in a *multiple-choice item*. Also known as a *decoy*. See also *non-functioning distractor*.

distributed practice Systematic incorporation of set rest periods into a learning sequence, or provision for rest periods to be undertaken by the learner as and when required.

ditto master Another name for a *hectograph master* (see *hectograph(ic) duplication*).

divergent thinking A creative approach to solving a problem or tackling a task that is aimed to produce a range of original solutions, procedures, etc; cf *convergent thinking*. See also *brainstorming*.

diverger A learner who is more proficient at *divergent thinking* than at *convergent thinking*; cf *converger*.

documentation In computing, a term for: 1. All the various *manuals, program* specifications, and other documents that the operators of a *computer* need to enable them to use the machine properly, 2. The various documents associated with a *software package*.

document reader A *computer terminal* that can read printed documents. See also *optical character recognition, magnetic ink character recognition*.

DOD See *digital optical disk*.

Dolby system An electronic system that is used to reduce high-frequency *noise* in *audio* recordings and transmissions. It involves artificially boosting the high frequencies in the signal prior to recording or transmission and then restoring the original balance during playback or post-reception decoding.

dolly 1. A moveable platform on which a film or television camera can be mounted in order to move it around a *set* during use; 2. To move a film or television camera towards the subject (*dolly-in*) or away from the subject (*dolly-out*) during a *shot*; cf *crab*.

dolly-in, dolly-out See *dolly*.

domain A limited but specified area of study or analysis related to: 1. Areas of learning (see *cognitive domain, affective domain, psychomotor domain*), or 2. A cluster of criteria (see *domain-referenced assessment*).

domain-referenced assessment A form of *criterion-referenced assessment* in which the assessment is associated with a group of criteria and is intended to overcome the problem of individual assessment items being related to more than one criterion (or *objective*).

dominoes test A type of *non-verbal intelligence test* that involves completing sequences of dominoes.

Donald Duck effect The increase in pitch and distortion that normally occur if a recording of speech is played back faster than the speed at which it was recorded. The effect can be avoided by making use of special equipment (see *compressed speech*).

doors See *barn doors*.

dot matrix printer A *printer* in which each character is made up of a series of dots produced by a pen (or set of pens) which moves across the paper. Such printers are widely used in *tractor-feed printers*. Also known as a *matrix printer*.

dotting test A test of the speed at which a person can tap dots with a pen or stylus or make patterns of dots on a moving piece of paper. It is used in personnel selection and aptitude testing.

double-band projector A *double system sound* film projector (usually 16 mm) that has separate linked channels for the picture film and the film that carries the *sound track*. See also *SEPMAG, SEPOPT*.

double-8 A type of *double run* motion picture film, 16 mm in width, which is slit down the middle after exposure to give a double length of *standard 8* or *super 8* film for projection.

double exposure The photographic recording of two (or more) sets of *images* on a single strip of *motion picture* film. The images may be either side-by-side (as, for example, in *double run* filming) or superimposed.

double-frame Another name for *full frame*, as applied to a *filmstrip*.

double (dual) projection A technique whereby two automatic *slide* projectors (which may be mounted side-by-side or one on top of the other) are operated through an electronic system that enables one slide in a sequence to be cross-faded into the next or allows instantaneous changeover between slides.

double run A term applied to a *motion picture* film that is first exposed down half its width and then reversed for exposure down the other half, eg *double-8* film.

double system sound The recording of *motion picture* images and sounds in synchronization but on separate media, usually using separate machines; cf *single system sound*. See also *SEPMAG, SEPOPT*.

down A term used to describe a *computer* or other system which is out of action due to malfunction, maintenance, etc.

down stage The performing area on a stage or *set* nearest to the camera or audience; cf *up stage*.

down-time The period (absolute or fractional) for which a *computer*, device or system is out of action (*down*) due to breakdown, routine maintenance, etc; cf *up-time*.

dowser A shutter in a projector or film printer used to shut off the light beam when not required.

draw-a-man test A *non-verbal intelligence test* for children that involves assessing the child's drawing of a human figure using a standard scoring system. Also known as the *Goodenough test*.

drexon A material used for storing optical data. It is used in *laser cards*, and can also be produced in tape and *disk* format.

drill An orderly, repetitive *learning* activity intended to help develop or reinforce a specific skill or aspect of knowledge. See also *drill and practice*.

drill and practice A method of *learning* and becoming familiar with the use of a procedure by repeating it over and over again until it is invariably performed correctly. This technique was used extensively in early *computer-assisted learning*, and is still widely used in *language laboratories*.

drive See *disk drive*.

drop-in In *audio recording*, insertion of a replacement section into an already-recorded tape by re-recording the section in question.

dropout A short loss of signal (or fall in signal strength) in a magnetic recording system due to temporary loss of contact between the *head* and the tape or faulty tape coating. See also *dropout compensator*.

dropout compensator A system that reduces the observable effect of *dropout* during the playback of a *videorecording* by repeating previously-stored *lines*.

drum 1. The rotating cylinder in a *helical-scanning* videotape recorder that carries the record/playback *heads* across the tape as it passes through the machine. 2. A rotatable cylinder round which a *motion picture* film with an *optical sound track* is passed during projection in order to control its speed.

dry carrel A 'bare' *carrel* which has no electrical connections and is fitted with no special equipment, being intended for individual study of *printed materials* only; cf *wet carrel*.

dry mounting A *mounting* process in which heat-sensitive intermediary paper is made to adhere both to the material being mounted (eg a *photograph*) and the material on which it is being mounted (eg a sheet of card) by the application of heat and pressure; cf *wet mounting*.

dry transfer lettering See *transfer lettering*.

dual 8 mm film projector An 8 mm film projector that is designed to project both *standard 8* and *super 8* films.

dual operation apparatus Instructional apparatus with two control systems, one operated by the learner and the other by the instructor, so that the latter can take over control from the former if necessary. It is used in training activities (such as flying training) that have an element of associated risk.

dubbing 1. Combining two or more *audio signals* into a composite recording. 2. Transferring an *audio signal* from one medium or machine to another. 3. Making a copy of a tape. 4. In film production, recording new dialog(ue) to be substituted for the original.

dumb terminal A *computer terminal* with no independent data processing capability; cf *intelligent terminal, smart terminal*.

dupe An abbreviation for *duplicate* (of a film, recording, etc).

duplicate An exact copy of a document, *slide, tape, film*, etc as opposed to the original.

dyad interaction A *group dynamics* term for an interaction involving only two people.

dynamic microphone A generic term for any *microphone* that works on electrodynamic principles, eg a *moving coil microphone* or *ribbon microphone*. Also known as an *electro-dynamic microphone*.

dynamic range The useable range between the *background noise* level of a system such as a *tape recorder* and the strongest signal that can be handled without distortion.

E

EA See *educational age*.

earphones Another name for *headphones*.

earplug A small *transducer* which fits directly into the ear, thus enabling the wearer to hear an *audio signal* fed into it.

easement A legal process whereby a *copyright holder* grants limited performance, reproduction, publication or other rights to another person, body, etc while still retaining ownership of the actual *copyright*.

EBR See *electron beam recording*.

echo 1. A single reflection of sound; cf *reverberation*. 2. An unwanted secondary television *image* produced by reflection of the *carrier wave* from a hill, building etc.

eclectic program(me) In *programmed instruction*, a *program(me)* that uses more than one type of programming technique.

edge numbers Groups of sequential numbers along the edge of a *motion picture* film at regular intervals — usually 1 foot apart. Also known as *footage numbers*.

edge stripe The narrow strip of magnetic oxide along one edge of a *COMMAG* motion picture film on which the *sound track* is recorded.

editing 1. Removing unwanted material from and/or inserting new material into a document, *file, computer program*, etc prior to storage, publication or use. 2. Selecting and rearranging recorded *audio signals* and/or *video signals* or *film* into a new continuity by manual or electronic means. See also *crash editing, electronic editing, editing 'in the camera', mechanical editing*.

editing bench A bench incorporating all the equipment need for the *mechanical editing* of

motion pictures of a particular *film gauge*.

editing block A device for cutting and splicing *audiotape* during *mechanical editing*.

editing 'in the camera' Shooting successive *scenes* of a *motion picture* in their script sequence, so that no further *editing* is required.

EDOD Erasable digital optical disk. A type of *digital optical disk* that is being developed as a possible replacement for *magnetic disks*. EDODs are being developed in a range of sizes, with storage capacities in the 40 *megabyte-gigabyte* range.

EDP See *educational development project, program(me)* or *electronic data processing*.

educational accountability 1. The principle that teachers and school systems may legitimately be held responsible for producing improvement in pupil achievement, and that such improvement can be measured by tests of teacher effectiveness. 2. The extent to which student performance is attributable to the nature and quality of the instructional process rather than to other factors such as maturing, selective admission, etc.

educational age (EA) Another term for *mental age*.

educational broadcast Any radio or television broadcast whose primary purpose is to contribute to the education of its listeners or viewers rather than to entertain.

educational development project, program(me) (EDP) A funded project or program(me) usually aimed at improving educational practice within a country, state, area, institution, etc. The 'National Development Programme in Computer-Assisted Learning' carried out in the UK during the mid

1970s was a typical example.

educational objectives The specific *objectives* which it is intended that a course, instructional program(me), exercise, etc should achieve. Largely as a result of the work of Bloom and his co-workers during the 1950s and 1960s, educational objectives are conventionally divided into three broad sets or *domains* — the *cognitive domain*, *affective domain* and *psychomotor domain* — although the addition of a fourth domain containing objectives associated with interpersonal and interactive skills has since been suggested.

educational quotient (EQ) A measure of a child's overall *mental ability* arrived at by dividing his/her *mental age* by his/her *chronological age*. See also *intelligence quotient (IQ)*.

educational station A US term for a radio or television station whose output is wholly or mainly devoted to *educational broadcasts*, and which accepts no advertising.

educational technology This has been 'officially' defined by a number of bodies, eg the Council for Educational Technology for the UK ('the development, application and evaluation of systems, techniques and aids to improve the process of human learning') and the (US) Commission on Instructional Technology ('a systematic way of designing, implementing and evaluating the total process of learning and teaching in terms of specific objectives, based on research in human learning and communication and employing a combination of human and non-human resources to bring about more effective instruction').

educational toy A play item which is capable of being used to develop educationally-useful skills rather than purely for recreational or pleasure purposes.

effects See *sound effects, special effects*.

effects box, generator Alternative names for a *special effects generator*.

egrul(e) An *inductive method* of instruction in which the learner is led through a series of examples (the 'eg's') before having to formulate the 'rule' that explains them or ties them together; cf *ruleg*.

EIAJ Electrical Industries Association of Japan. A body responsible for establishing standards in the field of *videotape* recording.

Most ½ inch and ¾ inch *videotape recorder* systems are based on EIAJ standards.

eidophor A type of *television projector* that first produces an intense primary *image* by electronic means and then projects this optically by means of a system of lenses similar to those used in a slide or film projector.

eight millimetre (8 mm) film A standard *gauge* of *motion picture* film 8 mm wide, with sprocket holes along only one edge. It is available in two formats — *standard 8* (or *regular 8*) and *super 8*.

eight track A term applied to an *audiotape* (usually in a *cartridge*) with eight separate *tracks* of sound recorded on it, or to a player or recorder used with such audiotapes.

electric board A generic term for a range of educational, training and demonstration devices that display questions on a board and employ simple electrical circuits to activate lights, buzzers, bells, etc when correct (or incorrect) *responses* are made to these questions. Also known as a *buzz board*.

electro-dynamic microphone Another name for a *dynamic microphone*.

electromagnetic loudspeaker Another name for a *moving coil loudspeaker*; cf *electrostatic loudspeaker*.

electromechanical A term applied to devices and systems (eg *tape recorders, record players, microphones* and *loudspeakers*) whose functions are accomplished by interrelated electrical/electronic and mechanical processes.

electron beam recording (EBR) A system of transferring a *video signal* directly on to *motion picture* film by means of an electron beam.

electronic blackboard A system which enables written text and/or drawings to be recorded in coded form on audiocassette together with an associated commentary. The material can be replayed via an ordinary television receiver or monitor using special playback and interfacing equipment.

electronic classroom A classroom (such as a *language laboratory*) in which instruction can be given to and *feedback* received from individual learners by electronic means, usually via individual *carrels* connected to a master *console* operated by the teacher or instructor.

electronic data processing (EDP) A general term for all forms of data processing that involve the use of electronic systems such as *computers*.

electronic editing 1. Audiotape *editing* that is carried out by *dubbing* recorded material from one tape recorder to another rather than by cutting and splicing the tape *(mechanical editing)*. 2. A form of videotape *editing* in which material is transferred from one *videorecorder* to another via special electronic equipment that ensures correct synchronization and compatibility; cf *crash editing*.

electronic flash A photographic flash system that produces repeated flashes using a special re-usable lamp. Electronic flash systems can be powered by ordinary batteries, rechargeable batteries or (in the case of large studio systems) the mains. They have largely replaced flash systems that use consumable *flash bulbs*.

electronic journal A journal that is produced and published using the methods of *electronic publishing* rather than by conventional publishing methods. Such journals are still at the experimental stage.

electronic mail A general term for systems that enable letters, memoranda, messages, etc to be sent from one individual, department, institution, etc to another solely by electronic means, without the use of a conventional postage or internal mail system. The most common type of electronic mail system is based on the use of a large multi-terminal *computer* or a *network* of *microcomputers*, and enables messages to be stored in each receiver's *file*, for perusal at a time convenient to the receiver. The use of such systems seems certain to increase dramatically during the later 1980's, both within individual organizations and between organizations.

electronic publishing The reproduction and distribution of documents using the electronic media of *new information technology* rather than by conventional printing and publishing methods. See also *electronic journal*.

electronic reproduction materials *Audiovisual materials* which rely on electronic means of reproduction for their use, eg *audiotapes* and *videorecordings*.

electronic stencil cutter An electronic device which can be used to produce *stencils* for use in *rotary stencil duplication* directly from line or tone illustrations, photographs, etc.

electronic video recording (EVR) A system developed during the mid-1960s for recording television signals on *film* in the form of optical *images* and playing them back via a special player connected to an ordinary television *receiver* or *monitor*. The system never achieved widespread use because of the appearance of inexpensive *videocassette recorders*.

electrostatic copying A reprographic process that first produces an electrostatically charged *image* of the original material on a plate or drum and then uses this to transfer pigment particles to the copy paper. Also known as *xerography*.

electrostatic loudspeaker A *loudspeaker* that operates on electrostatic rather than electromagnetic principles, its *transducer* mechanism consisting of an electrostatically-charged diaphragm (which may be several square feet in area) suspended between two perforated plates; cf *electromagnetic loudspeaker*.

electrostatic microphone Another name for a *condenser microphone*.

elliptic question A type of question (widely used in *program(m)ed instruction*) in which the learner is not asked a question directly but left to complete a statement by adding one or more missing words. See also *completion test*.

embossed screen A projection screen covered with raised dots of light-reflecting material, thus producing a high forward reflectivity. The *lenticular screen* is one common type.

emulsion The layer of photo-sensitive material on a *photographic film*, a *photographic plate* or *photographic paper* in which the *image* is produced.

emulsion speed Another term for *film speed*.

enabling objectives The component actions, skills, knowledge, etc that a learner must master or acquire in order to attain a specific *educational objective*.

enactive learning A term (first used by Olsen and Bruner) to denote *learning* through direct experience as opposed to learning via *media* of some sort *(mediated learning)*.

encryption Encoding of data to protect its privacy, particularly when being transmitted over public circuits or stored in a system such as a *computer* to which other users have access.

end spurt A final increase in effort or concentration made by an individual at the end of a learning sequence, shift, etc. See also *beginning spurt*.

end title The formal title which brings a *film, filmstrip, slide sequence*, television program(me), *computer-based learning* sequence, etc to a conclusion.

enhancement materials Instructional materials that are used to supplement the basic subject matter taught or studied in a course by extending the learner's knowledge, experience, etc in specific areas. Also known as *enrichment materials* and *extension materials*.

enlarger An optical device that can be used to produce *prints* or *transparencies* of increased or reduced size from an original transparency, which can be either *positive* or *negative*.

enrichment materials Another name for *enhancement materials*.

entry behavio(u)r The set of skills, *knowledge*, etc that a learner actually possesses at the time he/she enters or begins a course or program(me) of instruction; cf *assumed behavio(u)r, entry level performance*. Also known as *entry skills*.

entry level performance A set of statements specifying the prior skills and concepts necessary for entering a particular course or undertaking a particular learning task; cf *entry behavio(u)r*. Also known as *entry profile*. See also *assumed behavio(u)r*.

entry point Part of a system that is selected as a suitable place for introducing modifications to the system, eg because of its receptiveness to change or its key position in the system as a whole.

entry profile Another term for *entry level performance*.

entry skills Another term for *entry behavio(u)r*.

entry word The word by which an entry is positioned in a catalog(ue), bibliography, index, etc, usually the first word (other than the definite or indefinite article) of the heading or title.

epidiascope A device that can project *images* held on either opaque or transparent materials on to an external screen, ie a combined

episcope and *diascope*.

episcope A name for an *opaque projector* that is commonly used in the UK.

EPROM Erasable programmable read-only memory; A *PROM* (programmable read-only memory) from which the encoded *program* can be erased, thus allowing the device to be re-programmed; cf *read-only memory (ROM)*.

EQ See *educational quotient*.

equal-appearing interval scale Another name for an *interval scale*.

equalization A process whereby distortion of an *audio signal* or *video signal* is reduced by means of special electronic circuits that compensate for specific types of distortion, eg loss of *bass* in a recorded signal. See also *RIAA curve*.

equalizer An electronic device that enables the *balance* of an *audio signal* to be adjusted in a much finer way than is possible using ordinary bass and treble *tone controls*; typically this adjustment takes place octave by octave.

equivalency test A test that is used to measure the extent to which previous education or knowledge satisfies the *entry level performance* requirements of a given course.

equivalent form tests Tests which are similar in content and degree of difficulty, and which produce similar average *scores* and *variabilities* when used with similar *populations*.

equivalent groups Groups that yield essentially the same results when a particular *variable* or *factor* is measured or studied. Such groups are used as *experimental groups* and *control groups* in educational research, although they are sometimes difficult to find.

erase 1. In tape recording, to destroy the existing magnetic pattern on a magnetic tape using an *erase head* or *bulk eraser*. 2. In data processing, to empty a *store* of any existing data present in order to make it available for the storage of new data.

erase head The *head* in a *tape recorder* which removes any previous recording from the tape prior to new material being recorded via the *record head*.

ergonomics The application of anatomical, physiological and psychological knowledge and principles to the study of the relationship between man and all aspects of his work (environment, equipment, tasks, etc).

error rate In *programmed instruction*, the percentage of incorrect *responses* to an *item*, a set of items or an entire program(me). It is used as one of the criteria for determining whether the item, set of items or program(me) is satisfactory.

error score The difference between an individual's *raw score* in a test or *assessment* and his/her *true score*.

error variance The spread or *variance* of the *error scores* for all the people who undertake a test or other form of *assessment*.

essay test, examination A test or examination that involves writing essays on one or more topics. It assesses ability to discuss, evaluate, analyze, summarize, criticize, etc at speed.

establishing shot In film or television production, any *shot* that is used to orientate the audience with regard to some relevant aspect of the *action* (eg the time, the place, or the people involved). See also *re-establishing shot*.

ethnographic A term applied to an investigation, evaluation, study, etc where the investigator or evaluator attempts to become an integral part of the group being studied and approaches the work with as few preconceived ideas as possible. The investigator is also highly sensitive to those around him/her, appreciating that his/her presence may well influence people's behavio(u)r. See also *social/anthropological approach*.

ETV An abbreviation for educational television.

evaluation 1. A *cognitive* process which involves making judgements about the value or quality of ideas, works, solutions, methods, materials, etc for some specific purpose; the highest level (Level 6) of Bloom's *cognitive domain*. 2. A series of activities designed to determine the effectiveness or value of a course, instructional program(me), exercise, etc.

evaluation instrument Any method (eg a *questionnaire* or *structured interview*) by which information is obtained for the purpose of *evaluation*.

EVR See *electronic video recording*.

EWS See *experienced worker standard*.

examples class A teaching technique widely used in *tertiary education* establishments in which demonstrators, junior members of staff or (post)graduate students work through typical problems with small tutorial groups.

exciter lamp An incandescent lamp used as the light source for the sound scanning beam in an *optical sound projector*.

execute To carry out commands in a computer based system.

expectancy chart A chart which shows, in graphic form, the predicted level of attainment of a learner in different areas, based on his/her past record of *achievement*.

expendable materials Materials (such as exercise books, graph paper, chemicals and dissection samples) which are of necessity used up during a course, lesson, etc. Also known as *consumable materials*.

experience curve A type of *learning curve* which records improvement that takes place both during instruction and after formal instruction has been completed, eg when a trainee starts work in the job for which he has just been tained. Also known as an *improvement curve*.

experienced worker standard (EWS) An idealized statement of the *performance* of a trained and experienced worker that is used in setting standards and targets in industrial training.

experimental group The collection of subjects in a research sample that are actually subjected to *experimental treatment*; cf *control group*.

experimental treatment The conditions that are deliberately imposed on the *experimental group* in the course of an experiment or research study, eg manipulation of a particular *independent variable*.

expert system 1. A *computer* system which is programmed with all the knowledge that is currently available in a particular specialized field and is capable of making 'intelligent' evaluations; such systems are currently under active development. 2. Sometimes used as a synonym for an *artificial intelligence* system or intelligent learning system. Also known as a *knowledge based system.*

expert witness method A *group learning* technique in which students or trainees question or cross-examine one or more experts in a particular field.

expository display A display which simply presents information; cf *inquisitory display.*

expository organizer A preliminary lesson in which learners are introduced to material that is completely new and unfamiliar to them by using principles and concepts with which they are already familiar to form a '*cognitive* bridge' to the new material. See also *advance(d) organizer.*

expository teaching Teaching that is based on exposition, ie presentation of material to a class in a taught lesson, lecture, etc.

exposure 1. In photography, the process of subjecting a *photographic film*, a *photographic plate* or *photographic paper* to an amount of light that is sufficient to produce a *latent image* on the *emulsion*. 2. A measure of the total amount of light to which such a film, plate or paper has been subjected. See also *exposure index, exposure latitude, film speed.*

exposure index A number assigned to a *photographic film* by the manufacturer in order to indicate the *film speed*, and thus give guidance as to which combination of *shutter speed* and *f-number* should be used in given light conditions.

exposure latitude The range of *exposures* over which a particular *photographic film, photographic plate* or *photographic paper* will give an acceptable *image.*

exposure meter An instrument for determining the intensity of light incident on a camera from a scene or object to be photographed, filmed, etc. Such devices are now generally incorporated into the actual camera.

extension materials 1. Materials designed for use in *extension studies.* 2. Another name for *enhancement materials.*

extension studies 1. Studies that are designed to extend the normal range of treatment of a subject and/or allow for the pursuit of appropriate related interests by the students. 2. Teaching, instruction or training that is provided by an educational establishment for people other than its own regular students.

extension tube A threaded tube or ring which enables the lens to be mounted at a greater distance from the *image plane* of a camera than normal, thus increasing the *back focus* and enabling the camera to operate at a shorter object distance (hence producing a greater *image* size) than would otherwise be possible (see figure 17).

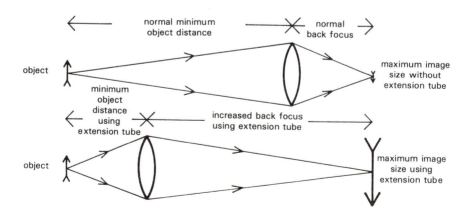

Figure 17 Use of a lens extension tube for close-up photography

external memory, store A *computer store* (such as a *disk store* or *tape store*) that is external to the actual *computer*.

external validity In research, the extent to which experimental results obtained by studying a particular *population* can legitimately be generalized to other populations of interest or to a wider population; cf *internal validity*.

extinction 1. A *behavio(u)ral psychology* term for the elimination or progressive reduction in magnitude or frequency of a *conditioned response* upon the withdrawal of *reinforcement*. 2. The disappearance of learned content from *memory* over a period of time.

extraneous variable In experimental research, an uncontrolled *variable*, sometimes unforeseen, which may influence the relationship between the particular *dependent variable* and *independent variable* that are under consideration.

extreme close-up Another name for a *big close up*.

eye light In photographic, film or television work, a special source of illumination that is introduced in order to produce desirable reflections from the eyes and teeth of a subject without substantially affecting the overall lighting conditions. It is usually a small *spotlight*.

extrinsic motivation The use of artificially-introduced *rewards* or *punishments* in an instructional program(me) in order to increase learner motivation; cf *intrinsic motivation*.

F

face validity Acceptance of the apparent suitability of a test or study for measuring that which it purports to measure without carrying out systematic objective investigations to determine whether this assumption is justified. See also *content validity*.

facilitator A leader of a group discussion or other group learning activity whose main function is to act as a catalyst in stimulating discussion rather than to provide the group with information. The term is also applied to someone who fulfils a similar role in situations where *illuminative evaluation* is being carried out.

facility index, value The fraction (expressed as a decimal between 0 and 1) of candidates choosing the correct answer (the *key*) in a *multiple-choice item*. Ideally, it should be between 0.35 and 0.85, the item being too difficult (or too ambiguous) if it is less than the former and too easy if it is greater than the latter.

facsimile An exact copy or likeness, eg of a document.

facsimile transmission (fax) An electronic system whereby a *facsimile* of a document can be produced at a distance. In such a system, the original (eg a signed document, drawing or photograph) is scanned and its contents converted into coded electronic signals. These are transmitted via a communications channel of some sort, and, at the receiving end, are used to drive a *printer* that produces the required facsimile.

factor A hypothetical entity (such as a skill, mental ability or personality trait) that is assumed to underlie and influence a *psychological test* such as an *intelligence test*. See also *factor analysis*.

factor analysis A statistical technique for analyzing patterns of *correlation* between the results of different *psychological tests* and describing the results in terms of the minimum possible number of *factors*. It is used in the measurement of *intelligence* and personality.

faculty development Another term for *staff development*.

fade A controlled decrease or increase in the strength of an *audio signal, video signal* or *television signal*, a projected *image*, etc. See also *fade-in, fade-out*. Should not be confused with *fading*.

fade-in The gradual appearance of a *video signal* or projected *image*, or an increase in strength of an *audio signal*; cf *fade-out*.

fade-out The gradual disappearance of a *video signal* or projected *image*, or a decrease in strength of an *audio signal*; cf *fade-in*.

fader A control used to produce *fade* effects.

fading 1. In *programmed instruction*, the gradual removal of the *prompts* in a sequence of *items* teaching a particular topic. Such sequences typically start with strongly-prompted items and end with items that are completely unprompted. Should not be confused with *vanishing*. 2. In radio and television reception, variation of the strength of a received signal due to changes in the propagation conditions. Should not be confused with *fade*.

fast film A *photographic film* with a high *film speed*.

fast forward A facility on a *tape recorder* or *audiotape player* for winding the tape rapidly forward. See also *fast (picture) search*.

fast motion Passage of a *film* through a *motion picture camera* at slower than the normal rate during *exposure* so that the action appears to be speeded up when the processed film is projected at normal speed. Also known as *undercranking*.

fast (picture) search A facility on a *videotape recorder* whereby the tape can be run forwards or backwards at high speed while still showing the pictures, thus enabling a desired point in the program(me) to be rapidly located.

fax See *facsimile transmission*.

feedback 1. In *programmed instruction*, the information supplied to a learner immediately after his/her *response* to an *item* which indicates whether or not the response was correct. 2. Communication of *responses* to a teacher by learners, as in a *feedback classroom*. 3. In general, the return of part of a system's output in such a way that it influences the input. See also *negative feedback, positive feedback*.

feedback classroom A type of *electronic classroom* where the teacher can monitor the *responses* of the students to *multiple-choice questions* or similar *items*.

feedforward A term applied to a systematic approach to instruction that is built round clearly-defined *objectives*, the instruction being based on these objectives and its success (or otherwise) being evaluated using the objectives as criteria.

feed reel, spool The *reel* (*spool*) from which film or tape is fed into a camera, projector, *tape recorder*, etc; cf *take-up reel, spool*. Also known as a *delivery reel, spool, supply reel, spool*.

feltboard A flat display surface covered with felt, flannel or similar material on to which pictures, symbols or shapes backed with the same or similar material will adhere. Also known as a *flannel board* or *flannelgraph*.

fibreoptic (fiberoptic) cable A type of signal-carrying cable in which the signal propagates along a narrow optical fibre (fiber) in the form of light rather than along an electrical conductor in the form of an electrical or conventional electromagnetic signal. Because of the extremely high frequency of light compared with that of electrical or conventional electromagnetic signals, such cables have a much greater signal-carrying capacity than electrical cables.

fibrevision (fibervision) A recently-developed

type of *cable television* system that makes use of *fibreoptic (fiberoptic) cables* to distribute the signal to users.

field In television picture production, a single complete scanning of the picture from top to bottom. Two interlaced fields are required to complete a *frame* of the picture, so that each field scans 312½ lines of a 625 line picture and 262½ lines of a 525 line picture. See also *interlaced scanning*.

field test, trial A trial run of a near-final system (eg an instructional program(me), exercise or instructional package) in the conditions in which the system is designed to be used. Such trials are often carried out to determine the *target population* with which the system is likely to be successful or useful.

fifth-generation computer A term applied to the new type of *computers* currently being developed to act as *expert systems*. It is hoped that such computers will display advanced *artificial intelligence* of a type that it has not so far proved possible to achieve; cf *first-generation computer, second-generation computer, third-generation computer, fourth-generation computer*.

figure-of-eight microphone Another name for a *bi-directional microphone*, the name being derived from the shape of its *polar diagram* (see figure 9 on page 22).

file 1. An assembly of documents fastened together or placed in the same container for archival or other purposes. 2. A computer program, collection of data, section of word processor text, etc that is stored on a *disk*.

fill light A secondary lighting source used to fill in shadow areas. It is usually placed roughly opposite or to the side of the *key light*, so that it fills in any strong shadows produced by this.

film 1. A general term for a thin layer of *emulsion* carried on a transparent flexible *base*. 2. A long strip of such material used for making *motion pictures*, or the completed motion picture itself. 3. A thin layer of material that is superimposed on another material, eg *frisket film, laminating film, transfer film*.

film chain A system comprising one or more fixed television cameras and appropriate projectors that is used to transmit projected materials (eg photographic *slides, frames* of *filmstrips* or *motion picture* sequences) into a television system. Also called a *telecine chain*.

film clip A short *motion picture* sequence that is used as an insert in a television or other program(me). Also called a *film insert*.

film gauge The width of a *motion picture* film or *photographic film*. The most commonly used gauges are 8 mm, 16 mm, 35 mm and 70 mm.

filming speed The rate (number of *frames* per second —*fps*) at which a *motion picture* film is run through the camera during *exposure*, usually 24 fps for sound films and 18 fps for silent films. Also called *camera speed*. Should not be confused with *film speed*.

film insert Another name for a *film clip*.

film loop Another name for a *loop film*.

filmograph A *motion picture* sequence made by filming motionless objects or systems using a *motion picture camera*, often employing *special effects*. Such sequences are often incorporated in motion picture films.

film speed The sensitivity of a *photographic film*, as measured using a standard scale such as *ASA, DIN* or *ISO*. Also known as *emulsion speed*. Should not be confused with *filming speed*.

filmstrip A strip of 35 mm *film* carrying a sequence of *positive* photographic images designed for projection or individual viewing. Such filmstrips can have two basic formats, namely *full frame* (in which the longer side of each 35 mm frame is parallel to the edge of the film) and *half frame* (where the frames are only half the size of a normal 35 mm frame, with the longer side at right angles to the edge of the film).

filter 1. A general term for any device or system with selective transmission properties. 2. In *programmed instruction*, a test which determines the future route of the learner. See also *gate frame* 3. A piece of tinted or treated glass or special plastic used to alter the quality of the light entering an optical system such as a camera or leaving a light source such as a *luminaire*. 4. An electronic circuit designed to let through or stop electrical signals in a certain frequency range.

fine control sensitivity A person's ability to make delicately-controlled muscular adjustments, particularly of large groups of muscles. One of the *psychomotor skills* that are

important in certain skilled occupations and are assessed using appropriate *aptitude tests*; cf *finger dexterity*.

finger dexterity A person's ability to make controlled manipulative movements with the fingers. One of the *psychomotor skills* that are important in certain skilled occupations and are assessed using appropriate *aptitude tests*; cf *fine control sensitivity*.

finger reading Reading by touch, as in the braille system.

firmware A term applied to a *computer program* that is recorded in a storage medium from which it cannot be accidentally erased, or to an electronic device containing such a program, eg a *ROM, PROM* or *EPROM*; cf *software*.

first-generation computer A term applied to any *computer* based on the technology of electronic *valves* (*vacuum tubes*). All the early computers, built during the late 1940s and 1950s were of this type; cf *second-generation computer, third-generation computer, fourth-generation computer, fifth-generation computer*.

fishbowl session A group discussion technique in which part of a class or group sit in an inner circle and hold a discussion while the remaining members sit around the outside and observe the proceedings. This is generally followed by a plenary discussion between the two groups, after which the roles are often reversed for a further session.

fisheye lens A *wide angle lens* with an extremely short *focal length* and abnormally wide *acceptance angle*. It is used for taking extra-wide-angle *shots*.

fishpole A hand-held microphone *boom*, typically of the order of 2 metres (meters) in length.

fixed focus A term applied to a camera in which the *back focus* cannot be varied, being set so as to give maximum *depth of field*. Many inexpensive cameras are of this type.

fixed-response item An *item* in an *objective test* or *programmed instruction* sequence which provides all the options from which the testee or learner must make his/her selection; cf *free response item*. Also known as a *forced-choice item*.

fixed tracking Use of tightly-structured,

inflexible program(me)s of study in a course, so that students have little or no scope for individual curriculum selection.

flannel board, flannelgraph Alternative names for a *feltboard*.

flare Unwanted exposure of part(s) of a *photographic film* due to internal reflections between lens components, 'leaky' camera turrets, doors or magazines, etc.

flash bulb An expendable bulb used to produce a single bright flash of light for photographic purposes. It has now been largely superseded by *electronic flash*.

flashcard A card or other opaque material carrying words, pictures or other information designed to be displayed briefly, usually by hand, during a lesson.

flat response The ability of a signal-handling system (especially an *audio* system or a component thereof) to handle all the frequencies that it is designed to handle without changing their relative strengths.

Flesch formula A standard formula that is used to give a quantitative measure of the *readability* of textual material based on the number of syllables in a typical sample of 100 words and the number of sentences (including any incomplete sentence) in the sample. It gives values of 'reading ease' that range from roughly 100 (very easy) to 0 (very difficult). See also *Cloze test, fog index*.

flexible curve Another name for an *adjustable curve*.

flexible schedule A system where the working day can be organized on an 'ad hoc' basis in order to meet particular instructional needs as opposed to one where instruction has to be fitted into a rigid timetable. Such a system enables the lengths and frequencies of teaching periods to be varied, and also enables different sizes of teaching group to be catered for.

flexicurve Another name for an *adjustable curve*.

flexistudy An *individualized learning* system in which students are provided with learning materials for home study, counsel(l)ing, tutorial support and access to college facilities (such as library, laboratory and *computer* facilities) as and when required. Flexistudy-type courses are becoming increasingly widely used in the UK,

particularly by the further education sector.

flicker Short-period variations, either of a regular or random nature, in the *luminous intensity* of a screen, eg during the projection of a *motion picture*.

flip chart A set of large sheets of paper attached to an easel unit so that they can be flipped over the top of the unit into or out of view as a presentation progresses.

flippy A term that is sometimes used to denote a double-sided *floppy disk*.

floating point notation A method of representing numbers by a decimal number (usually with a single digit before the point) multiplied by a power of ten, so that 324 million (for example) is expressed as 3.24×10^8. Many *computers* and electronic calculators display numbers in this way, converting them into standard notation by 'floating' the point to the appropriate position — hence the name. Also known as *scientific notation*.

flood, floodlight A *luminaire* that gives a wide spread of light, and can thus be used to illuminate a large area of a *studio, set*, etc.

floppy disk A small magnetically-coated *disk* used as a medium for storing data, eg as a computer *backing store*. Floppy disks come in various sizes, the most common being 8 inch, 5¼ inch, 3½ inch and 3 inch, and are relatively inexpensive, although they have much smaller storage capacities than *hard disks*. 5¼ inch floppy disks are sometimes referred to as *mini-floppy disks* or *diskettes*, while 3 inch or 3½ inch disks are sometimes referred to as *micro-floppy disks* or *minidisks*. See also *flippy*.

flow chart, diagram A graphical representation of the successive stages of a process or system, showing how each part relates to the whole. Such charts are used in a wide range of fields, including computer programming (where they are used to show the main structural units of *programs*), instructional design (eg for showing the various *modules* of a course or the various sections or frames of an instructional program(me)), work study, and planning. A typical flow chart (of a *computer based learning* program(me)) is shown in figure 18. See also *algorithm*.

fluorescent chalk Special chalk that becomes luminescent in a darkened room under ultra-violet lighting.

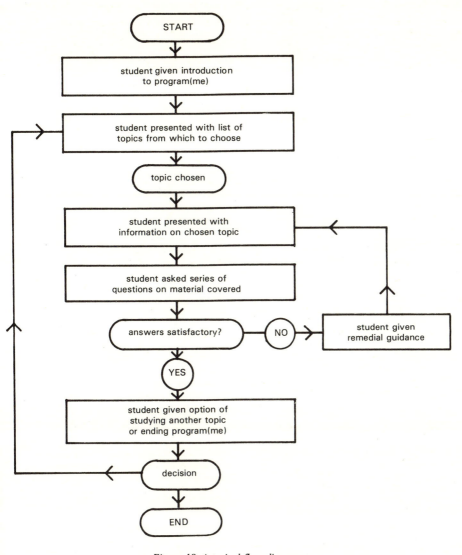

Figure 18 A typical flow diagram

flutter Periodic variations in the operating speed of a recording or playback system with a frequency above 10 Hz; cf *wow*.

FM See *frequency modulation*.

f-number A measure of the effective *aperture* size of a lens system, calculated by dividing the *focal length* of the lens by the aperture diameter.

focal length Loosely taken to mean the distance from a lens to its *focal plane* — the plane in which parallel light incident on the lens is brought to a *focus* (see figure 19). More precisely, used to describe the distance from the rear nodal point of a lens or lens system to the rear *focal plane*; cf *back focus*.

focal plane See *focal length*.

focus 1. To adjust an optical or optico-electronic system so that the *image* is sharply defined, ie is *in focus*. 2. The position in such

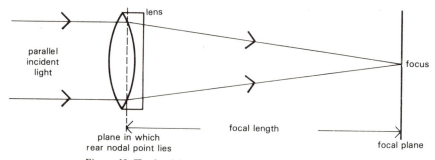

Figure 19 The focal length and focal plane of a lens

a system at which the sharpest *image* is formed (see figure 19).

fog Unwanted additional density in a processed photographic *image* caused by accidental exposure to light prior to or during *processing* or exposure to a chemical fogging agent.

fog index A quantitative measure of the *readability* of textual material based on the average sentence length and percentage of long and/or difficult words that it contains. One version, known as the *modified fog index*, gives a direct measure of the *reading age* of the material. See also *Cloze test, Flesch formula*.

foil 1. Another term for a *distractor*. 2. A term sometimes used to describe the acetate sheet used in the preparation of *OHP transparencies*.

follow-up activities Additional and/or enrichment activities that are used to build upon the work of a lesson, the content of a program(me), etc.

font Originally a set of printer's type of uniform style and size. It has now been extended to denote a particular alphanumeric *character set* available within a system such as a *visual display unit* or *word processor*.

foot The standard unit of *motion picture* film length, comprising 72 frames of 8 mm film, 40 frames of 16 mm film and 16 frames of 35 mm film.

footage numbers The *edge numbers* on a *motion picture* film.

forced-choice item Another name for a *fixed-response item*. Should not be confused with *forced-choice technique*

forced-choice technique A technique that is employed in the design of tests and *questionnaires* in order to counteract the

tendency to select *responses* which show up the respondee in the best possible light.

forcing A technique in *programmed instruction* whereby *prompts* are used to make it almost certain that the learner gives the required *response*.

forgetting curve A graphical representation of the rate at which recall of learned material degenerates (in the absence of *reinforcement*) until the material is completely forgotten.

formal prompt (cue) In *behavio(u)ral psychology* or instructional design, a *prompt (cue)* which provides information about the form of the expected *response*, by for example, providing the initial letter and/or number of letters of a required word, as in 'The capital city of France is P___'; cf *thematic prompt (cue)*.

format 1. The style or method of presentation 2. The configuration of any information-carrying system.

formative evaluation *Evaluation* of instructional program(me)s or materials that is carried out while they are still in the process of development; cf *summative evaluation*.

form perception test A test designed to measure *spatial ability*.

forward branching In *programmed instruction, branching* in which the learner is sent forward by several *frames* if he/she makes a correct *response*. Also known as *skip branching* or *washahead*.

fotonovella A narrative technique based on the use of a sequence of photographs with text superimposed as in a strip cartoon. Also known as *photonovel*.

foundation course, studies A course or program(me) of studies designed to provide a basis for more advanced or specialized studies.

four-look system A method of instruction used in a number of US colleges and universities whereby new material is first studied by making notes from a *textbook*, then taught in a formal lesson, then reinforced by further study of the textbook and class notes, and finally used on the basis of a student *assignment*.

fourth-generation computer A term applied to a *computer* based on the technology of integrated circuits. Such computers, which started to be built in the late 1970s, are much more compact than earlier computers and also have much greater calculating powers than earlier machines of comparable price; cf *first-generation computer*, *second-generation computer*, *third-generation computer*, *fifth-generation computer*.

four track A synonym for *quarter track*, as applied to an *audiotape* or *tape recorder*.

fps frames per second — the standard unit of *motion picture camera* or motion picture projector speed.

frame 1. An individual picture in a *photographic film*, *filmstrip* or *motion picture*. 2. In television, the picture formed by a pair of interlaced *fields*; see also *interlaced scanning*. 3. In *viewdata* or *computer-based learning*, a single screenful of information. 4. In *programmed learning*, one of the discrete stages (or *steps*) into which the instructional sequence is broken down. 5. A holder in which a transparency, photograph, etc is set for display purposes. See also *gate frame*, *practice frame*, *teaching frame*, *test frame*.

frame game A type of *game* or *simulation* which is structured in such a way that a variety of roles, ideas and relationships may be built in as and when required or appropriate.

frame lines The dark lines between the *frames* of a *filmstrip*, *motion picture* or exposed *photographic film*.

frame synchronizer A facility in a *video* system whereby a single *frame* of video sequence can be stored for display as a *still frame* in synchrony with the rest of the sequence.

framing Adjusting the film position in the *aperture* of a film or filmstrip projector so that the *image* is vertically centred (centered) on the screen.

free group discussion A group discussion in which the specific topics covered and the direction that the discussion takes are largely controlled by the participants rather than by the person in charge of the group; cf *controlled discussion*.

free-response item An *item* in a test or *programmed instruction* sequence in which the choice of *responses* is not limited as in a *fixed-response item*, the respondee being free to make any response that satisfies set criteria.

freeze frame A technique for stopping the action of a *motion picture* sequence by repeating the same *frame* as often as is necessary. Also called *hold frame* or *stop frame*.

French curve Another name for an *adjustable curve*.

frequency distribution A tabulation of the *scores* achieved or recorded in a test or study showing the numbers of occurrences of successive scores or the numbers of scores falling in different intervals. This is often presented in graphical form, eg as a *histogram* or *frequency polygon* (see figure 10 on page 23).

frequency-division multiplexing A form of *multiplexing* in which several different signals are transmitted down the same communication channel by using a different part of the bandwidth of the *carrier wave* or *carrier signal* to carry each; cf *time-division multiplexing*.

frequency modulation (FM) Adding a signal to a *carrier wave* or *carrier signal* by causing the frequency of the latter to vary in correspondence with the amplitude of the signal to be carried. The abbreviation 'FM' is widely used to denote systems or devices (such as channels in radio *receivers*, or the receivers themselves) that handle signals modulated in this way; cf *amplitude modulation*.

frequency polygon A graphical representation of a *frequency distribution* in which the number of scores in each frequency interval is plotted as a series of horizontal lines, these then being joined by vertical lines along the boundaries between the intervals to form a polygon — see figure 10 on page 23 for a typical example.

frequency range Another term for *bandwidth*.

frequency response A detailed (usually graphical) description of the performance of a recording or reproduction system (or a component thereof) at different frequencies throughout the *frequency range* handled (see figure 20).

the same side as the *projector*; cf *back projection*.

frosted acetate *Acetate* sheet with a frosted (*matt*) finish on one side, so that material can be written or drawn on it more easily.

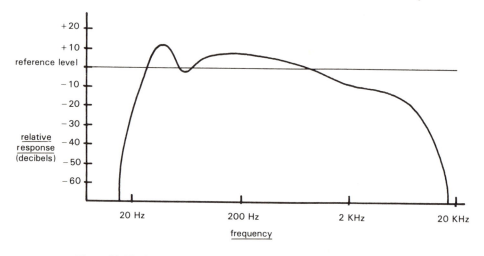

Figure 20 The frequency response curve of a (hypothetical) loudspeaker system

Fresnel lens A lens consisting of concentric stepped rings, each of which is a section of a convex surface. It is widely used as a *condenser lens* in *overhead projectors* and *spotlights*.

frieze A long *wallchart* on which scenes, images, etc are built up.

fringing False colo(u)ration around an *image* produced by a faulty or poorly-adjusted optical system, eg one that is not corrected for *chromatic aberration*.

frisket A *stencil* or *mask* which is placed on a *photograph*, piece of *artwork*, etc in order to protect certain areas during air brushing, aerosol can spraying, or similar processes.

frisket film Thin, self-adhesive *film* that can be cut up to make *friskets*.

front-end processor A separate processing system (such as an *analog-to-digital converter* or *microcomputer*) that is used to pre-process signals or data before they are fed into a *computer*.

front projection Projection of an *image* on to the front of an opaque *screen*, for viewing from

F-test A statistical test used in analyzing data, eg for determining whether two *populations* have equal *variances* by testing specific *samples* from each, or for testing the *statistical significance* of an observed *correlation coefficient*.

full frame A term applied to a *filmstrip* in which the horizontal axis of the *frames* is parallel to the length of the film; cf *half-frame*. Also known as *double-frame*.

full track A term applied to an *audiotape* with a single recording *track* covering almost the entire width of the tape.

functional relationship A situation in which two or more *variables* are known to be related, but in which causation is not implied; cf *causal relationship*.

fused curriculum A *curriculum* which combines two or more subjects and studies their inter-relationship.

G

gain 1. In general terms, the difference between the output and input levels of a system. 2. The ratio of the output signal level of a sytem such as an *amplifier* or *aerial* to the input signal level, usually expressed in *decibels*.

gain ratio A statistical coefficient that measures the *gain* achieved by an individual or system, eg the difference between a learner's *pre-test* and *post-test* scores divided by the pre-test score. See also *gain score*.

gain score The measured amount of favo(u)rable change in an individual in respect of some trait or *variable* brought about by treatment or instruction, eg the difference between a learner's *pre-test* and *post-test* scores. See also *gain ratio*.

game In an instructional context, any exercise that involves competition (either between participants or against the game system) and rules (arbitrary constraints within which the participants have to operate). See also figure 49 on page 178.

game chain A sequence of inter-related *games* where the end point or output of one becomes the starting point or input of the next member of the sequence.

Gantt chart A type of *bar chart* in which actual *performance* is plotted against target performance. Such charts are used in the planning and monitoring of *projects*.

gap See *head gap*.

garbage A computing term for incorrect, corrupted or meaningless data, *programs*, etc. See also *GIGO*.

gate 1. The *aperture* in *motion picture* equipment through which the film is exposed or projected. 2. The assembly that supports and positions the *slide* in a slide projector or the

frame being shown in a *filmstrip* projector. 3. A technical term for an electronic switching circuit. 4. A technical term for the codes or *software* which enable a user to access one *computer* system from another (eg when using *videotex(t)*). 5. See *gate frame*.

gate frame In *programmed instruction*, a *frame* in a *branching program(me)* that poses a key question, the answer to which determines the next frame to which the user is routed. See also *filter '2.'*.

gauge See *film gauge*.

Gaussian distribution (curve) A symmetrical, bell-shaped distribution curve first described by the nineteenth-century mathematician C.F. Gauss. The term is commonly used as a synonym for the *normal distribution (curve)*, which is shown in figure 32 on page 115.

gelatin duplication Another name for *hectograph(ic) duplication*.

general intelligence, mental ability The overall *intelligence* or mental ability possessed by an individual, as opposed to some specific aspect thereof (eg *numerical ability* or *verbal ability*). It is the basic *factor* that is assumed to underlie a wide range of *psychological tests*. See also *intelligence quotient*.

general purpose language A computer *programming language* whose use is not restricted to a single type of computer or to a small range of computers; examples are BASIC, COBOL, FORTRAN and PASCAL.

generation 1. A term used to denote the 'nearness to the original' of a series of copies of a film or tape, the original *master* film or tape being denoted 'first generation', a copy made directly from this as 'second generation', a copy made from this as 'third generation', and so on. 2. The production of *graphic* *materials* on a *visual display unit* using a *computer*.

generative CAL A type of *computer-assisted learning (CAL)* system in which a set of basic *algorithms* is provided for the teacher, who can make use of these to generate a wide range of specialized program(me)s geared to meet the needs of particular groups or to fit into particular courses.

genlock An electronic device that enables two or more *television signals* to be kept properly synchronized with one another, eg during multi-camera production, or *editing*.

geomatrix item, question An *item* (question) which incorporates a range of potential statements/answers from which the learner has to select those that seem relevant to the problem; it may also incorporate rows or columns relating to the level of difficulty of the learning materials, confidence levels of answers, etc. Such items are usually computer marked. See also *structural communication test*.

geometric mean See *mean*.

Gesell observation dome A chamber fitted with two-way mirrors through which subjects can be observed in particular situations or activities without being aware of the presence of observers. It is used in studying the behavio(u)r of young children, mentally retarded individuals, etc.

ghost, ghosting 1. A faint *image* that remains on a *chalkboard, markerboard*, etc after material has been rubbed or wiped off. 2. A secondary *image* on a television screen, caused by poor reception conditions or faulty equipment. 3. A double *image* produced by a faulty shutter mechanism during the projection of a *motion picture*.

gigabyte A unit of data size or data storage capacity equivalent to 10^9 (ie 1000 million) *bytes*; cf *kilobyte, megabyte*.

GIGO Garbage in; garbage out. A term used in computing to stress the fact that a *computer* will only produce a meaningful output if the information that is fed into it is meaningful, in the correct format, and free from programming errors.

glitch 1. A brief interruption or disturbance of the operation of a system such as a *computer* or *videoplayer*; cf *crash, hang-up*; see also *bug*. 2.

A flaw in a television picture consisting of a narrow horizontal bar moving vertically through the picture.

global learning *Learning* material as a whole unit rather than by splitting it up into managable sections as in *part learning*. Also known as *whole-part learning*. See also *holist*.

glossy A term used to describe *photographic paper* or other paper with a shiny surface; cf *matt(e)*.

goal A general statement of intent or aspiration; virtually synonymous with *aim*.

goal analysis A procedure for identifying indicators or behavio(u)rs which would be recognizable as evidence that a particular *goal* has in fact been achieved.

goal-free evaluation *Evaluation* in which the evaluator simply assesses the apparent effects of a program(me), course, etc without reference to the *aims* and *objectives* thereof. He/she may also attempt to deduce its *goals* for subsequent comparison with those specified by the designer.

goal specification Detailed specification of the desired outcomes of a program(me), course, etc prior to the implementation or use thereof.

gold transfer foil Thin gold leaf that can be transferred to *lettering*, embellishments, illustrations, etc by application of pressure and heat.

golf ball (printer) A *printer* system (used in typewriters, computer printers, etc) that employs interchangeable spherical *heads* each of which carries a particular *character set*.

Goodenough test Another name for the *draw-a-man test*.

graded approach A method of instruction that involves presenting materials, tasks, lessons, etc in progressively more difficult stages. See also *graded difficulty*.

graded difficulty A term applied to a series of tasks that are deliberately made progressively more difficult in order to extend a learner's capabilities gradually. This technique is commonly used in *programmed instruction*.

graded tests A hierarchy of tests that are increasingly demanding in terms of the skills that are assessed, eg the standard series of tests that are taken by pupils learning to play a musical instrument such as the piano.

grading on the curve A form of *norm-referenced assessment* in which grades or marks are allocated to students in a class or large group in such a way that they conform as closely as possible to a *normal distribution*.

graininess In photography, the tendency of the chemicals in the *emulsions* of *fast films* to gather into 'clumps' during *development*, thus reducing the *resolution* of the final *image* by producing a pattern of small dots or 'grains'.

gramophone A (somewhat old-fashioned) UK term for a *record player*, the equivalent US term being *phonograph*.

gramophone record A (somewhat old-fashioned) UK term for an *audio disc*.

graph A diagram that uses dots, bars, lines or other symbols to represent and display visually the relationship between an *independent variable* (which is usually plotted horizontally) and one or more *dependent variables* (usually plotted vertically) — see figure 20 on page 70 for a typical example. See also *band curve graph, histogram, historigram, scattergram, zone curve graph*.

graphic (graphical) material(s), graphics A general term for two-dimensional illustrative or representational material(s), and for *artwork, captions, lettering, photographs* etc that are incorporated into a presentation of some sort.

graphicacy A term suggested by Balchin to denote the graphical equivalent of 'literacy' and 'numeracy', ie the ability to think and visualize in graphical, pictorial and spatial terms and to communicate such ideas and concepts to others.

graphical plotter An electro-mechanical device that can draw *graphs*, diagrams, etc when fed with suitable signals from a *computer* or similar system. Also called an *autoplotter*.

graphics table, tablet A sensitive surface over which a device can be moved by hand in order to draw graphics and shade or fill in the spaces. Also known as a *data tablet*.

graphics terminal A general name for a *computer terminal* on which *graphical materials* can be created, altered, displayed, etc. See also *graphics tablet*.

grey scale 1. The variation in tonal value from white, through different shades of grey, to black on the screen of a *monochrome* television set. 2. A standard test chart incorporating such a scale.

grid paper Drawing paper with precision-printed grid lines.

group dynamics 1. The methods by which a group of people function as a collective, integrated whole. 2. The field of study that is concerned with such methods.

group examination An examination in which a number of specified subjects or papers have to be passed at a single sitting. Should not be confused with a *group test*.

grouping 1. In instructional organization, allocating learners into groups, bands, streams, etc for various purposes, eg for *group teaching*. 2. A term used in perception theory to denote the tendency to see objects as groups rather than as isolated elements.

group instruction The act of attempting to teach a number of learners the same lesson at the same time. Should not be confused with *group learning, group teaching or team teaching*.

group learning *Learning* that takes place through some form of interactive small-group activity, eg in a *fishbowl session* or *simulation*. Should not be confused with *group instruction* or *group teaching*.

group project A *project* that is carried out by a group of people working cooperatively rather than by individuals working independently. Also known as a *team project*.

grouprogram A *group learning* technique that uses an *audiotape* to provide a structure and input to, and also to regulate the timing of, a group activity of some sort (eg a *simulation* exercise or discussion).

group teaching Dividing a class of pupils into groups according to some aspect(s) of their ability, and then teaching them in these groups. Should not be confused with *group instruction, group learning or team teaching*.

group test 1. A test that is designed to give information about a group of people rather than about the individual members of the group. 2. A test that is administered to a number of subjects simultaneously, as opposed to an *individual test*. Should not be confused with a *group examination*.

group training A general term for training in which the trainees work in groups, either to receive instruction (as in *group teaching*) or to carry out some form of *group learning* or *group project*.

g-test A test of overall mental ability, ie of *general intelligence*.

guided decision making A system of learning where students are given a progressively demanding series of carefully-designed open-ended problems to solve, so that they are helped to develop decision-making skills as they do so.

guided discovery learning A form of *discovery learning* in which the activities of the learner are partly structured by the teacher in order to help ensure that the former achieves the desired *objectives*.

guided reading Another term for *directed reading*.

guided response A *psychomotor* process that involves carrying out a particular psychomotor activity under direct or indirect guidance; Level 3 of Harrow's *psychomotor domain*.

guide path The system of wheels, posts and guides that define the path of the tape through a *tape recorder* or *audiotape player*.

guide track A *speech track* recorded in a situation where the *background noise* level is high in order to serve as a guide for the actor or presenter to re-record the same material under *studio* conditions at some later time.

Guilford's model of intelligence A model of *intelligence* or structure of intellect proposed by J.P. Guilford. It consists of a three-dimensional plot of three factors, namely, (i) the kind of 'content' of information, (ii) the kind of mental 'operation' involved, and (iii) the kind of 'product' or form in which the information occurs, thus producing a multi-cell cube each cell of which represents an intellectual ability defined by the particular factors associated with it (see figure 21).

gun microphone A highly-directional, highly-sensitive *microphone* in which a long interference tube is used to eliminate all sounds other than those emanating from the direction in which the tube is pointed. Also called a *rifle microphone* or *shotgun microphone*.

Guttman scale A type of *attitude scale* that requires the respondee to make 'yes/no' or 'agree/disagree' *responses* to a series of questions or statements of progressively increasing severity or extremism.

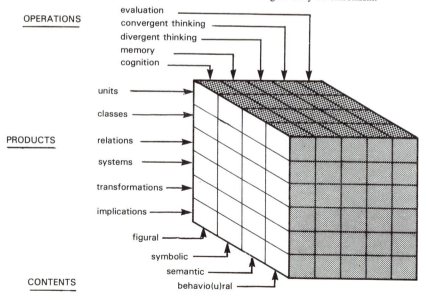

Figure 21 Guilford's model of intelligence

H

halation 1. Unwanted *exposure* in the area surrounding an intense photographic *image* produced by scattering of light within the *emulsion* or back reflection from the *base* of the film. 2. Unwanted darkening of the area surrounding an over-loaded bright *image* on a television screen.

half-frame A term applied to a *filmstrip* in which the horizontal axis of the *frames* is perpendicular to the length of the film; cf *full-frame*. Also known as *single-frame*.

half-tone A term applied to *images* where tonal gradation is produced by printing evenly-spaced dots of different sizes, the density within the dots being constant. This technique is commonly used to reproduce *monochrome* photographs in books, leaflets, etc.

half-track A term applied to *audiotapes* with two separate recording *tracks*, each approximately half the width of the tape, and to *audiotape recorders* and *audiotape players* that use such a track configuration. Also known as *two-track*.

'halo' effect In *assessment, bias* resulting from the assessor being influenced by favo(u)rable traits or behavio(u)r on the part of the person being assessed, eg good manners. See also *Pygmalion effect*.

handbook 1. A treatise on a particular subject or subsection thereof, often giving a simple but all-embracing treatment suitable for newcomers to the field. 2. A set of instructions on how to use a particular piece of equipment, eg a *microcomputer*.

hand control A small hand-held device whereby an automatic slide projector, television set or similar system can be controlled from a distance.

handout Any printed or duplicated item run off

in multiple copies for issuing to learners, conference delegates, etc.

handshaking In data transmission, the exchange of alerting signals between the transmitting and receiving systems prior to full transmission between the two.

hang-up A non-scheduled halt in the operation of a *computer* or similar system due to improper coding or programming; cf *crash, glitch*.

haptic (learner) A term applied to a learner who, in a visual sense, analyzes the visual presentation of material into discrete elements (the visual version of an *atomist* or *serialist*); cf *visual learner*.

hard copy Information printed, typed or otherwise reproduced on paper, as opposed to information temporarily displayed on a screen, held in a store, coded on tape, etc (*soft copy*).

hard disk A large, rigid *disk* (or stacked system of disks) with a high data storage capacity — typically of the order of tens or hundreds of *megabytes*; cf *floppy disk*.

hardware A generic term for the equipment used in *instructional technology*, computing, etc; cf *software*.

Harvard case method A method of teaching management and business studies through the systematic use of case histories and *case studies*, thus providing concentrated practical experience in a classroom situation.

Hawthorne effect A situation where improvement in *learning* apparently brought about by the use of a new technique is wholly or partly due to the (often temporary) increased interest and motivation that are produced by the new technique rather than to the intrinsic properties of the technique itself.

head 1. A component of an *audiotape recorder, audiotape player, videotape recorder,* etc that is used to transfer a signal to or from the tape or to erase an existing signal. 2. A component of a *compact disc player* or *videodisc player* used to scan the signal carried on the disc. 3. A device used to *read* data into or out of a data storage medium such as a *disk*. 4. The system that carries the characters in a *daisy wheel printer, golf ball printer* or similar device.

head demagnetizer A device used to reduce the residual magnetism in tape *heads*. Also known as a *degausser*.

head drum A rotating drum that carries one or more *heads*, as in a *helical-scanning* videorecorder.

head gap The narrow gap between the poles of a magnetic *record head* or *playback head*. The width of the gap determines the maximum frequency that can be handled at a given tape speed, this frequency being inversely proportional to the gap width.

head out A term applied to a *motion picture* film, *videotape* or *audiotape* that is wound on a *reel* with the start on the outside, so that it is ready for immediate projection or playback.

headphones A pair of small *transducers* mounted on a headband for individual listening to an *audio signal*. Such headphones can be *monophonic* (with the same signal being heard in both ears) or *stereophonic* (with different

signals being fed into the left and right transducers); cf *headset*.

headset A combined *headphone/microphone* system of the type used by film or television production personnel for two-way communication.

hectograph, hectographic duplication A reprographic process that involves first preparing a reverse-image *master* of the material to be reproduced (a *hectograph master* or *ditto master*) by typing, writing or drawing on a sheet of glossy paper, the back of which is in contact with special colo(u)red carbon paper (*hectographic carbon*). Multiple copies are then produced by pressing the master against sheets of paper whose surface has been lightly moistened with spirit, thus causing some of the pigment on the master to be transferred to the paper. The process is also known as *spirit duplication, gelatin duplication* or *Banda*.

hectograph master See *hectograph, hectograph(ic) duplication*.

hectographic carbon See *hectograph, hectograph(ic) duplication*.

helical scanning The *scanning* system used in most *videotape recorders* and *videocassette recorders*; it involves moving the tape diagonally across the curved face of a rapidly-rotating *head drum*, which scans the tape in a series of parallel *tracks*, each of which contains one complete *field* of the picture signal, as in the *U-wrap* system shown in figure 22; cf *transverse scanning*. Also known as *slant track recording*.

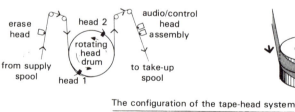

The configuration of the tape-head system

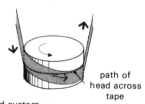

path of head across tape

The pattern of tracks on the tape

Figure 22 The principle of helical-scanning videorecording using the U-wrap tape configuration

heuristic approach A method of instruction or problem solving that involves using successive evaluations of trial and error in an attempt to arrive at a final result. See also *discovery learning*.

hidden curriculum The informal and subtle ways in which a school, college, or similar establishment mirrors and supports the accepted values of the social system or organization that runs it, eg by encouraging hard work and self-reliance. See also *informal curriculum*.

hierarchy An arrangement of elements containing subordinate and superordinate relationships, eg the pyramidal authority structure within a school or college or the structures of the various *domains* into which *educational objectives* are conventionally divided. See also *learning hierarchy*.

hi-fi An abbreviation for *high-fidelity*.

high-angle shot In photographic, film or television work, a *shot* taken with the camera above the subject, looking down on to it. Such shots place the subject in an 'inferior' position, reducing its apparent size and slowing down any motion that it possesses; cf *low-angle shot*.

high-band (U-matic) A ¾ inch *videocassette recorder* system that has an extended *band-width* compared with standard *U-matic*, and thus gives a better picture quality; cf *low-band (U-matic)*.

high-contrast (photographic) film Special *photographic film* used for reproducing *line drawings* or similar materials. As its name suggests, it gives particularly high contrast between the dark and light parts of the resulting *image*.

higher cognitive A term applied to *educational objectives*, learning skills, etc that fall in the upper part of the *cognitive domain*, generally taken to encompass the four highest levels (*application, analysis, synthesis* and *evaluation*); cf *lower cognitive*.

high fidelity A qualitative term used to describe a sound recording or reproduction system capable of handling the full audible range of frequencies (20Hz–20kHz) with low distortion, or a high-quality *audio recording* on disc or tape.

high-level (programming) language A *programming language* (such as ALGOL, BASIC, COBOL or FORTRAN) which provides a range of facilities and standard constructions designed to simplify the writing of *computer programs*; cf *low-level (programming) language*.

highlight Emphasis of part of an illuminated scene or object produced by the use of *highlighting, back lighting* or *cross lighting*.

highlighting 1. In photographic, film or television work, lighting used to emphasize the central point of interest in a *set* or *scene*, eg by use of a *kicker*. 2. The emphasis of a point, issue, word, etc in any context.

hiss high-frequency *noise* in an *audio signal* or reproduced sound due to a faulty recording, faulty equipment, poor reception, etc; cf *hum*.

histogram A graphical representation of a *frequency distribution* in the form of a vertical *bar chart*, the widths of the bars representing the sizes of the different classes into which the distribution is divided and the heights of the bars the corresponding frequencies. A typical example is shown in figure 10 on page 23. Should not be confused with a *historigram*.

historigram A statistical term for a *graph* that shows the change in a *variable* over a period of time. Should not be confused with a *histogram*.

hitch-hiking Using existing ideas or systems as a basis for stimulating new ideas.

hither plane In a three-dimensional *computer graphics* display, the (imaginary) plane that defines the front limit of the display; cf *yon plane*.

hold frame Another term for a *freeze frame*.

holist A term applied by Pask to a person who learns, remembers and recapitulates material as a whole; cf *serialist*. See also *global learning*.

hologram A visual recording, produced using a *laser*, which presents the illusion of three dimensions, including *parallax* effects.

home experiment kit A *package* supplied or sold to learners so that they can perform experiments at home, eg as part of a *distance learning* course.

home instruction Instruction that is provided in a learner's home rather than in a school, college, etc, eg by radio or television or as part of a *distance learning* course.

homing A facility in some automatic slide projectors for returning the *magazine* to the 'start' or 'home' position (usually the 'zero' position in the case of *carousel*-type projectors).

hook-and-loop board A *non-projected display* system in which items are attached to a display surface covered with tiny loops by means of pads or strips carrying tiny hooks. Such boards can be used to display much heavier items than other adhesive display systems such as *feltboards* or *magnetic boards*. Also known as a *teazle board* or *teazlegraph*.

horizontal (format) See *landscape (format)*.

horizontal panel book A *programmed text* in which pages are divided into panels which are not read in sequence, the reader being directed to a particular panel on the basis of his performance in the work of the program(me).

horizontal transfer (of learning) A form of *transfer of learning* in which no new higher-order skills are learned, but in which existing skills are applied to a new task (or set of tasks) of similar level of difficulty; cf *vertical transfer (of learning)*. Also known as *lateral transfer*.

host 1. An entrepreneur or organization that provides access to a number of *data bases* through his/its own *computer*; also known as an *information vendor*. 2. A *computer* that provides the same service.

hot metal (composition) In printing, mechanical typesetting in which new metal type is cast from hot metal for each job.

hotpress printing machine A type of printing machine (used extensively for producing showcards, television *captions*, etc) in which a heated *platen* and brass type are used to transfer ink from pigmented white, black or colo(u)red foil on to card.

housekeeping (routines) The *software* responsible for the processes by which a *digital computer* keeps up-to-date track of all relevant information regarding addresses, availability of store space, file numbers, etc, ie the software that controls the internal 'housekeeping' of the computer system.

house style In publishing, a set of standard practices governing design and composition associated with a particular publishing house. More widely, the term is used to cover distinctive styles of design and layout in documents produced by a particular body, organization, etc.

howl round See *acoustic feedback*.

hue The subjective quality of a particular colo(u)r as perceived by an individual.

hum A continuous low-frequency sound, often corresponding to the mains frequency of 50 or 60 Hz or one of its harmonics (*mains hum*), produced when an electrical or electronic device is in operation. This is one of the main types of *noise* that occurs in sound reproduction systems; cf *hiss*.

humanist psychology A school of psychology that emphasizes the concepts of 'self' and 'person' and the study of man's 'humanness' in an integrated and holistic manner, as opposed to the analytical and psychometric approach adopted in *behavio(u)ral psychology*. Humanist psychology came to the fore during the 1960s as a result of the work of psychologists like Carl Rogers, and was in some ways a reaction to the 'dehumanization' often associated with the behavio(u)ral school.

hum bars Slowly-moving horizontal bars on a television picture caused by unwanted *mains hum* getting into the *video signal*.

hunting 1. In *video* playback, low-frequency instability of picture and sound caused by periodic variations in the tape throughput speed. 2. A cyclic error in a servo system.

hypercardioid microphone A *microphone* with a *polar response* curve intermediate in shape between that of a *bi-directional microphone* and that of a true *cardioid microphone*.

hyperfocal distance The closest focusing distance at which a lens can be set without throwing distant objects noticeably out of focus, thus producing the greatest possible *depth of field* for the lens. See also *fixed focus*.

hypnopaedia Literally 'education in sleep' (from the Greek). *Learning* carried out while the learner is asleep, eg by playing *audiotapes*. Also known as *sleep teaching*.

hypothetical construct An abstract concept which, though not observable, is inferred as actually existing. The various *factors* that are assumed to constitute *general intelligence* are examples of such constructs.

hypothetico-deductive method A research or reasoning method that starts with the formulation of a hypothesis, then deduces testable consequences of this hypothesis, and finally tests these predictions by observation, experiments, 'thought experiments', etc; cf *inductive method*. See also *deductive method*.

I

ice breaker 1. An activity designed to establish rapport and generate a receptive atmosphere in a group of people who are about to take part in an exercise, course, etc. 2. A preliminary question or short paper taken by students before starting an examination in order to accustom them to the examination room environment and help overcome nervousness; it is not usually marked as part of the examination proper.

icon In computing, a pictorial representation of a *menu* function, eg use of a picture of a pencil to indicate a drawing facility.

iconic model, sign A *model* or sign that resembles or has some of the properties of the object, event or situation that it represents.

ideograph A *character* or figure which represents an object, idea, etc, as, for example, in the Chinese writing system. See *ideography*.

ideography A system of writing that is based on the use of pictures or symbols to represent different objects, concepts, etc rather than on the use of letters or syllable sounds to build up words. The Chinese writing system is a typical example.

idiot board, sheet Colloquial names for a *teleprompter*.

IKR See *immediate knowledge of results*.

illuminance A measure of the amount of light falling on a surface, the unit of illuminance being the *lux*. Should not be confused with *luminance*.

illuminative evaluation Another name for the *social/anthropological approach (to evaluation)*.

image 1. In *reprography*, photography, television, projection, etc a reproduction of the subject matter being copied, photographed, shown, transmitted or projected. 2. In psychology, a perception that is retained or recalled after the *stimulus* that originally produced it has ceased. See also *image association*.

image association A phenomenon encountered in the study of *memory* whereby recall of one *image* or idea causes the spontaneous recall of another (often apparently unrelated) image or idea.

image modifier A camera-like device used for enlarging or reducing the *image* in graphical or textual material during preparation for printing, etc.

image plane The plane perpendicular to the *optical axis* in which a lens produces its *image*. In the case of distant objects, the image plane corresponds to the *focal plane* (see figure 19 on page 68), but, in the case of near objects, generally lies beyond the focal plane.

immediate experience A term used to denote first-hand sensory experience of the world as it is here and now, as opposed to second-hand or mediated experience of the type available through the techniques of *instructional technology*, eg by watching a *video* or *film*.

immediate knowledge of results (IKR) In *programmed instruction*, *feedback* that is supplied immediately after an *item*, thus maximizing the *reinforcement* value.

immediate response A facility available in some *audio-active comparative language laboratories* whereby short segments of program(me) *stimulus* and student *response* can be played back immediately without rewinding the tape.

impact printing A term applied to all printing systems in which *images* of *characters* are produced by hammering an inked ribbon on to the copy paper using a hard die, the various systems used in typewriters being typical examples.

impression method of marking A technique of marking a composition, essay, *project*, etc purely on the basis of the overall impression that it creates; cf *analytical method of marking*.

improvement curve Another name for a *learning curve* or *experience curve*.

inaudible advance A term applied to a synchronized sound/vision presentation (such as a *tape-slide program(me)* or *sound filmstrip*) with inaudible *synchronizing signals* that cause the *frames* to advance automatically at the appropriate times; cf *audible advance*.

in-basket (in-tray) technique A method of training or instruction in which an individual is called upon to play a specific role and must, in isolation, respond to a number of hypothetical situations as they arise. The technique was originally used in the field of business management training — hence the name.

incentive An external motivation that is provided to a learner in order to encourage him/her to carry out a task, work program(me), etc, eg marks or gradings provided for written work.

incident process A type of participative *case study* in which the participants are not supplied with all the necessary information at the start, having to obtain further information themselves as the work of the exercise progresses.

in-company, in-house, in-plant training Training provided for the employees of an organization on the organization's own premises; cf *in-service training*.

incrust Another name for *super(im)position*.

independent learning, study An instructional system in which learners carry out the main part of their studies working on their own, only meeting instructors or tutors in order to receive direction, guidance or assistance or to review progress; cf *directed learning*.

independent samples *Samples* in educational or other forms of statistically-based research which do not interact in any way to influence the particular *variable(s)* under study.

independent variable In experimental work, research studies, etc, a *variable* which is under the direct control of the experimenter or researcher; cf *dependent variable*.

index 1. A systematic guide to a document, part of a document or group of documents, comprising a series of entries generally arranged in alphabetical order; see also *author index, citation index, keyword index, subject index, syndectic*. 2. A quantitative measure of some property or quality of a system, process, individual, etc; see, for example, *discrimination index, facility index*. 3. To label items in a systematic manner or to prepare '1.'.

indirect teaching A teaching approach that relies on creating situations in which students are motivated to learn for themselves rather than relying on direct instructions supplied by the teacher.

individualized instruction, learning, teaching, training The tailoring of instruction, learning, teaching or training to meet the specific needs of individual learners rather than the average needs of the learning group as a whole. Also known as *personalized instruction*. See also *individually-prescribed instruction*.

individually-paced instruction, learning A form of *individualized instruction (learning)* in which each learner is allowed to proceed at his/her own natural pace. See also *Keller Plan, mastery learning*.

individually-prescribed instruction (IPI) A form of *individualized instruction* in which each learner is allowed to plan and direct his/her own program(me) of study, within certain constraints; cf *autodidaxy*.

individual test A test that is designed to be administered to a single person rather than to a group; cf *group test*.

induction See *inductive method*.

inductive method 1. A method of instruction that involves presenting the learner with a sufficient number of specific examples to enable him/her to arrive at a definite rule, principle, fact, etc embracing the examples by the process known as *induction*. The *egrul(e)* system used in *programmed instruction* is a well-known example of the method. 2. A research or reasoning method that uses the process of *induction* to infer general principles, laws, etc from specific instances; cf *deductive method, hypothetico-deductive method*.

in focus See *focus*.

informal curriculum Material learned informally by association with fellow pupils, students or trainees. See also *hidden curriculum*.

informal education 1. Education in which the traditional teacher/learner roles become blurred. 2. Education that an individual acquires by his/her own efforts (eg via private reading) or through real-life experience rather than through a formal course of some sort.

informatics The study of information, the way in which it is created, manipulated and used, and its impact on society.

information explosion A term used to denote the unprecedented rapid increase in knowledge that has taken place in the second half of the 20th century and the consequent problems of information exchange, storage and retrieval.

information picture Another name for a *pictogram*.

information technology (IT) A relatively recent term covering all the different methods of storing, retrieving, transmitting, receiving and using information; cf *informatics*. See also *new information technology* (which is generally implied when the term is used).

information vendor Another name for a *host*.

inhibition 1. In *behavio(u)ral psychology*, the failure of a *stimulus* to produce its associated *response* due to some external or internal factor that affects the *S-R bond* without actually destroying it, as in *extinction*. 2. In computing, prevention of an operation from being performed when not required by supplying a suitable signal to the appropriate part of the system.

initial ability, behavio(u)r The ability or behavio(u)r of a learner at the start of a program(me) of instruction, before he/she takes part in an exercise, etc.

initial teaching alphabet (ita) An alphabet system that uses 43 visual symbols. It is used in teaching reading to beginners, thus avoiding many of the problems of irregularity and inconsistency that may arise when the normal 26 letter alphabet is used in such teaching (eg problems that arise from the different possible sounds of the various vowels and vowel combinations).

ink jet printing A high-speed printing method in which the characters are produced by a jet of ink that is broken up into droplets which are then electrostatically charged and directed on to the copy paper by means of a variable electric field.

inlay An *image* that is incorporated in another (larger) image, etc in one corner, or in a circle or rectangle within its area. This technique is widely used in television production. Should not be confused with *insert*.

innovation A process of change which enables a new idea, strategy or concept to be introduced into practice.

inquisitory display A display which asks one or more questions; cf *expository display*.

insert In film or television production, a short *shot* (usually a *close-up*) that is inserted into the main shot at some point (ie used to replace the latter temporarily) in order to show detail, provide dramatic effect, etc. Should not be confused with *inlay*. See also *noddy*.

in-service training, education Training or education that is provided for a person while he/she is actually in employment, not necessarily on the premises of the organization for which he/she is working; cf *pre-service training, education*.

instant lettering Another term for *transfer lettering*.

instructional aid Any item (*hardware* or *software*) used to support instruction.

instructional development The systematic development of instructional resources in order to bring about changes in behavio(u)r.

instructional system A combination of appropriate *instructional system components* and an overall management or organizational pattern for their use that is designed to bring about systematic learning. An example of such an instructional system might be a complete *distance learning* course.

instructional system component (ISC) An integrated set of *learning resources*, together with the method in which they are intended to be used, which form an identifiable part of an *instructional system*. See also *delivery system*.

instructional technology A term that is sometimes used to denote the combined fields of *educational technology* and training technology, but is also used to denote a subset of educational technology (based on the idea that instruction is a subset of education).

instrumented laboratory training (IT) A form of *T-group training* which places great emphasis on systematic *feedback* via *check lists, rating scales,* etc.

intaglio Printing from a metal *plate* (usually copper) on which the *image* has been produced by engraving or etching with acid. *Photogravure* is an example of such a process.

integrated experience approach A 'gestalt' approach to education that involves using a range of varied experiences to achieve an integrated, comprehensive set of *objectives* covering a particular field or subject area.

intelligence See *general intelligence, intelligence A, B, C, intelligence quotient.*

intelligence A, B, C A distinction between three types of *general intelligence* made by Hebb: (i) intelligence A, which represents an individual's innate potential, depending entirely on his/her natural neurological facilities, (ii) intelligence B, which is a hypothetical level of development of intelligence that has resulted from the interaction of intelligence A with the individual's external environment, (iii) intelligence C, v hich is the sample or component of intelligence B that is actually measued by standardized *intelligence tests.*

intelligence age Another term for *mental age.*

intelligence quotient (IQ) The ratio (multiplied by 100) of an individual's *mental age,* as measured by *intelligence tests,* to his/her *chronological age.* IQ appears to obey the *normal distribution curve,* with almost 70 per cent of the population having IQs between 85 and 115. Also known as *mental ratio.*

intelligence test A *psychological test* that is administered in order to measure an individual's *general intelligence* or some specific aspect thereof.

intelligent terminal A *computer terminal* which can be used to perform a certain amount of data processing itself, without having to make use of the facilities of the *central processing unit* to which it is connected. Such terminals are, in effect, *microcomputers;* cf *dumb terminal, smart terminal.*

interaction analysis 1. In *group dynamics,* the systematic study, recording and analysis of the interactions that take place between each member of a group and every other member. 2. The systematic study and analysis of the interaction of a teacher with a class.

interactive 1. A term applied to instructional materials (such as *computer-assisted learning* materials) which vary the material presented according to the *responses* and /or decisions made by the learner. 2. A term describing a learning environment or exercise where learners are required to interact with one another in some way, eg by taking part in *role play.*

interactive courseware development A technique whereby a teacher or trainer plans, writes and evaluates a computer-based course or instructional program(me) by carrying out *on-line* dialog(ue) with a *computer* via a suitable *terminal.*

interactive mode A method of using a *digital computer* whereby the user engages in *on-line* dialog(ue) with the computer via a suitable *terminal;* cf *batch mode.*

interactive video A hybrid *individualized learning* system in which a random-access *videotape recorder* or *videodisc player* is linked to a *digital computer* through a special interfacing system that enables television material stored on *videotape* or *videodisc* to be incorporated into *computer-based learning* program(me)s administered via the computer; in such a system, the user has some control over what he/she sees and hears, the level of interactivity depending on the design of the system, and (in the case of *videodisc*-based systems) being measured on a scale known as the *Nebraska scale.*

interactive videotex(t) *Videotex(t)* in which the user is connected to a computerized *data base* by cable (usually a telephone line) and can therefore engage in *on-line* dialog(ue) with the data base. The British PRESTEL system is a typical example; cf *broadcast videotex(t).* Also known as *viewdata.*

intercutting A technique used in film and television *editing* in which different *shots* of the same subject are combined in sequence in order to add variety, dramatic effect, etc to the presentation.

interdisciplinary A term used to describe a course, instructional program(me), exercise, etc that draws its material from a number of different subject areas and illustrates the links and relationships that exist between them.

interest area, interest/discovery area Other names for a *discovery area.*

interest test A test used in areas such as personnel selection and career guidance to obtain information about the personal and/or leisure interests of pupils, candidates for jobs, etc.

interface A general term for the area or method of linkage between two systems, eg between a system that is feeding data into a *computer* and the actual computer. See also *buffer*.

interference 1. In *learning* theory, the *inhibition* of one piece of learning by another, a process that is thought to be one of the main causes of forgetting. 2. In a communications system, data processing system, etc, confusion, *noise* or loss of clarity in a signal being handled.

intergram A *hologram* of a moving system that can be viewed without the need for special *laser* illumination.

interlaced scanning The *scanning* procedure used in most television systems. It involves building up each *frame* of the picture in two stages (or *fields*), each of which scans alternate *lines* in the picture. The process is illustrated (in greatly simplified form) in figure 23.

intermediate In photography and cinematography, any *film* (other than a camera original) that is only intended for use in making duplicates. See also *internegative, interpositive*.

internal conditions of learning The prior or prerequisite conditions that have to exist within a learner before a new skill, ability, etc can be learned.

internal consistency The extent to which all the items of a test measure the same ability. See also *Kuder-Richardson reliability coefficient*.

internal validity In research, the extent to which changes in a *dependent variable* in a particular *experimental group* are in fact due to the experimental treatment to which the group is subjected rather than to the effects of extraneous factors acting within the group; cf *external validity*.

internegative 1. A duplicate *negative* of a colo(u)r *motion picture* that is used solely for preparing other copies of the motion picture. 2. A *negative* of a colo(u)r *photograph* that is used in producing *positive* copies of the photograph.

interpositive A duplicate *positive* of a colo(u)r *motion picture* that is used solely for preparing other copies of the motion picture.

interpreter A *computer program* which controls the execution of another program which has not previously been compiled or assembled, translating the latter program into *machine code* instructions one line at a time.

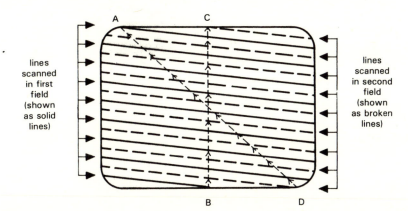

In the British 625 line system, the scanning of the first field begins at A (the start of line 1) and ends at B (half way along line 313); the scanning of the second field starts at C, beginning by completing line 313 and finishing at D (the end of line 625). In the American 525 line system, the scanning process is similar, with the transition between fields taking place half way along line 263.

Figure 23 A greatly simplified illustration of interlaced scanning

interrupt 1. A computing term for a temporary halt to the *processing* of a job while another process (usually associated with *system software*) is initiated or completed. 2. To so halt the processing of a job.

interval scale The second most sophisticated of the four main types of *scale* used in educational measurement, having all the essential properties of an *ordinal scale* and also having equal intervals between the ranked *scores*. Also known as an *equal-appearing interval scale* or a *cardinal scale*. See also *nominal scale, ratio scale*.

interview schedule A *check list* of questions or points to be raised that is used to give structure to an interview and/or ensure that it follows a pre-determined or standard pattern.

intrinsic motivation Motivation based on the pleasure produced by the performance of a task rather than on the use of external reinforcers; cf *extrinsic motivation*.

intrinsic program(me) See *intrinsic programming*.

intrinsic programming In *programmed instruction*, a programming technique (developed by Crowder) that is characterized by the use of relatively lengthy *items, multiple choice questions* and extensive use of *branching*; *intrinsic program(me)s* are so named because they adjust the presentation to suit the needs of the user without the use of an extrinsic device such as a *teaching machine* or *computer*.

inventory test 1. A general term for a *personality test* or *questionnaire* designed to assess or identify attitudes, traits or personality characteristics. 2. A diagnostic test used to determine the level of prior knowledge or later achievement in respect of a short component of a course or program(me) of instruction. See also *pre-test, post-test, psychological inventory*.

inverse correlation Another name for *negative correlation*.

inverted file A type of *file* frequently used in *data bases*. In such a file, the attributes of items are identified by index terms, which are then collected in so-called inverted files that list all items possessing that particular attribute; cf *serial file*.

invisible college An informal group of individuals exchanging information in a specific field of common interest. Membership is generally flexible, is often widely scattered, and tends to be exclusive.

in vision In television or film production, a term that is applied to activity that takes place within the field of view of the particular camera that is in operation at the time; cf *out of vision*.

IPI See *individually-prescribed instruction*.

IQ See *intelligence quotient*.

iris diaphragm A device for enabling the size of a circular *aperture* (such as the aperture in a camera) to be varied continuously by altering the positions of a set of curved shutters that are positioned symmetrically around its periphery.

iris in, out See *iris wipe*.

iris wipe In television production, a *wipe* effect in the form of a circle that either expands to fill the screen (*iris in*) or contracts and eventually disappears (*iris out*).

ISC See *instructional system component*.

Ishihara Test One of the most commonly-used colo(u)r vision tests. It involves identifying letters, numbers or forms in colo(u)rs that become confused with, or lost in, the background colo(u)rs if there is a vision defect involving the two sets of colo(u)rs used (eg reds and greens).

ISO International Standards Organisation. An international body that operates standards in a wide range of fields, including *film speed*. The ISO rating of a film is a combination of the *ASA* rating and the *DIN* rating.

IT 1. See *information technology*. 2. See *instrumented laboratory training*.

ita See *initial teaching alphabet*.

italic A *typeface* that slopes to the right (as in *italic*); cf *roman*.

item 1. In *programmed instruction*, another name for a *frame*. 2. In *assessment*, a single question or component in a test (see, for example, *completion item, multiple-choice item*). 3. A computing term for a unit of information, relating to a particular document, person, etc, held within a *data base*.

item analysis *Analysis* of *objective items* using standard statistical and mathematical techniques in order to determine whether they are valid, reliable, fair and useful. See also *item bank* (1.).

item bank A large collection of validated *objective items* from which sets of items may be culled as required in order to make up a particular *objective test*. 2. An alternative name for a *data bank* or *data base*.

item base An alternative name for a *data bank* or *data base*.

item difficulty gradient The extent to which *items* in a test or examination are arranged in order of increasing difficulty (a common

practice in tests that contain large numbers of items, particularly *objective tests*).

item editing See *shredding*.

item sampling Administering random subsets of *items* from a test to randomly-selected students in order to build up a picture of the overall *validity, reliability,* etc of the test.

item trial testing See *shredding*.

ITV 1. Instructional television. 2 Independent Television. The commercial television broadcasting system that operates in the UK.

J

jack plug A single plug-type connector that can carry two or more electrical or electronic lines. It is used in connection with a *jack socket*.

jack socket A single-hole socket into which a *jack plug* fits or can be fitted.

jelly A colo(u)r *filter* or *diffuser* placed in front of a light source.

jitter 1. Slight irregular unsteadiness of the film in a *motion picture camera* or film projector. 2. A similar effect in *video* playback caused by *flutter* in the playback machine.

job aid Any form of 'aide memoire' designed to facilitate either the learning or the performance of a task.

job analysis Detailed study of a job in order to identify the various tasks of which it is composed. See also *skills analysis*.

job description 1. A summary of the main characteristics of a job of work, and of the worker characteristics required for effective performance thereof; cf *job specification*. 2. In computing, information about a job specifying how it is to be processed by the computer.

job engineering Altering the responsibilities, methods, procedures and equipment associated with a job, thus changing its skill level. See also *de-skilling*.

job evaluation Establishing the relative worth or importance of the various jobs within a *hierarchy* of jobs by using appropriate *assessment* and *evaluation* techniques.

job knowledge test A test carried out to assess an individual's achievement in, and knowledge of, a job for which he has been trained. Also known as a *trade test*.

job rotation Systematic movement of people between jobs in a given organization in order to widen their experience and know-how.

job sample test A test (based on *simulation* of part of a job) that is used to measure present *performance* in the job or aptitude for jobs of that, or similar, type.

job specification A detailed statement of the activities associated with a job and of the qualifications, experience and personal qualities needed to carry it out; cf *job description*.

joint frequency The frequency with which two or more *variables* in a statistical *population* occur together. See also *correlation*.

joystick A lever that can be moved freely in any direction in order to control a *cursor*, 'write' on a *graphics terminal*, etc.

jumbo slide 1. Another name for a *superslide*. 2. A photographic *slide* with a somewhat larger *mount* and *image* area than a standard 2'' × 2'' *compact slide*.

jump In cinematography, a discontinuity in the *action* caused by momentary stopping and re-starting of the camera motor, incorrect editing, deliberate use of a *jump cut*, etc.

jump cut In film and video *editing*, deletion of a section within continuous *action* so that the action moves discontinuously forward.

justification In printing, typesetting, etc, arrangement of the *characters* and spaces so as to produce text *lines* of equal length corresponding exactly to the required page or column width, thus producing *justified* text.

justified See *justification*; cf *unjustified*.

K

k 1. In conventional scientific usage, an abbreviation for kilo; used as a prefix to scientific units to denote multiplication by 1000, as in kW (1000 watts). 2. In computing, an abbreviation for 2^{10} (ie 1024, not 1000 as is sometimes mistakenly supposed); used as the standard unit in which capacity of computer *memory* is measured, 1k of memory corresponding to a storage capacity of 1024 *bytes* (or in some systems, 1024 *words*).

Keller Plan A type of *individualized learning* strategy based on the self-paced study of (mainly) *printed materials* backed up by tutoring (including tutoring carried out by peers called *proctors*) and monitored by means of mastery tests at the end of each unit. See also *personalized system of instruction*.

key 1. The correct answer to a *multiple-choice question*; cf *distractor*. 2. In data processing, another name for a *tag*. 3. An explanation of the sign convention used on a map or diagram. 4. A lever that is depressed on a *keyboard* to register a given *character*.

keyboard A typewriter-like facility used to feed data or instructions into a *computer*, *word processor* or similar system. See also *blind keyboard, qwerty keyboard, palantype, soft keyboard, tactile keyboard*.

keyboard terminal A *computer terminal* that incorporates a *keyboard* of some sort.

keyboard trainer A system for teaching *keyboard* skills to an individual learner using a *keyboard terminal* and *visual display unit* in conjunction with a suitably-programmed *computer*, often a dedicated *microcomputer* that is built into the keyboard/VDU system to form a free-standing unit.

key light The principal light illuminating the central subject in a *set* or *scene*.

keypad 1. A small hand-held *keyboard* of the type used to control a remote-control television set, call up pages of a *videotex(t)* system, etc. 2. A small subsidiary section of a larger *keyboard* (eg in a *computer terminal*) that is used to enter particular types of *characters* or commands.

key punch A *keyboard*-type machine used to punch holes in *punched cards* or *paper tape* in order to feed data into a *computer*.

keystone distortion, keystoning Distortion of a rectangular projected *image* arising from the plane of the screen not being at right angles to the axis of projection. The two most common types are shown in figure 24.

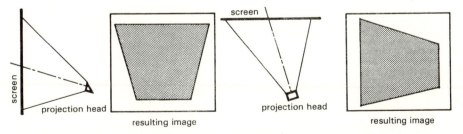

incorrect alignment in vertical plane

incorrect alignment in horizontal plane

Figure 24 The two most common types of keystone distortion

keyword In indexing, a significant word selected from the *text* of a document for use as an entry in a *keyword index*, an alphabetical index of such keywords designed to help readers locate sections that deal with specific topics. Also known as a *descriptor*.

keyword index See *keyword*.

kicker A *spotlight* used to produce a *highlight* effect.

kilobyte A unit of data size or data storage capacity equivalent to 10^3 (ie 1000) *bytes*; cf *megabyte, gigabyte*.

kinematograph See *cinematograph*.

kinescope A US term for the equipment used to make a film recording of a television program(me) from the *image* displayed on a picture tube, or for a recording thus made. The corresponding UK term is *telerecording*.

kinesthetic method A method of teaching basic reading or basic number work in which the pupil traces the form of the letters or numbers, or writes them, while at the same time sounding them out. Also known as the *tracing method*.

kinetographic symbols Standard systems of symbols used to chart movements of the human body, eg in *work study* or choreography. See also *therblig*.

kit 1. A set of components for constructing something, together with instructions for putting them together. 2. A *package* of materials and/or equipment designed for use in a particular teaching or learning activity or set of activities (see, for example, *home experiment kit*).

knowledge 1. A *cognitive* process which involves the remembering of facts, ideas, etc without necessarily understanding or being able to make use of them; the lowest level (Level 1) of Bloom's *cognitive domain*. 2. More generally, a body of facts, ideas, etc that is (or may be) acquired through *learning*.

knowledge based system A term applied to an *expert system* of the 'intelligent *data base*' type. It is often used as a synonym for an expert system.

Kuder-Richardson reliability coefficient A standard statistical formula used to calculate the average intercorrelation between *items* in a test in order to determine the *internal consistency* of the test and thus give an indication of one aspect of its *reliability*. Two versions of the formula are commonly used, namely the full formula (KR20) and a simplified but less accurate version known as KR21.

kurtosis A statistical measure of the shape of the peak of a distribution, ie of the degree to which it is flat or pointed.

Kurzweil reading machine A reading aid for the blind that converts printed matter into *digital* form using *optical character recognition*, and hence into spoken form using *speech synthesis*.

L

label 1. In data processing, a *character* (or group of characters) that is written on, attached to or added to a set or *string* of data in order to identify or give information about the set of data. 2. Identifying information that is attached to, written on or added to an object, diagram, etc.

laboratory 1. A room designed and equipped for carrying out scientific or technological experiments and demonstrations, or a room specially equipped for carrying out practical work in a non-scientific subject. 2. See *language laboratory*.

laboratory method An instructional method based on experimental, practical or investigative work carried out in a *laboratory* of some sort.

lacing The UK term for the process of feeding a tape or film into an item of equipment such as a recorder, player or projector by threading its *leader* through the appropriate channel. The equivalent US term is *threading*; cf *channel loading*.

laminating film Transparent acetate or similar film for use in *lamination*.

lamination The process of strengthening and/or protecting a document by sticking or sealing a sheet of *laminating film* on to its surface, or, in some cases, to both sides of the document.

landscape (format) A term used to describe the *format* of a page, book, document, photograph, drawing, etc with an *aspect ratio* greater than 1 : 1, ie one whose horizontal length is greater than its vertical length. The term originates from photographs and paintings of landscapes, which are normally produced in such a format; cf *portrait (format)*. Also known as *horizontal (format)*.

language laboratory A language instruction room fitted with individual *carrels* in which

tape recorder/headphone systems and other devices are used to present material to learners, enable the learners to respond, provide *feedback*, etc. See also *audio-active language laboratory, audio-active comparative language laboratory*.

language translator 1. A *computer program* used to convert other programs from one *programming language* to another, eg from BASIC to FORTRAN. 2. A *computer program* which can be used to translate material from one natural language to another, eg from English to French. See also *interpreter*.

lantern slide A *slide* of size $3\frac{1}{4}'' \times 3\frac{1}{4}''$, or $3\frac{1}{4}'' \times 4''$, in which the *image* fills virtually the entire area. The name derives from the *magic lantern*, the original name of the type of projector which was used to show such slides. Lantern slides have been superseded by the more convenient *compact slide*.

lantern slide projector A slide projector designed to show *lantern slides*. Such projectors (which were originally known as *magic lanterns*) have been superseded by $2'' \times 2''$ slide projectors.

LAP See *learning activity package*.

lapel microphone Another name for a *clip-on microphone*.

large-type reading materials Books and other reading materials that are printed in 18 *point* or larger type of clear, simple design. Such materials are produced for use by people with poor eyesight and by very young children.

laser An optico-electronic device that produces an intense, coherent, monochromatic beam of light using the process of light amplification by stimulated emission of radiation (of which its name is an acronym). Such devices are becoming increasingly widely used in audiovisual and *information technology* systems, eg for reading the signals on *compact discs* and *optical videodiscs*, and in *laser holography* and *laser printers*.

laser card A rectangular card of similar size to a credit card that can be used to store information recorded by *laser* optics. See also *drexon*.

laser disc A widely-used name for an *optical videodisc* from which information is read by reflecting a *laser* beam from its surface.

laser holography The production and use of *holograms* using *lasers* as light sources.

laser printer An ultra-high-speed *printer* system that uses a *laser* to produce the *characters* on the copy paper. Such printers can operate at a rate of several thousand *lines* per minute.

LaserVision The trade name for what seems likely to become the standard *optical videodisc* system, developed by a consortium of companies including Philips, MCA, Pioneer and Sony. The system encodes *television signals* in the form of a continuous spiral *track* on one surface of a plastic disc 300 mm in diameter, the track consisting of a series of pits of varying length and separation that are read by reflected light from a finely-focussed *laser* beam.

latency 1. In *learning*, the time that elapses from the display of an instructional *stimulus* to the start of the student *response*. 2. In computing and data processing, a waiting time associated with the delay in gaining access to data held in a *store*. See also *response time*.

latent image The invisible *image* recorded on a *photographic film*, a *photographic plate* or *photographic paper* that has been exposed but not yet developed. See also *developing*.

latent learning *Learning* that occurs without actually manifesting itself in *performance* at the time, only becoming evident at some later time.

laterally reversed A term used to describe an *image* that is reversed from left to right, ie a mirror image; cf *right reading*.

lateral thinking A term that denotes the process of solving a problem by indirect methods, often involving *divergent thinking*, rather than by adopting a direct, logical approach. See also *brainstorming*.

lateral transfer Another term for *horizontal transfer*.

Lavalier microphone A small *microphone* that is suspended from a halter so that it can be hung round the neck of a speaker or presenter. Such microphones have now been largely replaced by *clip-on microphones*. Also known as a *throat microphone*.

layout A visualized plan for a display, poster, publication or other presentation. It is usually produced on the same scale as the final product, and includes sufficient detail to show how the latter will look.

LCD See *liquid crystal display*.

leader 1. A length of non-usable film or tape at the beginning or end of the usable main section of a film or tape; leaders are used for *lacing* purposes, and also serve to protect the main section during handling of the film or tape. 2. A person who acts as chairman, coordinator, facilitator, etc for a group of learners. See also *leaderless group*.

leaderless group A group of learners who are required to carry out some activity on their own without any member of the teaching staff being present to act as *leader*. Such a group may, however, choose a leader from within itself.

lead lecture A *lecture* designed to present material and information for later discussion or given in preparation for participative work (eg an exercise of the *game/simulation/*participative *case study* type or a practical activity of some sort).

learner-based (-controlled, -managed) education, instruction Education or instruction in which the individual learner has considerable influence over what is taught, how it is taught, the pace of instruction, etc, with each learner's program(me) being effectively tailored to meet his/her individual needs and make the most of his/her ability and experience.

learning 1. In *behavio(u)ral psychology*, a change in the stable relationship between (i) a *stimulus* that an individual perceives, and (ii) the *response* that is made, either covertly or overtly. 2. A relatively permanent change in behavio(u)r that results from past experience or purposeful instruction.

learning activity package (LAP) An integrated set of self-instructional materials (often including a variety of media, such as a set of slides, an *audiotape* and *printed materials*) that is specially designed to meet the needs of individual learners in a particular instructional sequence or learning situation. This is sometimes simply described as a *learning package*.

learning (aids) laboratory An alternative name for a *resource(s) centre (center)*.

learning block A flaw or weakness in an individual's *cognitive* function that causes him/her to have difficulty in mastering a particular item, subject, group of subjects, etc.

learning-by-appointment A system in which individual learners can obtain access to instructors, tutors, self-instructional materials, instructional *hardware*, etc as and when they need them by making appropriate appointments or booking arrangements with the institution through which they are made available.

learning centre (center) Another name for a *resource(s) centre (center)*.

learning contract A formal or informal agreement between an individual learner and an instructor, department, institution or organization which specifies the *educational objectives* to be attained, the method(s) of instruction and the way in which the eventual *performance* of the learner will be assessed. See also *contract-based learning, teaching, training; contract plan; negotiated learning.*

learning curve A graphic presentation of the rate of progress of a learner (or group of learners) produced by plotting some appropriate measurable *variable* against time (see figure 25 for a typical example). Also known as an

experience curve or improvement curve.

learning environment The total environment (arrangement of campus, nature of building, nature of room, facilities in room, etc) in which *learning* takes place.

learning hierarchy Arrangement of *educational objectives*, sections of a course etc into a *hierarchy* that shows how they relate to and build upon one another.

learning package See *learning activity package*.

learning pattern A summary of the main features of the content and instructional methodology of a course, lesson, program(me), etc. The term is used particularly in connection with *programmed instruction* systems and other highly-structured forms of instructional system.

learning plateau A temporary flattening out in the *learning curve* of a trainee or student, sometimes representing a period of consolidation in the acquisition of skills.

learning resources Any resources (people, instructional materials, instructional *hardware*, etc) which may be used by a learner to bring about or facilitate *learning*.

learning resources centre (center) Another name for a *resource(s) centre (center)*.

learning structure The pattern in which an individual teacher or trainer organizes a *learning* sequence for his/her pupils, students or trainees, usually according to an overall plan.

learning style The preferred mode of *learning*

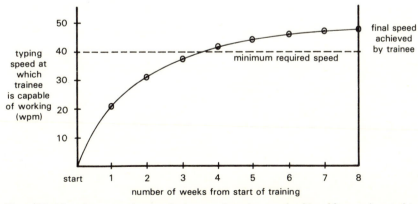

Figure 25 A learning curve showing the increase in typing speed achieved by a trainee typist over the period of a basic training course

that is employed by an individual. Also known as *cognitive style*.

lecture An expository instructional activity in which a teacher or trainer gives a systematic oral presentation of facts or principles (often supported by illustrative material) to a class, with the class generally being responsible for taking notes on the material covered. See also *lecture method, lead lecture*.

lecture method A teacher-centred (centered) approach to instruction which relies solely or heavily on *lectures* to impart information to learners.

LED See *light-emitting diode*.

LED display A display (eg of numbers, as in the time displays on a digital alarm clock or *videorecorder*) that is produced using a system of *light-emitting diodes* which can be individually energized to produce the required pattern. Such displays differ from *liquid crystal displays* in that the *characters* actually emit light.

lens aperture The effective *aperture* size of a lens or lens system. It is often expressed in terms of the *f-number*.

lens barrel The light-proof cylindrical support in which the lens of a projector, camera, etc is mounted, usually incorporating a facility for focusing.

lens cap A protective cap used to cover a lens when not in use.

lens hood A conical extension of a camera's *lens barrel* designed to prevent unwanted light from entering the lens from the side.

lens mount The part of a *lens barrel* by which it is attached to the camera, projector, etc with which it is being used. It may be of the screw-in type (as in a *C-mount*) or some sort of *bayonet mount* or clip-on system.

lens turret A rotatable mounting carrying two or more different lenses, each of which can rapidly be brought into use. Such lens turrets are mounted on many television cameras and *motion picture cameras*.

lenticular screen A *silvered screen* with tiny corrugations on its surface designed to increase the luminous intensity of the *image* when viewed from a direction close to the axis of projection. It is used as a *daylight screen*.

lesson plan An outline of the important points of a lesson arranged in the order in which they are to be presented together with a statement of the instructional methods to be used, the *objectives* that it is intended to achieve, etc.

lesson unit A discrete individual lesson designed to form part of a larger course or sequence of lessons.

Letraset One of the most common types of *transfer lettering*. It is widely used as a generic term for such lettering.

lettering 1. The activity of adding letters, numbers and other *characters* to *graphic materials* to create *labels, captions, titles, keys*, etc. 2. The resulting arrangement of *characters*.

lettering device, system Any system designed for use in adding *lettering* to graphic or other materials, eg the various forms of *transfer lettering, mechanical lettering systems* and *photographic lettering systems*.

letterpress (printing) A printing process in which the *image* is produced by the transfer of ink from the surface of raised type or blocks by pressing the latter against the copy material.

letter-quality printer A printer that produces output of similar quality to a standard typewriter. Such printers usually have *golf ball* or *daisy wheel* printing *heads*, and generally print on to single sheets of paper; cf *tractor feed printer*.

level indicator A device that is incorporated in a component of a sound recording or reproduction system (eg an *amplifier* or *tape deck*) to give a continuous indication or measure of the strength of the signal being handled, eg by the position of a needle on a meter scale or the length of a linear display of lights. Also known as a *vu-meter*.

level 0 The lowest level of the *Nebraska scale*. It represents a domestic *videoplayer* which has no potential for interactivity.

level 1 The first practical level of the *Nebraska scale*. It represents a *videoplayer* with the following basic features: *remote control, freeze frame*, forward and reverse, quick scan, slow motion, *frame* by frame replay, and *search*.

level 2 The middle level of the *Nebraska scale*. It represents a *videoplayer* which uses an integral *microprocessor* to offer *branching* facilities, *multiple-choice* format and scorekeeping facilities.

level 3 This is effectively the top current level of the *Nebraska scale*. It represents a *videoplayer* (either industrial or domestic) which is linked to an external *computer*, and offers the greatest versatility of any interactive configuration now available.

level 4 The theoretical peak of the *Nebraska scale*. It represents a complete *work station* incorporating all appropriate *video, computer* equipment and associated furniture, but represents possible future developments rather than any system that is currently available.

library media specialist (LMS) A person with particular expertise in *audiovisual materials* who is employed by a library. Such a person may have either a passive role, ie simply responding to queries and requests for help from library users, or may take a more active role such as promoting the development of learning materials within the institution for which he/she works.

lie scale A type of *item* that is sometimes incorporated into a *psychological inventory* of attitude or personality in order to detect cheating on the part of the testee. It often deals with socially-unacceptable attitudes or behavio(u)r.

lifelong education, learning The concept that education is not a one-off process undertaken during the early part of an individual's life but an on-going process that should continue throughout his/her life. See also *recurrent education*.

light board Another name for a *lighting console*.

light box A back-illuminated translucent surface used for viewing and working with transparent graphic and photographic materials. Also known as a *mimeoscope*, or *viewing light box*.

light-emitting diode (LED) A solid-state electronic component which emits light when an electric current is passed through it. It is used as a light source in *fibreoptic (fiberoptic) cable* systems and *LED displays*.

lighting console A *console* whereby the lighting in a *studio, set*, etc can be remotely controlled once the desired arrangement of light units has been set up. Also known as a *light board*.

lighting grid A grid suspended below the roof of a *studio* from which individual lighting units can be hung.

light pen A pen-like implement that can be moved across the surface of a computer *data tablet* or *visual display unit* screen in order to enter new data, alter existing data or otherwise interact with the system. Also known as a *pen* or *stylus*. See also *mouse*.

Likert scale An *attitude scale* involving the use of a list of statements to which an individual has to respond, normally from a range of four or five degrees of agreement/disagreement (see figure 26); cf *semantic differential scale*.

line 1. A cable connecting a *computer peripheral* or *remote terminal* to a central *computer*. 2. A wire or cable through which an *audio signal, video signal* or other signal is passed. 3. A horizontal row of *characters* forming part of a *page*, column or section of text, the *listing* of a *computer program*, etc. 4. One of the horizontal scans by which a television picture is built up, a UK picture consisting of 625 such lines and a US picture 525.

linear A term applied to an instructional program(me), *computer program*, exercise, etc that consists of a number of specified sequential stages, each of which has to be completed before proceeding to the next; cf *branching*.

linear notes A systematic way of organizing notes that involves using main headings, sub-headings, further subsidiary headings, and so on.

linear program(me) A *programmed instruction* sequence in which no *branching* occurs, all learners working systematically through exactly the same *linear* sequence of *frames*, generally at their own pace; cf *branching program(me)*.

linear programming 1. In *programmed instruction*, a programming technique based on the principles of *behavio(u)ral psychology*; it makes use of short *frames*, arranged in a rigid *linear* sequence (ie employs no *branching*) and makes heavy use of techniques such as *prompting* and *reinforcement*; cf *intrinsic programming*. 2. A mathematical model(l)ing technique for breaking down complex problems into a form whereby they can be handled by a *digital computer*.

linear relationship A relationship between two *variables* such that a plot of one against the

	Strongly agree	Agree	Disagree	Strongly disagree
1. I find the course easy				
2. The course contains too many lectures				
3. The course does not include enough practical work				
4. The course provides safisfactory facilities for individual tutorials				
5.				

Figure 26 Part of a Likert scale used in a course evaluation questionnaire

other is a straight line. If the two variables are x and y, such a relationship can be expressed in the form y = mx + c, where m and c are constants.

line drawing, diagram A drawing or diagram in which there is no gradation of tone and in which shading or texture (if any) is produced using patterns of lines or screen overlays (see, for example, most of the figures in this book).

line printer In computing and data processing, a *printer* that produces rapid *hard-copy* printout of textual material, *listings* of *programs*, etc by printing entire *lines* at a time as the paper is fed through the system. See also *bi-directional*.

line-up slides Special *slides* that are used to align the different components of a dual- or multi-projector system so that the resulting images are properly *registered*.

lining up Setting up a camera, projector, system of projectors, etc ready for use.

linkage model A model of the process whereby a user of instructional resources (eg a teacher or trainer) and a resource person (eg a media specialist in a *resource centre (center)*) interact in order to identify the needs of the former and meet them using the resources available through the latter. It involves each in making use of a *problem-solving model* centred (centered) on his/her situation and the on-going exchange of 'problem messages' and 'solution messages' between the two.

linked course A course that is run jointly by two or more educational establishments, eg by a secondary school and a further education college. See also *bridge course*.

lip sync In film and television production, simultaneous recording of pictures and sound in order to give exact correspondence between lip movements and speech; cf *wild sound*.

liquid crystal See *liquid crystal display*.

liquid crystal display (LCD) A data display technique that builds up visible *characters* by producing patterns of opaque *liquid crystals* (regions of a liquid that have had their optical properties changed by application of an electric field). Such displays are used in a wide range of electronic devices, eg pocket calculators and digital watches; cf *LED display*.

list A computing term for a series of *records* in a *file*; cf *listing*.

listening centre (center) A multi-outlet system that enables several people to listen to the same *audio* material (usually an *audiotape*) simultaneously using *headphones*. A typical listening centre has 6–8 outlets. Also known as a *multiple-head-set unit*.

listen-respond-compare laboratory See *audio-active comparative language laboratory*.

listing A computing term for a line-by-line *readout* or *printout* of a *program* (or section thereof), a set of data, etc; cf *list*.

lith film Abbreviation for lithography film — a high-contrast *photographic film* used for making *plates* for *lithographic printing*.

lithographic printing, lithography A printing process in which the *image* areas of the (flat) printing *plate* are made water-repellent (and hence ink-receptive) and the non-image areas ink-repellent. Thus, ink adheres to the image areas only, and is subsequently transferred to the paper on which the image is printed. See also *offset lithographic printing*, and figure 33 on page 118.

live program(me) A term applied to a radio or television *program(me)* that is broadcast or distributed at the time it is made.

lm See *lumen*.

LMS See *library media specialist*.

load 1. To enter information, instructions, etc into a *computer*. 2. To insert a tape or film into a recorder, player, projector, camera etc prior to use, eg by *lacing* or *channel loading* or by inserting a suitable *cassette* or *cartridge*.

location mark A coded group of *characters* that indicates the precise location of a book or other item in a library, *resources centre (center)*, archive, etc.

locus of control The term 'locus of control' refers to who does the adapting in an instructional system — the learner or the system. In the case of a learner-controlled system, the choice of the next step is made by the learner.

log book A record or diary of work, impressions, experiences, etc kept by a pupil, student, trainee, teacher or class.

logging in (on), logging out (off) The procedure by which a user initiates or terminates a particular session of *on-line* interaction with a *digital computer*. It is often abbreviated to *long in (on), log out (off)*.

log in (on), log out (off) See *logging in (on),*

logging out (off).

logistics A term which originally referred to the process of making victualling and other arrangements for troops, but which is now used to denote all the various organizational and other arrangements associated with the operation of a course or program(me), use of an exercise, distribution of a resource, etc.

long-focus lens A term applied to a lens with a longer than normal *focal length*, eg to a *long-throw projector lens* or a special camera lens that is used for photographing distant objects or for producing magnified images of very close objects. See also *bellow lens, telephoto lens*.

long-playing (record) (LP) A term that was introduced during the early 1950s to distinguish the (then) new *microgroove* 12 inch and 10 inch *audio discs* that played at $33\frac{1}{3}$ rpm from the coarse-grooved 78 rpm records that had been standard until that time. The new records had a much longer playing time — hence the name.

long shot (LS) In photographic, film or television work, a *shot* that shows a scene or object as it would be seen from a distance; cf *close-up, medium shot*. See also figure 29 on page 106.

long-term memory That part of the human *memory* in which material is stored on a long-term or permanent basis as opposed to a short-term, temporary basis; cf *short-term memory*.

long-throw (projector) lens A term applied to a *projector* lens with a longer than normal *focal length* and hence a longer than normal *throw* (see figure 27). In the case of a 35 mm slide projector, the most common standard lens has a focal length of 100 mm and the most common long throw lens a focal length of 200 mm, thus

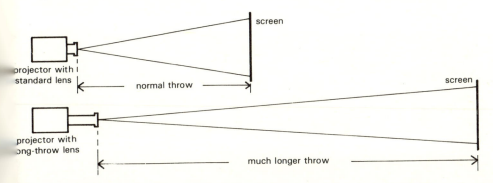

Figure 27 Use of a long-throw lens to increase the effective throw of a projector

loop film An endless loop of *motion picture* film contained in a *cartridge* that enables it to be shown or viewed continuously without rewinding. Also known as a *film loop*. See also *single concept loop film*.

loops Slack lengths of film immediately above and below the *gate* of a *motion picture camera* or film projector that enable the film to be moved intermittently through the gate without tearing it.

loose-leaf A term applied to a notebook or book in which the individual sheets are held in place by a mechanism (eg split metal rings or a spring binder) that enables them to be removed, rearranged, etc with the minimum of difficulty.

loudspeaker A device that enables an electrical *audio signal* to be converted into actual sound by means of a suitable electromagnetic *transducer* (see *moving coil loudspeaker*) or system of electrostatic transducers (see *electrostatic loudspeaker*). Loudspeakers may be self-contained units, or, in many cases, are incorporated in other devices such as television sets, *tape recorders* or *record players*. Also called a *speaker*.

low-angle shot In photographic, film or television work, a *shot* taken with the camera below the subject, looking up at it. Such shots place the subject in a 'dominant' position, exaggerating its height and speeding up any movement; cf *high-angle shot*.

low-band (U-matic) The $\frac{3}{4}$ inch *videocassette recorder* system that is most widely used in education and training for sub-broadcast-quality work. It is based on the original *EIAJ* specification, having a lower *bandwidth* than the more-expensive *high-band (U-matic)* system that is also available.

lower case A printers' term for 'small' letters like a, b, c, - - -. The corresponding capitals A, B, C, - - - are described as *upper case*. See also *x-height*.

lower cognitive A term applied to *educational objectives*, learning skills, etc that fall in the lower part of the *cognitive domain*, generally taken to encompass the two lowest levels (*knowledge* and *comprehension*); cf *higher cognitive*.

low-level (programming) language A *computer programming language* which requires the programmer to specify his/her *program* in minute detail, but which provides access to more specialized facilities of the *hardware*. It also produces programs which are much more rapidly executed than those written in a *high-level (programming) language* because they are closely related to the *machine code* instructions that actually make the computer operate. Low-level languages are usually specific to a particular make or range of machines, and are generally much more difficult to learn and tedious to work in than high-level languages.

LP See *long-playing (record)*.

LS See *long-shot*.

lucite Thick, clear plastic that can be moulded, carved, machined, etc. It is used for making and mounting visual display items.

lumen (lm) The S1 unit of *luminous flux* (the rate of flow of visible light from a source), one lumen being the luminous flux radiated through unit solid angle (1 steradian) from an isotropic point source with a *luminous intensity* of 1 *candela*.

luminaire A *studio, set* or theatre lighting unit that enables the colo(u)r, size, shape and sharpness of the light beam to be controlled by means of *barn doors, filters* and *diffusers*. Examples of luminaires are *broads, floods* and *spots*.

luminance A measure of the amount of light emitted by a surface, whether by reflection or scattering or by self-luminous emission or transillumination. It is measured in *candelas* per square metre (meter). Should not be confused with *illuminance*.

luminous flux The rate of flow of visible light from a source. This is measured in *lumens*.

luminous intensity The amount of light emitted by a body. This is measured in *candelas*.

lux (lx) The S1 unit of *illuminance* (the amount of light falling on a surface), one lux being an illuminance of 1 *lumen* per square metre (meter).

lx See *lux*.

M

McDade Plan A course system based on the use of short units of *personalized instruction* that are adaptable to the needs of individual students.

machine code The *binary code* in which the actual instructions that cause a particular *digital computer* to operate are written, and in which the computer communicates internally with its various systems and parts. *Programs* that are written in other *programming languages* have to be translated into machine code using a suitable *compiler* or *interpreter* before they can be executed by the computer; cf *high-level (programming) language, low-level (programming) language.*

machine-dependent instruction A term applied to an instructional process or system in which *hardware* of some sort (eg a *computer*, or tape-slide study facility) is so integral to the process or system that its removal or non-availability would render the system or process inoperable; cf *machine-independent instruction.*

machine-independent instruction A term applied to an instructional process or system that does not depend on the availability of specialized *hardware* for it to operate effectively; cf *machine-dependent instruction.*

machine-paced instruction A type of *programmed instruction* in which the pace at which instruction proceeds is controlled by the *teaching machine* or *computer* by which the *program(me)* is administered.

machine-readable A term used to describe a document, *label*, set of data, etc that is in such a form that it can be 'read' directly by a suitable *computer peripheral* using a technique such as *optical character recognition* or *magnetic ink character recognition.*

macro lens A generic term for a lens (such a *bellow lens* or *macrozoom lens*) designed for use in *macrophotography.*

macrophotography Photography of small objects at reproduction scales between life size and roughly 10 times magnification; cf *microphotography, photomicrography.*

macrozoom lens A *zoom lens* designed for use in *macrophotography.*

magazine 1. A light-proof *film* container for use with a camera, processor, etc. 2. A container for *slides* or a *filmstrip* designed for use in conjunction with a suitable *projector* or *viewer.*

Magerian objective A rigorously-specified *behavio(u)ral objective* of the type advocated by R.F. Mager and his followers. Such objectives specify what the learner should be able to do, under what conditions, and at what level of competence.

magic lantern An early name for a device used to project *lantern slides*, the name of which was derived from the term.

magnetic board A flat sheet of ferromagnetic material (eg mild steel) on to whose surface magnetic objects or objects backed with small magnets or *magnetic tape* can be stuck for display purposes. See also *magnetic chalkboard, magnetic markerboard.*

magnetic card A card coated on one side with a thin layer of magnetic oxide that can be used to record *audio* material or data.

magnetic cartridge A medium-quality *record player* pick-up *cartridge* that uses a moving magnet as a *transducer.*

magnetic chalkboard A *chalkboard* made of ferromagnetic material so that it can also serve as a *magnetic board*, thus combining the advantages of the two types of board. See also *magnetic markerboard.*

magnetic disk See *disk.*

magnetic film 1. Any *motion picture* that has a *magnetic sound track*. 2. Sprocketted *film* coated with magnetic oxide that is used to carry the sound recording of a *SEPMAG* motion picture film. 3. A data storage medium consisting of a thin layer of magnetizable material on a non-magnetizable film-like substrate; cf *magnetic tape*.

magnetic film projector A *projector* designed for showing *motion pictures* with *magnetic sound tracks*.

magnetic ink character recognition (MICR) A technique that enables *characters* printed in special magnetic ink to be *machine-readable*.

magnetic letters, figures, characters Pre-cut letters, figures or *characters* with magnetized backs designed for use in making up *magnetic board* displays.

magnetic markerboard A *markerboard* made of ferromagnetic material so that it can also serve as a *magnetic board*, thus combining the advantages of the two types of board. See also *magnetic chalkboard*.

magnetic/optical sound projector A *motion picture* projector capable of showing films with either a *magnetic sound track* or an *optical sound track*.

magnetic recording film See *magnetic film* (2.).

magnetic sound projector A *motion picture* projector capable of showing films with *magnetic sound tracks* but not those with *optical sound tracks*; cf *magnetic/optical sound projector*.

magnetic sound track A thin stripe of magnetic oxide along one edge of a *motion picture* film that is used to carry the associated sound signal; cf *optical sound track*. See also *COMMAG*.

magnetic tape 1. Thin magnetic oxide-coated plastic tape on which *audio signals, television* signals or *digital* data can be recorded. 2. Heavy magnetized tape used for attaching light materials to *magnetic boards* or for preparing displays for such boards.

MAG-OPT A term applied to a *motion picture* with both a *magnetic sound track* and an *optical sound track*.

mag track An abbreviation for *magnetic sound track*.

main entry The principal entry in a catalog(ue), bibliography, *index*, etc relating to a particular document or item. It gives the fullest information about the document or item, and (usually) details of any other entries.

mainframe See *mainframe computer*.

mainframe computer A term that is applied to any large *digital computer* system of high capacity and power to distinguish such machines from smaller *minicomputers* or *microcomputers*. The name derives from the term *mainframe*, which originally referred to the *central processing unit* of such a large computer.

main store The fast, *random-access memory* system incorporated in the *central processing unit* of a *digital computer*. Until recently, such memory was generally built-up of tiny magnetizable magnetic rings (*core memory*), but this type is now being largely superseded by various forms of semiconductor-based memory, which are becoming cheaper, faster and more powerful.

main title 1. The name of a *film, program(me)*, etc, generally shown at the start. 2. The principle title by which a book or other document is known; cf *subtitle*.

mains hum See *hum*.

maintenance costs The total on-going expenditure of funds that is required to keep a system in an operational state after the initial purchase, acquisition or construction costs have been met. Should not be confused with *running costs*, of which they form one component.

management game Another name for a *business game*.

manipulation test A test of *psychomotor skill* designed to assess manual dexterity. It is used in personnel selection, vocational guidance, etc.

manipulative materials *Learning resources* such as model-making *kits, educational toys*, and tools that are actually handled and manipulated by the person using them.

manual 1. A detailed and comprehensive guide to practice, use, manufacture or service, usually in book or booklet form. 2. Relating to the use of the hands. 3. A term applied to an exercise such as an educational *game* or *simulation* that does not involve the use of a *computer* or similar system.

manual entry Entering data, instructions, etc into a *computer* via a *keyboard terminal*.

markerboard A board with a smooth, light-colo(u)red surface on which display material may be written or drawn using crayons, felt pens or other easily-erased markers. See also *magnetic markerboard*.

marking scale A *scale* that is established by an examining body, school, etc in order to guide examiners in marking tests or examinations, particularly in subjects or areas where a large element of subjective judgment has to be employed.

mark-up In publishing, to provide detailed instructions of the requirements regarding typesetting on printer's copy.

married print A *print* of a *sound film* that carries both the pictures and the sound. Also known as a *combined print* and a *composite print*.

mask 1. An opaque plastic, cardboard, paper or acetate *overlay* used for covering part(s) of an *OHP transparency* for the purpose of progressive disclosure. 2. An opaque *frame* used to define the picture area of a *slide* or *transparency*. 3. In word processing or computing, a display that includes blank areas to be filled in by the operator.

massaging Manipulation of material (eg on the screen of a *visual display unit* or *word processor*) until the required *format* and/or content is obtained.

mass media A generic terms for means of communication such as newspapers, radio and television that are capable of reaching large numbers of people simultaneously with a common message. Also known as *media*.

master 1. A copy of a document, tape, film, etc (or, in some cases, the original) from which further copies (or extracts) can be made, or a specially-prepared *plate*, *stencil*, etc used for printing such copies. 2. A device or machine which controls other devices or machines; cf *slave unit*.

mastering The use of a *disk, tape* or other form of stored information as a master from which others are copied. In *computer* storage on disk, such a master is made to ensure that the working disk is not the only copy available.

mastery learning An approach to instruction based on the assumption that mastery of any task, skill, topic, subject, field, etc is (in principle) possible for all individuals provided that each is provided with instruction appropriate to his/her particular experience and ability and is given all the time that he/she needs. See also *no-failure course, program(me)*.

mastery model A *model* for correct, error-free or minimally-acceptable *performance* of a task or set of tasks that is used as a standard during instruction.

mastery requirement See *unit-perfection requirement*.

masthead The most prominently displayed and typographically distinct title of a periodical such as a journal, generally found on the front cover and/or the first page of main content.

matched action shots In film production, two related, adjacent *shots* that are taken in such a way that the *action* proceeds naturally from one to the other, without any impression of discontinuity, after they have been edited together.

matched groups In an educational or other experiment, an *experimental group* and *control group* that are selected so as to be as nearly as possible identical in respect of all relevant qualities or *variables*. In some cases, this may be done by ensuring that all the individuals in each group are as near as possible identical in respect of these variables or qualities (eg all girls of age 14 with an IQ in the range 85–115). In other cases, it may be necessary to use the *matched pairs* technique, whereby each subject placed in one group is matched by a similar subject in the other.

matched pairs See *matched groups*.

matching item A type of *objective item* which requires the testee to arrange the members of two sets of words, symbols, pictures, etc in corresponding pairs, as in the example shown in figure 28.

materials development The development of instructional materials, generally within the context of a *behavio(u)ral objectives*-based approach.

mathetics A method of presenting information used in *programmed instruction*. It involves the systematic use of *reinforcement*, and is based on the *backward chaining* theories of T.F. Gilbert. See also *demonstrate, prompt, release*.

For each country in Column A, select the capital city from Column C and write it in the appropriate space in Column B		
A. Country	**B.**	**C. Capital City**
France		Warsaw
Spain		Oslo
		Copenhagen
Belgium		Belgrade
Norway		Budapest
		Berlin
Sweden		Paris
Switzerland		Moscow
		Prague
Italy		Brussels
Hungary		Madrid
		Lisbon
Russia		Berne
Czechoslovakia		Stockholm

Figure 28 A typical matching item

mathmagenic information Additional or augmenting information that is provided in order to facilitate *learning*, eg use of devices such as *prompts*, questions in text, *feedback* and *algorithms*.

matrix printer See dot matrix printer.

matrix, matrices test See *progressive matrices test*.

matt (matte) A term applied to a surface with a dull, non-reflecting finish, eg matt *photographic paper* or a *matt screen*; cf *gloss*.

matt (matte) screen A projection *screen* with a *matt* surface that provides even brilliance over a wide range of viewing angles; cf *beaded screen, silvered screen*.

maze test A test or test *item* in which the subject has to find the most direct route through a maze of some sort.

mean (μ) A statistical measure of the *central tendency* of a statistical distribution or set of *scores*. Usually taken to refer to the *arithmetic mean* (the sum of the individual scores divided by the total number of scores) as opposed to the *geometric mean* (the n'th root of the product of the n individual scores), and is regularly used as an abbreviation for the former; the term is used both as a noun and as an adjective; cf *median, mode*.

meaningful learning A term used to denote *learning* which involves relating new content to previously-learned content or to previously-integrated experience. It is used particularly in the context of *advance(d) organizers*.

mean square A statistical term for the *arithmetic mean* of the squares of the *scores* in a distribution.

mechanical aptitude test A test designed to assess an individual's ability to understand how movement can be transmitted mechanically through a system. Such tests are used in vocational guidance and personnel selection.

mechanical binding A method of holding the sheets of a book, booklet or other document together using mechanical devices other than sewing or adhesive, eg by using *comb binding* or a *slip binder*.

mechanical editing A general term for the various *editing* methods used with *audiotapes* or *motion pictures* that involve cutting them up and physically joining the pieces into the required continuity, cf *electronic editing*.

mechanical lettering device, system A device (system) used to add *lettering* to graphic or other material by mechanical means, eg by use of *stencils* or templates.

mechanism A *psychomotor* process in which a

learned *response* has become habitual, ie is automatically exhibited as a response to an appropriate *stimulus* or situation; Level 4 of Harrow's *psychomotor domain*.

media 1. The physical tools of *instructional technology*, including *printed materials, audiotapes, videotapes, films, filmstrips, slides* and all the various combinations thereof. 2. A synonym for the term *mass media*.

media centre (center) Another name for a *resource(s) centre (center)*.

media mobile A term of Australian origin for a bus or van equipped as a mobile *resource(s) centre (center)*.

median A statistical measure of the *central tendency* of a statistical distribution or set of *scores*. The *median* is the exact mid-point in a distribution, ie the point above and below which fall exactly 50 per cent of the measures or scores; cf *mean, mode*.

mediated learning A term (first used by Olsen and Bruner) that denotes *learning* that takes place via *media* of some sort (eg by reading about something in a book or seeing it depicted on film or television) as opposed to learning that is brought about through direct experience (*enactive learning*).

mediated observation Observation of a situation (eg activities in a classroom, an interview or a role-playing *simulation*) that is carried out indirectly using a medium such as television or film rather than by direct observation. Use of such a technique enables the situation to be recorded for future discussion, analysis, etc.

mediated self-confrontation Use of a suitable recording medium (such as *audiotape, videotape* or *film*) to show a learner or trainee how he or she is coping with a particular task or situation. See also *microteaching*.

media transfer Transposing material from one medium to another, eg from *film* on to *videotape* or from *artwork* to a *slide*.

medium close-up In photographic, film or television work, a *shot* intermediate between a *close-up* and a *medium shot*.

medium long shot In photographic, film or television work, a *shot* intermediate between a *medium shot* and a *long shot*.

medium shot (MS) In photographic, film or television work, a *shot* about half way between a *long shot* and a *close-up*, ie one that shows the subject as it would normally be seen by an observer. The relationship between the three types of shot, which together constitute the basic visual 'building bricks' of film and television program(me)s, is illustrated in figure 29.

megabyte A unit of data size or data storage capacity equivalent to 10^6 (ie one million) *bytes*; cf *kilobyte, gigabyte*.

memory 1. The part of the mind/brain system in which impressions, facts, etc are stored; see also *long-term memory, short-term memory*. 2. In computing and data processing, a generic term for any system in which data can be stored in *digital* form. See also *random-access memory, read-only memory, main store, backing store, working memory*.

memory card Another name for a *punched card*.

memory span 1. The period of time during which learned material is retained in the *memory*; see also *long-term memory, short-term memory*. 2. The number of related or unrelated items that can be recalled after a single presentation of the items.

mental ability See *general intelligence, mental ability*.

mental age An estimate of the intellectual development of an individual given in terms of the *chronological age* of the average population to which he/she is equivalent in mental terms. An exceptionally bright child of chronological age five, for example, might have a mental age of seven, while a backward child of the same age might have a mental age of only three or four. Also known as *intelligence age*. See also *educational quotient (EQ), intelligence quotient (IQ)*.

mental ratio Another name for *intelligence quotient (IQ)*.

menu A list of options presented by a *computer* to a user, usually via a *visual display unit*. See also *menu-driven program*.

menu-driven program A *computer program* that presents the user with a *menu* from which the section required at the time can be selected. Such programs are extensively used in *computer-based learning*; cf *command-driven program*.

meta-analysis 1. A term used in connection with *advance(d) organizers*, whose effective use enables a learner to achieve a higher level of abstraction, generality and inclusiveness known as meta-analysis. 2. A method of identifying common strands or features in a large number of *case studies* by carrying out a systematic *analysis* of qualitative data relating to same.

meta-cognition Use by a learner of his/her own individual 'how to learn' model (*learning style*) in a learner-controlled *learning* situation. See also *locus of control*.

long shot

medium shot

close-up

Figure 29 The long shot/medium shot/close-up sequence

meta-language A language that is used to specify or describe another language and can therefore be thought of as being of a 'higher level' than the latter. The term (which originated in semantics) is used in indexing and classification.

metal interlocking stencil letters Individual metal *stencil* letters, numerals and other *characters* that can be joined together to form complete words, *titles*, *captions*, etc.

metronome A mechanical device that can be used to produce a regular series of ticking noises of any required frequency. It is used in music teaching and psychological research.

MICR See *magnetic ink character recognition*.

microcard A rectangular card on which a matrix of *microimages* (such as pages of text) is recorded. See also *micro-opaque*. Recent versions of microcard, *microfiche*, *microfilm* and *microform* can also be read using computer-assisted retrieval. Computer-assisted production has now become widely used.

microcard, microfiche, microfilm reader A device whereby an eye-readable *image* of one of the pages of a *microcard*, *microfiche* or *microfilm* can be produced for individual or small-group study, usually by *back projection*.

micro-cassette A miniature audiotape *cassette* roughly one third the size of a *compact cassette*. Such cassettes are used for dictation, data recording, etc.

microcomputer A small, portable *digital computer* of the 'desk top' type; cf *mainframe computer*, *minicomputer*. Also known as a *desk-top computer*.

microcopy A copy of a page of text, diagram, etc that is so reduced in comparison with the original that it cannot be read or studied with the naked eye, eg one of the *microimages* on a *microfiche* or *microcard*.

microfiche A transparent sheet of *photographic film* (usually $4'' \times 6''$) on which a matrix of *microimages* (such as pages of text) is recorded. Such cards generally have an eye-readable title strip along the top edge. See also *microcard*.

microfilm 1. A roll or strip of transparent *photographic film* carrying a series of *microimages* (such as pages of text) which can be viewed one at a time by winding the film through a suitable device (a microfilm *reader*).

2. *Photographic film* with the characteristics required for recording *microimages*. See also *microcard*.

micro-floppy disk Another term for a *minidisk*.

microfolio A set of parallel strips of *microfilm* contained in a transparent jacket about the same size as a standard *microfiche*.

microform A generic term for any medium used to record *microimages*, eg *microcard*, *microfiche*, *microfilm*.

micrographics A generic term for all aspects of *microform* technology.

microgroove A term used to describe a conventional *black disc* with more than 350 grooves to the inch. The term was introduced during the early 1950s when such discs started to replace the coarse-grooved '78s' that had been the standard type of gramophone record up till then.

microimage An *image*, so reduced in comparison to the original, that it cannot be read or studied with the naked eye. See also *microcopy*.

micro-opaque A general term for a set of *microimages* stored on an opaque medium such as card (see *microcard*) or *photographic paper* (see *microprint*).

microphone A device that contains a *transducer* capable of converting incident sound waves into an electrical *audio signal* in *analog(ue)* form, usually for feeding into an amplifying, mixing or recording system of some sort.

microphone characteristic The directional properties of a *microphone*, usually given in terms of a *polar diagram* that indicates its relative sensitivities in different horizontal directions — see, for example, figure 9, on page 22 and figure 12 on page 28.

microphotography Producing microscopically-small photographic *images* of objects, pages of text, drawings, etc using extreme optical reduction techniques as, for example, in the production of *microfilms* or *microfiches*. This is the conventional meaning of the term in the UK and the USA, but in most European countries the term microphotography is used instead of *photomicrography*; cf *macrophotography*.

microprint A sheet of *photographic paper* on which a matrix of *microimages* is recorded.

microprocessor 1. An integrated system of digital logic circuits built into a single wafer of silicon; single microprocessors form the heart of modern microelectronic devices such as electronic watches, calculators and *microcomputers*, and are also used to build up more complicated systems such as larger computers. 2. A term sometimes used as a synonym for a *microcomputer*.

microprojector A device designed to enlarge and project transparent *microimages* or microscope *slides* for viewing by large groups.

microsleep A term for a type of short attention break that a learner periodically undergoes during a lecture, talk, etc that lasts longer than his/her *attention span*.

microteaching A range of techniques used in training teachers (and others concerned with interpersonal communication) in specific skills or sets of skills in scaled-down teaching situations. A typical microteaching session might involve one student teaching a small section of a lesson to a simulated class, with his/her performance being recorded on *videotape* for subsequent discussion and criticism by the rest of the trainee group. See also *mediated observation, mediated self-confrontation*.

microwave link A telecommunications link that involves beaming signals encoded on microwaves (electromagnetic waves in the frequency range $10^9 - 10^{12}$ Hz) between *aerials* connected by line-of-sight.

mid-range speaker A *loudspeaker* unit designed to handle the middle frequencies of the *audio spectrum*, often forming part of a multi-speaker system designed to cover the whole range; cf *tweeter, woofer*. Also known as a *squawker*.

mid-shot Another term for a *medium shot*.

mimeographing A widely-used US term for *stencil duplication*, derived from the name of one the leading US manufacturers of the equipment and consumable software used in such duplication.

mimeoscope Another name for a *light box*.

minicourse 1. A self-contained *package* of materials used in teacher training, designed so that it can be used by the trainee without supervision and enables self-evaluation to be carried out. 2. A US term for any course that

is shorter than normal, eg a short intensive course on a single topic or concept.

minicomputer A term that is used to denote a *digital computer* intermediate in size and power between a *microcomputer* and a *mainframe computer*.

minidisk An extra-small *floppy disk* 3½ or 3 inches in diameter. Such disks, which can hold roughly one A4 page of text, are used in some *word processor* and *microcomputer* systems. Also known as a *micro-floppy disk*. Should not be confused with a *mini-floppy disk*.

mini-floppy disk A term sometimes applied to a 5¼ inch *floppy disk* to distinguish it from the larger 8 inch variety or the even smaller 3½ or 3 inch varieties (*minidisks* or *micro-floppy disks*).

minischool A US term for a unit within a school that has adopted alternative or progressive instructional methods not yet used in the school as a whole.

miscue A *cue* which leads a reader to perceive a message, meaning, implication, etc which is not actually contained in the material being studied.

mix 1. In sound recording or television work, to combine two signals from different sources into a single signal; see also *sound mixer, vision mixer*. 2. A visual effect similar to a *dissolve*.

mix down To mix *audio signals* from a larger to a smaller number of *tracks*, eg from *eight track* to *stereo*.

mnemonic A system that serves as an aid to *memory*, eg use of an easily-remembered acronym to represent a list of items.

mobile A three-dimensional *non-projected display* composed of elements hung from a system of threads so that they can rotate and move about — effectively a dynamic *wallchart*. Mobiles like the one shown in figure 30 can be extremely useful as *reinforcement* aids, particularly with younger children.

mobile unit A van fitted with television or radio equipment that is used to shoot or record program(me)s 'in the field', ie away from the *studio*.

mock broadcast A method of language instruction in which students produce a script

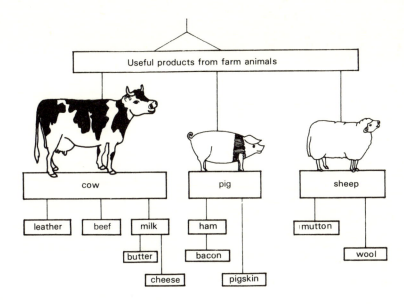

Useful products from farm animals

cow | pig | sheep

leather | beef | milk | ham | mutton

butter | bacon | wool

cheese | pigskin

Figure 30 A typical mobile of the type used for reinforcement purposes with young children

for and act out a radio program(me) as if it were being broadcast.

mock examination An examination that is organized for its students by a school or college in order to simulate an external examination that they are due to face some time after, thus giving them a 'rehearsal'.

mode 1. A statistical measure of the *central tendency* of a distribution, being the value or *score* that occurs most frequently, ie the value or score at which the peak of the distribution occurs; cf *mean, median*. 2. A particular method of operating or using a system such as a *computer* (see, for example, *batch mode, conversational mode, interactive mode*) or carrying out an operation (see, for example, *mode of instruction, learning, teaching*).

mode of instruction, learning, teaching Terms used to describe the way in which instruction is organized, eg as a large-group presentation, a small-group exercise, independent study, etc.

model 1. A physical or conceptual representation of an object or system, incorporating certain specific features of the original; see also *simulation*. 2. An example held up for imitation — see, for example, *mastery model, skill model, model(l)ing, observational teaching*.

model(l)ing 1. In *microteaching*, the use of live or recorded demonstrations of good teaching as *models* for students to aim at. 2. In language instruction, speech therapy, etc, use of examples of correctly-spoken material as *models* that the learners have to try to copy; this technique is particularly widely used in *language laboratory* work. 3. In *studio* or *set* lighting, use of *back lighting* in order to produce a three-dimensional effect.

modem A computing term for a device that is used to convert a *digital* signal into an *analog* signal capable of being transmitted along an ordinary telephone line or to re-convert an analog signal back into digital form after such transmission. The word is an abbreviation of *modulator-demodulator*. Also known as a *data set*. See also *acoustic coupler*.

moderator An internal or external referee who checks the standard of an examination paper, the standard of marking, etc.

modern typeface A *typeface* in which there is a marked contrast between the thick and thin strokes of letters.

modified fog index See *fog index*.

modular course A flexible course that allows individual learners to select the course program(me) that best suits them from a structured hierarchy of *modules*, some of which are generally compulsory (*core modules*) and some optional.

modular examination An examination in which candidates can elect to take a number of optional papers or sections of equal difficulty in related subjects, topics or areas — eg they may have to take any three out of six such optional elements.

modular system 1. A piece of electronic (or other) equipment that is built up of easily-replaced or interchanged units or *modules*. 2. A term sometimes applied to a *modular course*.

modular training A method of training that involves building up the trainee's skills and/or knowledge in discrete stages, each based on a specific *module* of learning.

modulation The addition of information to an electromagnetic wave or electrical signal by varying its amplitude, frequency or phase in correspondence with the signal to be added. See also *amplitude modulation, frequency modulation*.

modulator-demodulator See *modem*.

module 1. An organized collection of learning experiences assembled in order to achieve a specified group of related objectives. 2. A self-contained section of a course or program(me) of instruction. See also *modular course*. 3. See *modular system*.

moirée patterns, fringes Patterns produced when two separate regular patterns (eg parallel

lines or arrays of squares) are superimposed at an angle to one another. Such patterns can (inadvertently) occur in television pictures that include striped images, and are also used to create an illusion of movement in animated *transparencies* by forming fringes of the type shown in figure 31 using a moving roll placed behind the transparency.

monaural Another term for *monophonic*.

monitor 1. See *television monitor*. 2. A person who acts as a tutor, supervisor or assessor in an *individualized learning* system such as the *Keller Plan*. 3. To check the quality of an *audio signal* or *television signal* during recording, broadcasting, etc using a *monitor loudspeaker* or *television monitor*. 4. To carry out an on-going quality check or appraisal of a system while it is actually in operation. 5. See *monitor program*.

monitor loudspeaker A high-quality *loudspeaker* used to *monitor* a sound signal during recording, broadcasting, etc.

monitor program A *computer program* that acts as an *operating system* for a *computer*, ie controls and monitors the sequencing and processing of programs, directs responses to the appropriate users, etc.

mono An abbreviation for *monaural* or *monophonic*.

monochrome Of a television picture, photographic *image*, etc in black and white as opposed to colo(u)r.

monophone A single *earphone* with a handle.

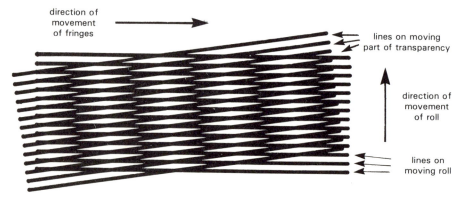

Figure 31 Use of the moirée fringes to produce animation in a transparency

Such devices are sometimes attached to exhibits in museums, etc in order to provide a spoken description or commentary.

monophonic A term used to describe a sound recording or sound reproduction system with only a single sound channel; cf *stereophonic, quadraphonic*. Also known as *monaural*.

montage 1. Combination of several *images* to produce a complex or multi-faceted composite image, eg on a television or cinema screen. 2. A series of short scenes in a film or television program(me) used to condense time or distance or show a series of related activities, events, places, etc.

Monte Carlo technique A *simulation* technique based on the use of a mathematical *model* (often computer-generated) that incorporates random elements or occurrences.

motion picture A *reel* (or set of reels) of *photographic film*, with or without an associated sound recording, bearing a succession of gradually-changing *images* which create an illusion of movement when projected in rapid succession (usually at either 18 or 24 frames per second). This is commonly referred to as a *film*.

motion picture camera A special camera designed for use in shooting *motion pictures*. See also *cine camera*.

motor ability, skill Other names for *psychomotor skill*.

mount A *frame* in which a single still *transparency* is set.

mounting The activity of attaching one surface, layer or material to another using heat and/or pressure and/or an intermediary paper or adhesive. See also *dry mounting, wet mounting*.

mounting press An electrically-heated press that is used in the *mounting* and/or *lamination* of flat graphic or photographic materials.

mouse A hand-held device by which the user of a *digitizer* or *data tablet* can enter graphical information into the system, alter existing material, etc. See also *light pen*.

mouth-to-ear instruction A generic term for traditional expository methods of instruction such as the *lecture* and taught lesson.

moving coil cartridge, loudspeaker, microphone A *cartridge, loudspeaker* or

microphone in which the *transducer* is a coil of wire that moves between the poles of a magnet. The *moving coil loudspeaker* is also known as an *electromagnetic loudspeaker*.

Moviola A system used to view *motion picture* film during *editing*. The term was originally the brand name of one of the leading manufacturers of such systems, but is now used as a generic name.

MTBF Mean time between failures — a measure of the *reliability* of equipment, etc.

MTBM Mean time between maintenance — a guide to the serving requirements of *hardware*.

multi-ability battery Another term for a *multi-factor battery*.

multi-access A term applied to a *digital computer* system with multiple *terminals* that enable several people to use its facilities simultaneously. See also *time sharing, virtual machine*.

multi-channel learning *Learning* that involves the use of more than one *perception channel*, eg the simultaneous use of hearing and sight. See also *multi-sensory learning (teaching) aids*.

multi-choice item, question See *multiple-choice item, question*.

multi-choice test See *multiple-choice test*.

multi-disciplinary A term applied to a course, instructional program(me), exercise, *package*, etc that covers or makes use of material from a number of different academic subject areas.

multi-element lens See *multiple-element lens*.

multi-factor battery A *battery* of tests, *scales*, etc which is designed to assess or measure several discrete *factors*. Such tests are constructed in conjunction with *factor analysis* techniques. Also known as a *multi-ability battery*.

multi-image A term applied to a presentation that makes simultaneous use of two or more *images*, usually projected and often on the same screen. See also *multi-screen*.

multi-media 1. A term describing a collection or group of documents or materials in several different *media*, eg a *multi-media kit*. 2. A term describing a single work designed to be presented through the integrated use of more than one medium, eg a *tape-slide program(me)* or *sound filmstrip*.

multi-media kit, package A *package* of materials in different *media* dealing with a specific topic or subject area and forming an integrated whole.

multiple bar chart Another name for a *component bar chart*.

multiple-choice item, question A type of *objective item* in which in testee/respondee has to choose the correct or most appropriate answer or *response* from a number of alternatives supplied — usually four or five. An example of a multiple-choice item in an objective test might be:
Question: What is the capital city of Rumania? *Alternative answers supplied*: (a) Belgrade; (b) Bucharest; (c) Budapest; (d) Sarajevo; (e) Sofia. See also *multiple-response item, question*.

multiple-choice test A test consisting entirely of *multiple-choice items*.

multiple-cutoff approach A technique used in multiple-test or multiple-paper *assessment* to ensure that weakness in one particular test or paper is not compensated for and/or obscured by high *scores* in the other tests or papers. It involves establishing a minimum cutoff (ie pass) score in each test or paper.

multiple-element lens A lens that is made up of several separate optical components; most camera lenses are of this type.

multiple-head-set unit Another name for a *listening centre (center)*.

multiple-limb coordination A *psychomotor skill* involving the ability to coordinate the movements of a number of limbs in performing tasks that require such coordinated action, eg driving a car.

multiple marking Marking of an essay, *project*, examination, etc that is carried out independently by two or more people in order to arrive at a collective mark that has greater *reliability*.

multiple-response item, question A type of *multiple-choice item* or *multiple-choice question* in which two or more of the *responses* are correct.

multiple track 1. A term applied to *magnetic tapes* with four or more (separate) parallel recording *tracks*, and to the equipment used with such tapes. 2. A term applied to *programmed instruction* materials or sequences with more than one *track* through them, ie *branching program(me)s*.

multiplexing A technique whereby several different signals can be transmitted down the same communications channel or line by combining them in such a way that they can be re-separated at the other end. One such technique involves encoding the signals in *digital* form and transmitting the pulses representing the different signals at different times (*time-division multiplexing*); another involves using different parts of the *bandwidth* of the *carrier signal* to carry different signals (*frequency-division multiplexing*).

multi-screen A term applied to a *multi-image* presentation that makes use of more than one screen; cf *split screen*.

multi-sensory learning (teaching) aids Learning or teaching aids which utilize or bring into play more than one of the physical senses, for example, film, television and tape-slide.

multi-track See *multiple-track*.

multivision A general term for presentations of the *multi-image* or *multi-screen* type.

mute 1. A term applied to a *film* or *video* with no associated *sound track* on the same film or tape. 2. To suppress the sound in a system.

N

N See *numerical ability*.

narration The verbal comments that are written to accompany a visual presentation such as a *film* or *video*.

narrowcasting A term sometimes applied to *cable television* and similar systems where distribution of the signal is restricted to those connected to the *network* (to distinguish them from broadcasting systems, where anyone can pick up the signal provided that he/she has the appropriate receiving equipment).

natural light *Ambient light* originating from natural as opposed to artificial sources.

nature table A display and working area in a primary or secondary school having exhibits and examples (often of local origin) relevant to nature study.

NBM See *non-book media*.

Nebraska scale A scale devised by the Nebraska Videodisc Design/Production Group to describe the degree of interactivity of *videodisc players*, and hence their usefulness in *interactive video* systems. See also *level 0, level 1, level 2, level 3, level 4*.

needs analysis A training term for a systematic investigation that is carried out in order to determine the type of instructional program(me) that a particular trainee requires in order to bring him/her up to the standard required for a particular job.

negative A photographic *image* with the tonal values reversed in relation to those of the subject depicted, or, if colo(u)red, complementary to those of the subject. The term is used both as a noun and as an adjective; cf *positive*.

negative correlation A type of *correlation* between two *variables* which indicates that an increase in one is associated with a decrease in the other, ie one where the *correlation coefficient* is between 0 and −1.0; cf *positive correlation*. Also known as *inverse correlation*.

negative feedback A type of *feedback* in which an increase in the output of a system causes the rate or level at which the system operates to decrease; cf *positive feedback*.

negative reinforcement A type of *reinforcement* which makes use of the termination of the reinforcing event to increase the probability that a desired *response* will be produced by a particular *stimulus*; cf *positive reinforcement*. Should not be confused with *punishment*.

negative skew See *skewness*.

negative transfer A reduction in the efficiency of *learning* because of earlier or related learning carried out in a different situation; cf *positive transfer*. See also *proactive inhibition*.

negotiated learning A form of *contract-based learning* in which the details of the contract are negotiated between the learner and the teacher/tutor/trainer.

network 1. A general term for any *system* consisting of a number of physically separated but interconnected *sub-systems*. 2. A system of interconnected agencies, organizations or institutions which can distribute or interchange resources, information, etc. 3. A group of radio or television broadcasting stations connected by cable, *microwave links*, or re-broadcast links so that all stations can broadcast the same program(me) simultaneously. 4. A system of *computers* or *word processors* (which may be in the same room or geographically dispersed) that are interconnected in such a way that they can exchange information and/or interact with a central master system, data base, etc. 5. A *cable television* or *CCTV* signal distribution system.

network analysis The name given to a particular formalized style of presenting a chart of relationships, eg the concepts in a course; cf *critical path method*.

new information technology The application of new electronic and other technologies (*computers, communications satellites, fibreoptic (fiberoptic) cables, videorecording,* etc) to the creation, storage, retention, transformation and distribution of information of all kinds. See also *information technology*.

Newton's rings Optical interference patterns in the form of alternate light and dark rings that are produced when two surfaces very close to one another are illuminated, eg the film surface of a photographic *slide* and its cover glass. See also *anti-Newton*.

nitrate film *Film* made of cellulose nitrate (celluloid), a highly inflammable plastic. Such film has now been largely superseded by the much-safer *acetate film* for most purposes.

Nixie A commercial name for a gas-filled digital display tube capable of showing numbers from 0–9. It is widely used as a generic term for such tubes.

noddy In television production, a type of *insert* used during interviews that shows the interviewer nodding agreement or otherwise expressing interest in what is being said by the interviewee.

no-failure course, program(me) A course or program(me) of instruction that is designed so as to eliminate outright failure by tailoring instruction to meet individual needs, providing *remedial instruction*, allowing transfer to less-demanding courses, etc. See also *mastery learning*.

noise 1. Unwanted background to a signal, *image*, etc, usually of a random nature; examples are the *hiss* and *hum* that can occur in *audio signals* and the *snow* effect that can detract from the quality of television pictures if the signal is weak; see also *background noise, signal-to-noise ratio*. 2. Any non-pertinent or irrelevant information that is retrieved during a search of some sort, eg interrogation of a *data base*.

noise reduction Reducing the subjective effect of *noise* on sound or picture quality by means

of electronic processing. The *Dolby system* (which is used to reduce noise in *audio signals* and *audio recordings*) is one of the best-known examples of a noise reduction system.

nominal group technique A way of organizing groups so as to enable individuals to express personal views with some anonymity. It is so named because individuals sometimes act on their own, so that such a group is only 'nominally' a group.

nominal scale The lowest of the four *scales* used in educational measurement. It consists of a set of identifying *labels* that are assigned to different categories, groups, etc, labels that may also be assigned numbers. See also *interval scale, ordinal scale, ratio scale*.

non-bibliographic data base A *data base* that offers direct access to factual data without referring to specified sources which contain the data; cf *bibliographic data base*.

non-book material Strictly speaking, any document (including a printed document) other than a book. It is now widely used to describe documents in *non-book media*.

non-book media (NBM) *Media* that transmit or carry information or instructions by other than typographic means, eg by sound, pictorial representation, projected *images*, etc. Also known as *non-print media*.

non-destructive readout *Readout* of data from a *computer store* that does not cause the record of the data in the store to be lost; cf *destructive readout*.

non-directive interview Another name for an *unstructured interview*.

non-directive tutorial A *tutorial* in which students are encouraged to contribute views and questions spontaneously, with the tutor acting as a leader and guide but not to the extent of dominating the group or firmly structuring the course of the discussion.

non-functioning distractor A *distractor* which attracts less than 5 per cent of the *responses* to a *multiple-choice item*, and which is therefore virtually ineffective.

non-print media Another term for *non-book media*.

non-projected display Any display that does not involve the use of a *projector, television* *monitor* or other optico-electronic device. See also *non-projected display materials, visual aids.*

non-projected display materials, visual aids Display materials (*visual aids*) such as *feltboards*, charts and *models* that do not require a *projector* for their use. Also known as *self-display materials.*

non-readers' intelligence test A UK term for a *verbal intelligence test* that is presented orally, thus enabling it to be used with children or adults who cannot read. Should not be confused with a *non-verbal intelligence test.*

non-reproducing A term used to describe guide lines, instructions, etc on printer's copy or *artwork* that do not show up when the copy or artwork is photographed or reproduced. A special light blue pencil (known as a *non-reproducing pencil*) is often used for this purpose.

non-reproducing pencil See *non-reproducing.*

nonsense figure A pattern of lines, marks or shapes that has little or no intrinsic meaning. Such figures are frequently used in the study of *intelligence*, personality, etc.

nonsense syllables Artificial letter combinations, often consonant-vowel-consonants (CVCs), which do not represent meaningful words. Such syllables are used in the study of *learning* and *memory.*

non-verbal communication The meaningful transfer of information through methods which do not involve the use of normal spoken or written language; eg by facial expression or *body language.*

non-verbal intelligence test An *intelligence test* that requires little or no use of language (written or spoken). Examples of such tests are the *draw-a-man test*, *maze test* and *progressive matrices test*. Should not be confused with a *non-readers' intelligence test.*

non-zero-sum game A type of *business game* or other game in which the success of the winner(s) is not necessarily at the expense of the loser(s); cf *zero-sum game.*

norm 1. The average performance or measure shown by a particular homogenous *population* in respect of a particular function, *factor, variable*, etc, eg the average *intelligence quotient*, which is defined as 100. 2. The behavio(u)r expected of members of a particular group, class, *population*, etc.

normal distribution (curve) A symmetrical bell-shaped distribution that has (or approximates to) the shape of a *Gaussian distribution*. Such a distribution has 68.2 per cent of scores within one *standard deviation* (σ) of the *mean* (μ), with a further 27.2 per cent being between one and two standard deviations from the mean (see figure 32).

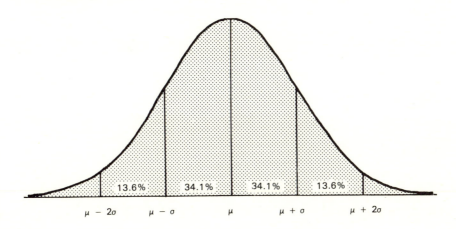

Figure 32 The normal distribution curve

norm line A smooth curve which passes through the *mean* or *median* scores of several successive groups when these are plotted graphically.

norm-referenced assessment *Assessment* that is designed to determine an individual's achievement or potential in comparison with the *norm* for the group, class or *population* to which he/she belongs (see, for example, *grading on the curve*); cf *criterion-referenced assessment*.

NTSC National Television System Committee. This is the body responsible for specification of television standards in the USA. It provides the colo(u)r television coding system used in the USA, Japan and many countries in South America. See also *PAL, SECAM*.

null hypothesis In statistics, research, etc, a statement which asserts that any differences observed between *samples* are attributable to random differences that occur naturally within the *population* from which the samples are drawn rather than to any significant difference between the samples.

number completion test A test of *numerical ability* that involves completing or continuing a series of numbers that are related by some definite principle or principles that can be inferred from the information provided. A typical *item* from such a test might be 'Give the next three numbers in the following series: 1, 2, 3, 5, 7, 11, —, —, —, - - -' (Answers: 13, 17, 19).

numerical ability (N) The ability to manipulate numbers. This is one of the basic abilities measured in *intelligence tests*, and is also one of the *primary mental abilities* thought by Thurstone to constitute *intelligence*.

O

OB See *outside broadcast*.

objective 1. A desired outcome of an instructional process or program(me) expressed in highly specific (generally behavio(u)ral) terms; see also *behavio(u)ral objective*. 2. Carried out in a detached, impartial manner without allowing subjective factors or personal prejudice to interfere. See also *objective assessment, examination, test*.

objective assessment, examination, test An *assessment*, examination or test that can be marked with total *reliability* by anyone, including non-subject specialists, or (in some cases) by a *computer*. This is made possible by designing the individual *items* in such a way that there is no need to apply subjective judgement over whether the answer is right or wrong, eg by using *multiple-choice items* or *matching items*.

objective evaluation 1. *Evaluation* carried out via formal measurements, usually of a quantitative nature. 2. *Evaluation* which is only concerned with establishing whether specified *objectives* have been achieved; cf *subjective evaluation*. See also *agricultural/botanical approach (to evaluation)*.

objective item, question An *item* or question in an *objective examination* or *objective test*.

object teaching Teaching that is based on observation, study of real objects and oral guidance rather than on the use of *textbooks*.

observation A research, *assessment, evaluation* or *learning* method in which the researcher, assessor, evaluator or learner carries out direct study of the phenomenon or system under investigation without interfering with or influencing the subject(s), in so far as this is possible. See also *classroom observation, mediated observation, observation schedule, observational learning*.

observation schedule A pro-forma that is used during *observation* (eg of trainee teachers carrying out teaching practice or *microteaching*) enabling the observer to note down his/her findings in coded or short-hand form.

observational learning *Learning* that takes place through the observation of a *model* system. See also *discovery learning*.

observed score Another term for a *raw score*.

obsolescence time 1. The length of time after which an item of *hardware* or other learning resource becomes so outdated that it is no longer of any real use. 2. The time over which the cost of purchasing a capital item is progressively 'written off' (amortized) for accountancy purposes.

occupational analysis The process of identifying those jobs which have a sufficient number of central tasks and skills in common to be grouped under a common occupation name. See also *occupational classification*.

occupational classification Using the results of *occupational analysis* to classify occupations into related groups or categories.

occupational guidance Offering guidance to individuals regarding the types of occupation for which they are suitable, often based on the use of *psychological tests* and/or *psychological inventories*.

OCR See *optical character recognition*.

off-air recording Recording a broadcast radio or television program(me) for later use.

off-campus study Education carried out outside the formal school/college/university system, eg by a *correspondence course* or other *distance learning* technique.

off-line Not connected to a *line, central processing unit*, system, etc at the time in question; cf *on-line*.

off-screen (OS) In film or television production, not seen, but (presumably) not far from the *action*. See also *out of vision*.

offset lithographic printing, lithography A *lithographic printing* process in which the *image* is transferred to the copy material via an intermediate surface such as a rubber blanket (see figure 33).

microphone, loudspeaker system or *aerial* with the same sensitivity or output in all horizontal directions.

OMR See *optical mark reader*.

one-to-one position Arrangement of a camera and the subject being photographed so as to produce an *image* the same size as the subject,

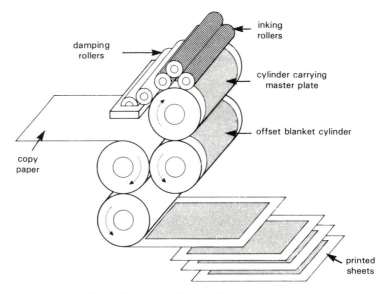

Figure 33 The offset lithographic process

off-the-job training Training that is organized and provided in a training centre (center) or other establishment away from the work/production situation of the trainees; cf *on-the-job training*.

OHP See *overhead projector*.

OHP transparency A large *transparency* (typically roughly 10 inch square) designed for display using an *overhead projector*.

omega wrap A tape path in a *helical scanning* videotape system shaped like the Greek letter Ω, thus giving slightly less than full 360° contact between the tape and the *head drum*; cf *alpha wrap, U-wrap*.

omnibus test A test which covers a range of different skills or mental operations in an extended sequence of *items*, but which produces a single overall *score*.

omnidirectional A term applied to a

eg during *slide* copying.

one-two-four snowball technique A *snowball group* technique in which the members are first asked to respond individually to a question or *stimulus*, then to form pairs in order to look for differences in these responses, then finally to form groups of four in order to arrive at a consensus response.

one-zero mark scheme A test marking scheme in which one mark is given for a correct answer to an *item* and zero marks for an incorrect answer or no answer. The scheme thus gives no credit for a partly-correct answer; cf *differential weighting*.

on-line Connected to a *line, central processing unit*, system, etc at the time in question; cf *off-line*.

on-the-job training The supervision and other supportive instruction that is given to a trainee or beginner in a particular job or position within the actual factory, plant etc at which he/she works; cf *off-the-job training*.

OOV See *out of vision*.

opaque projector The US name for a device that can be used to produce an enlarged projected *image* of opaque flat material such as the page of a book. In the UK, such a device is generally referred to as an *episcope*.

open access 1. A practice whereby users are given *direct access* to the stock of a library, *resources centre (center)*, etc, or to parts thereof; cf *closed access*. 2. A system whereby admission to a course is open to anyone who wishes to participate, regardless of qualifications or experience. 3. An informal *individualized learning* system in which students can make use of the facilities of the host institution at virtually any time.

open-book examination, test An examination or test in which students are allowed to bring into the examination room, and consult, specified reference material. The purpose of such an examination or test is to assess the testees' powers of interpretation, application, etc, rather than their powers of factual recall.

open classroom A classroom regime that is based on the principles of *open education*, generally incorporating a system of *discovery areas*. See also *open plan*.

open college An institution designed to enable adults to have access to courses which would not normally be available to them due to lack of formal qualifications. Such colleges tend to employ *open learning* methods. See also *open school, open university*.

open corridor A method of operating an *open education* system in a conventional 'separate classroom' school by using the corridor connecting a number of classrooms as a common learning area, area of contact, etc.

open education An approach to education where entry is not restricted by previous achievements. It may include an emphasis on learning rather than teaching, fostering of personal and affective growth, and encouragement of exploration and questioning; also, the teacher generally acts as a partner and guide rather than as an authoritarian figure. See also *open learning*.

open-ended A term applied to a question, test, examination, exercise, *project*, etc in which many acceptable answers or outcomes are possible rather than just one single correct solution or outcome; cf closed question.

open learning An instructional system which removes the traditional barriers to learning such as fixed times and places of instruction and rigid entry requirements, placing many aspects of the learning process under the control of the learner. The latter usually decides what, how and when to study — usually under some form of guidance. See also *individually-prescribed instruction, open college, open school, open university*.

open plan A term applied to a learning environment that is designed in an open, flexible manner rather than divided into traditional 'closed door' classrooms, thus allowing a wide range of teaching and learning methods to be employed (traditional 'face-to-face' teaching, *team teaching, group learning, individualized learning*, etc).

open reel, spool A term applied to an unenclosed tape or film *reel* (as opposed to the enclosed reels in *cassettes* and *cartridges*) and to the *hardware* used with such tapes or films.

open school An institution designed to offer adults access to education at secondary and lower-tertiary level regardless of their formal qualifications. Such institutions generally employ *open learning* methods.

Open Tech A UK program(me), funded by the Manpower Services Commission, which supports a large number of diverse projects mostly aimed at providing opportunities for adults in work to update or enhance their knowledge and/or skills. It uses a wide range of *open learning* approaches.

open test 1. A test that is generally available for use by persons other than professional psychologists or qualified test users. 2. A test that can be taken by anyone, not merely people who have undergone a particular course; cf *closed test*.

open university A term (originating from the name of the UK Open University, which was established during the 1960s) for an institution which provides adults with access to higher education regardless of their formal qualifications. Such institutions generally make heavy use of *distance learning* methods backed up by personalized counsel(l)ing and some face-to-face teaching.

operant conditioning A type of *conditioning* based on the direct *reinforcement* of desired *stimulus-response bonds.* It constitutes the theoretical basis of *linear programming* as originally developed by Skinner and his followers; cf *respondent conditioning.*

operating costs 1. A term used virtually synonymously with *running costs.* 2. On-going costs incurred once a project, program(me) etc has been launched; cf *start-up costs.*

operating system A *computer program* that controls the overall operation of a *computer* by controlling the sequencing and processing of programs, directing responses to the appropriate users, etc. Also known as a *monitor program.*

opportunistic teaching An unstructured, 'ad hoc' style of teaching which is based on acting on inspiration, seizing opportunities as they occur and working towards general *aims* as opposed to explicitly-defined *objectives*; cf *structured teaching.*

optical axis The axis of symmetry in an optical system such as the one shown in figure 34.

optical mark reader (OMR) A device that uses *optical character recognition* to recognise and record visible marks made by a respondee on a response sheet of some sort, eg in a *multiple-choice test* or survey.

optical pointer An electrically-operated torch which projects a small arrow or spot of light. It is used in place of a conventional pointer during projection, especially in darkened rooms.

optical sound projector A *motion picture* projector capable of showing films with *optical sound tracks* but not those with *magnetic sound tracks*; cf *magnetic/optical sound projector.*

optical sound track A *sound track* which has been recorded and/or printed on a *motion picture* film in the form of an optical strip along one edge of the film. Light passing through the strip from an *exciter lamp* to a *photocell* has its intensity modulated and hence produces an electrical signal that represents the original sound; cf *magnetic soundtrack.* See

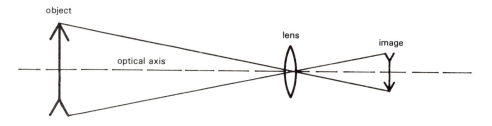

Figure 34 The optical axis of an optical system

optical character recognition (OCR) A system whereby *characters*, symbols or marks that are legible to the naked eye (eg numbers and letters on cheques) can also be read automatically by a machine using optico-electric methods; cf *magnetic ink character recognition (MICR).*

optical disc A general term for *audio discs* and *videodiscs* that are read by optical rather than electrical means. See also *compact disc, optical videodisc.*

optical fibre (fiber) See *fibreoptic (fiberoptic) cable.*

optical film projector A *projector* designed for showing *motion pictures* with *optical sound tracks.*

also *variable area sound track, variable density sound track.*

optical transmission, communication Use of visible light rather than microwaves or other radio waves as the vehicle for carrying signals, generally using *fibreoptic (fiberoptic) cables.*

optical videodisc A type of *videodisc* in which the signal is read by optical rather than electrical means, generally employing a *laser* to scan the signal; cf *contact videodisc, capacitance, capacitive videodisc.* See also *LaserVision.*

oral examination An examination in which the examinee gives spoken answers to spoken questions, as opposed to written answers to written questions. Also known, especially in the UK, as a *viva* or *viva-voce (examination)*.

ordinal scale The second lowest of the four types of *scale* used in educational measurement. In such a scale, the objects or items under investigation are simply placed in rank order and assigned rank values. See also *interval scale, nominal scale, ratio scale*.

organization An *affective* process that involves the conceptualization of values and the formation of ordered relationships between values; Level 4 of Krathwohl's *affective domain*.

organizer See *advance(d) organizer*.

organizer's guide A set of instructions produced for the guidance of the organizer of an educational or training exercise such as a *game, simulation* or participative *case study*.

orientation course A short course designed to introduce students, trainees or employees to a subject, course, institution, organization, industry, etc.

original A term applied to the actual *film* that is exposed in the camera during still or motion picture photography, or the actual *audiotape* or *videotape* on which sound or television signals are recorded, as opposed to any copies, prints or edited versions that are subsequently produced from them.

origination A *psychomotor* process that involves developing new motor acts or ways of manipulating materials by building on previously-learned *psychomotor skills*; Level 6 of Harrow's *psychomotor domain*.

OROM Optical read only memory. A type of *digital optical disk* that is used in the *constant angular velocity* mode. A 5.25 inch disk of this type can store roughly 300 *megabytes* of data.

orthochromatic A term used to describe *photographic film* that is sensitive to ultraviolet, blue and green light but not to red; cf *panchromatic*.

orthogonal factors A statistical term for *factors* which are completely independent and, in graphical representation, are generally shown at right angles to one another. Such factors are identified using *factor analysis*.

OS See *off-screen*.

outcome specification In instructional design, a statement of desired *terminal behavio(u)r* in terms that can be measured or assessed.

out of focus A term used to describe an *image* produced by a lens, camera, etc that is not sharply defined, ie not *in focus*.

outlier library A branch or section of a library other than the main central branch or section, eg in one of the outer buildings of a multi-site institution.

out of sync A term used to describe a situation where the sound and picture components of a *television signal* or *sound film* are not properly synchronized.

out of vision (OOV) In television or film production, activity that takes place outside the field of view of the particular camera that is in operation at the time; cf *in vision*.

outside broadcast (OB) A radio or television program(me) produced 'on location' rather than in a *studio*.

overcranking Shooting a *motion picture* sequence at a higher speed than the intended projection speed in order to slow down the action; cf *undercranking*.

overexposure In photography or *reprography*, *exposure* of sensitive material to light or heat at too great an intensity or for too long a time to produce a properly-formed *image*; cf *underexposure*.

overhead camera In television production, a camera fitted in a vertical position pointing down at a flat surface on which *captions*, *artwork*, etc may be placed. Also referred to as a *TV-reader*.

overhead projector (OHP) A device designed to project easily-visible *images* from large *transparencies (OHP transparencies)* on to an external screen in an undarkened room.

overhead transparency See *OHP transparency*.

overlay A transparent or translucent sheet that is superimposed on a *transparency* or opaque item of *artwork* in order to provide additional or alternative information, eg to add information to an *OHP transparency*.

overlearning, overtraining Memorizing or *learning* material beyond the point needed to ensure satisfactory recall or skilled performance.

overload 1. To feed into a system an input greater than that which it is designed to handle, thus causing distortion, breakdown, etc. 2. A situation where '1.' has occurred.

overstriking Substituting one *character* for another on a *visual display unit* screen.

over-the-shoulder shot In film or television production, a *shot* taken over the shoulder of a person involved in the action, thus simulating the view that he/she has of what is going on.

overt response A *response* that takes the form of an oral, written, manipulative or other act on the part of a learner which can be directly observed and/or recorded by an observer; cf *covert response*.

overt stimulus Any *stimulus* that can be directly observed and/or recorded by another person; cf *covert stimulus*.

overwriting Entering new information into a *computer store* so as to replace information already held there.

P

paced operative training The training of operatives on an increasing-speed basis in order to bring them up to the speed of a standard production line, the speed of the machine that they are to operate, etc.

pacing The process of indicating the speed to be achieved by an individual learner, group or class in carrying out a given task or program(me) of work. See also *individually-paced instruction, learning, machine-paced instruction, self-pacing*.

package 1. A collection of all the materials needed to organize, run or participate in an exercise, course, program(me), etc. 2. A computing term for a generalized *program* or set of programs (often with supportive *documentation*) designed to meet the needs of several users or to fulfil a specific user-oriented function (see *applications program, package*). Also known as a *software package*.

packet switching A method of routing data, or a message, from a transmitter to a receiver which involves dividing the data or message into small units or 'packets' of standard size and format, each labelled with the source and the destination. The packets are then transmitted in a way that makes the most efficient use of the communication network being used.

pad An alternative name for a *data tablet*.

paddle A manual control device used in conjunction with a *computer*, eg in video games and *interactive video*.

page 1. One side of a sheet of paper in a document. 2. A specific section within a *computer store*. 3. A *viewdata* term for a collection of information that can be called up by means of its particular page number; such a page may consist of several *frames*.

pagination 1. The process of numbering the

pages in a document. 2. In catalog(u)ing, stating the number of *pages* in a document.

paired comparison An experimental or research method in which subjects are compared with one another in pairs, each with each, until all relevant *variables* or *factors* have been covered.

PAL Phase Alternate Line — the colo(u)r television coding system that is used in the UK, most of Western Europe (except France) and many other parts of the world. See also *NTSC, SECAM*.

palantype A term applied to a *keyboard* which produces phonetic *characters* for subsequent transcription, often by a *computer*.

pan 1. In film and television production, a *shot* in which the camera is rotated about a vertical axis, thus moving the direction of the shot across the scene from left to right or vice versa. 2. To move a camera as in '1.'; cf *crab*. 3. An abbreviation for *panchromatic*.

panchromatic A term used to describe *photographic film* that is sensitive to all the colo(u)rs of the visible spectrum; cf *orthochromatic*.

panel 1. A collection of *resource materials* made available to a learner while he/she is working through a particular instructional program(me). It may include *printed materials, audiovisual materials, laboratory* equipment, *computer* facilities, etc. 2. A group of people selected to act as a team or jury for some purpose. 3. A board or surface in which instructions, switches, etc are mounted.

pan-tilt handle An extension rod attached to a *pan-tilt head* to enable the operator to *pan* and *tilt* the camera manually.

pan-tilt head A mechanism attached to the top

of a camera *pedestal* or *tripod* to enable the operator to *pan* and *tilt* the camera using a *pan-tilt handle*.

pantograph 1. A drawing aid (consisting of a hinged metal or wooden frame with adjustable joints) that can be used to make enlargements or reductions of original material. The user traces over the material to be copied with a *stylus*, and, as he/she does so, a pen or pencil attached to another part of the pantograph draws an *image* of the required size. 2. A system of hinged rods used to raise or lower a light source suspended from a *lighting grid*.

paper and pencil test Any educational or psychological test which involves only question papers, answer papers and writing instruments.

paper tape A long, narrow strip of paper, usually 1 inch wide and wound in thousand foot *reels*, in which a pattern of holes can be cut to represent *digital* data (eg for feeding into a *computer*, control system, etc). Also known as *punched tape*.

paradigm An operational *model* that can serve as an example or guide. The term is especially associated with the US philosopher and historian of science T.S. Kuhn, who uses it to describe the underlying theoretical model on which a particular branch or sub-branch of science is currently based together with the techniques, conventions and standards associated with the practice of that particular branch or sub-branch of science.

parallax The apparent displacement of an object in relation to its background due to observation of the object from more than one point in space (see figure 35). Parallax is an important factor that has to be taken into account in photography, television production, etc.

parameter 1. In research and measurement, a quantity which is constant in the circumstances or case being considered but which can have different values in other circumstances or cases, ie a 'variable constant'. 2. A statistical value such as the *mean, mode, median, range, standard deviation* or *variance* that is obtained in respect of a particular *variable* for a particular *population*.

parent page A *viewdata* term for the *routing page* immediately prior to the *page* containing the information that the user requires.

partial correlation A measure of *correlation* where the influence of a third *variable* on the main *independent variable* and *dependent variable* is eliminated by keeping the third variable constant.

participant classroom observation A *classroom observation* technique in which the observer actually takes part in the activity or activities being observed; cf *systematic classroom observation*.

participative simulation A *simulation* one of whose main purposes is to provide a vehicle for participation in some activity or group of activities, eg *role-play*; cf *predictive simulation*.

part learning Remembering material by breaking it down into easily-digested units and

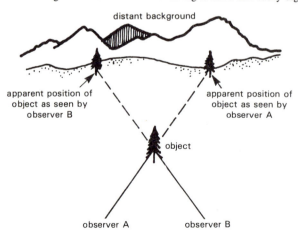

Figure 35 Parallax between an object and the background against which it is viewed

learning each of these separately before attempting to learn the whole sequence; cf *global learning*. See also *part (-progressive) method*.

part (-progressive) method A training technique whereby a complex operation is broken down into easily-learned parts which are mastered separately before being brought together and practised and developed as a whole; cf *cumulative-part method, whole method*. See also *part learning*.

part-publication A publishing term for a large work (such as an encyclopaedia or set of encyclopaedias) that is published in separate parts issued at regular intervals, the various parts eventually building up the complete work.

passe partout A type of picture *mounting* in which glass, picture and backing are bound together using gummed paper or adhesive tape along the edges.

passive learning *Learning* in which the learner has a purely passive role, receiving information from the instructor or materials being studied without taking any active part in the proceedings; cf *active learning*.

password A coded (often personalized) recognition signal that a user of a time-sharing *computer, data base*, etc employs to gain access to the system.

paste-up Assembly of different visual components (*text, graphical materials*, etc) on a common base, eg during the preparation of *camera-ready artwork*.

patch 1. A transparent piece of thin *film* used to repair a break or tear in a *motion picture* film. 2. See *patch method*. 3. See *patch panel*.

patch cord See *patch panel*.

patch method A method of teaching history that involves in-depth study of significant periods rather than a systematic chronological approach.

patch panel A panel containing two rows of *jack sockets* by means of which variable interconnections can be made between items of equipment using *patch cords* — short pieces of cable with a *jack plug* on each.

pathway scheme A method of organizing a *modular course* that allows each student to choose the path through the course units that best suits his/her requirements.

pattern drill A type of *drill* used in language instruction. It involves exposing the learner to a sequence of *model* utterances in which small, systematic changes are made in sound, form, order and vocabulary in order to help him/her master the topic being dealt with.

pause control A control on a *tape recorder* that allows the motion of the tape to be temporarily halted without disengaging the *head* system in use at the time, thus ensuring continuity when the motion is resumed by releasing the control.

Pavlovian conditioning See *respondent conditioning*.

payment by results A system whereby a teacher or trainer is paid on the basis of how his/her pupils, students or trainees perform in examinations or tests.

PCM See *pulse code modulation*.

pedagogy A word re-emerging in educational circles as a term for educational science, ie the study of classroom methodology and teaching techniques.

pedestal A support for a film or television camera that allows the height of the camera to be continuously adjusted during use. See also *ped up, down*.

ped up, down Movement of a film or television camera vertically up or down using a *pedestal*.

peer group A group of individuals of similar age, background, qualifications, etc, eg the students at a particular stage of a course.

peer (group) assessment A method of *assessment* that is based on the consensus opinion of a *peer group*, eg allocating marks for the contributions made by individual members of a group to a *group project* by asking each member to rate the contribution made by every other member and then taking the average of the marks awarded.

peer teaching, tutoring A technique in which teaching or tutoring of learners is carried out by other learners, usually older or of the same age, who have already met the learning objectives involved. See also *coach-and-pupil method*, cross-age teaching.

pegboard test A test of manual dexterity and coordination that involves fitting pegs into holes on specially-designed boards. It is used in personnel selection, job aptitude testing, etc.

pen See *light pen*.

perception A *psychomotor* process that involves becoming aware of objects, qualities, relationships, etc through the medium of the sense organs; Level 1 of Harrow's *psychomotor domain*.

perception channel One of the senses through which *perception* can occur (sight, hearing, etc); cf *cognitive channel*.

perceptual learning *Learning* which results from direct contact with information, experiences, events, etc through the senses.

perceptual motor skills *Psychomotor skills* which depend basically on the coordination of hand and eye.

perceptual set Readiness to see or perceive things and relationships in a certain way, generally in accord with a pattern of some sort.

perfect negative correlation Having a *correlation coefficient* of −1.0.

perfect positive correlation Having a *correlation coefficient* of +1.0.

perforated screen A projection screen that incorporates a pattern of small (invisible) holes in order to transmit sound from a *loudspeaker* mounted behind the screen.

perforations Holes along the edge(s) of a *photographic film, motion picture* film, *filmstrip*, etc used for its registration in, and transport through, a camera, projector, etc.

performance The actual behavio(u)r emitted by a person or group when given a learning or other task. It is often used (incorrectly) as a synonym for *achievement*.

performance analysis Systematic study of the current *performance* of an individual or group in a particular job, task, etc in order to identify any areas where improvements could be made.

performance-based instruction A loose term for any instruction that is based on mastery criteria, ie instruction in which the learner has

to demonstrate mastery of each successive unit before being allowed to move on to the next.

performance objective Another name for a *behavio(u)ral objective*.

performance standard The absolute or comparative level of *performance* required to demonstrate *achievement* of a specified set of *behavio(u)ral objectives*, mastery of a particular task or job, etc. See also *mastery model*.

performance test 1. A test which requires some sort of motor or manual *response* as opposed to a purely verbal or written response, eg the standard driving test. 2. A test which requires the testee to demonstrate behavio(u)r consistent with the satisfactory *performance* of a particular job, occupation, etc. 3. A test of current *performance* as opposed to potential. See also *achievement test*.

peripheral (equipment, unit) An ancillary item of equipment that is used in association with a *computer* or other major item of equipment, eg a *terminal* or *backing store*.

peripheral transfer The transfer of data between two *peripherals* of a computer system, eg from one *backing store* to another, or between two *intelligent terminals*.

persistence The time taken for an *image* or the subjective impression of same to die away after the signal or *stimulus* giving rise to it is removed. Both *motion pictures* and television rely on the *persistence of vision* that occurs in the human eye to produce a subjective impression of continuous movement using a succession of still pictures.

persistence of vision See *persistence*.

personality profile A graphical representation of an individual's personality, broken down into its various aspects or *factors*.

personality scale, test A *rating scale, inventory test* or *projective test* that is designed to measure some aspect(s) of personality, eg extroversion/introversion.

personalized instruction Another term for *individualized instruction*.

personalized system of instruction (PSI) A generic name given to *individualized instruction* systems of the *Keller Plan* type.

phonodisc Another name for an *audio disc*.

phonograph A (somewhat old-fashioned) US term for a *record player*, the equivalent UK term being *gramophone*.

phonotape Another name for an *audiotape*.

photocell, photoelectric cell An electronic device that produces an electrical output that depends on the amount of light falling on it.

photocopy A copy of a document produced on or via sensitized material by the action of light or heat. See also *photostat*.

photogram An *image* recorded on *photographic paper* without the use of a camera or similar device; cf *photograph*.

photograph An *image* recorded on *photographic film*, *photographic paper*, etc by use of a camera of some sort; cf *photogram*.

photographic film, paper, plate Plastic *film*, paper or glass one side of which is coated with photosensitive *emulsion* on which visual *images* may be recorded by *exposure* to light and subsequent *developing*.

photographic lettering system A system used to produce *lettering* for *artwork*, etc by photographic means.

photographic sound track Another name for an *optical sound track*.

photogravure A printing process that makes use of an etched *plate* or cylinder (produced by photographic means) to pick up ink from a roller and transfer it to the copy material.

photolithography *Lithographic printing* that uses *plates* produced by photographic means.

photomicrography Still or motion picture photography of minute objects or systems viewed through the optical system of a microscope. Should not be confused with *microphotography*, although this term is used instead of *photomicrophotography* in most European countries. See also *macrophotography*.

photonovel See *fotonovella*.

photostabilization process A rapid photographic process such as the *Polaroid* system which makes use of *developing* and fixing agents incorporated in the actual *film* to produce a finished *positive* photograph almost immediately after an *exposure* is made. See also *diffusion transfer process*.

photostat 1. A generic term applied to a type of camera used to make copies of documents, drawings, etc. 2. A copy made using such a camera.

phototypesetting (photosetting) The process of composing *text* or other material by projecting the *characters* directly on to a photosensitive surface.

pick-up A mechanism for reading signals from an *audio disc* or *videodisc*, ie the *tone arm* and *cartridge* mechanism in a conventional *record player* and the *head* mechanism in a *compact disc player* or *videodisc player*.

pictogram A graphical display in which items or objects are drawn in different sizes or quantities in order to represent actual sizes or quantities more forcefully. Also known as an *information picture*.

pie chart, diagram A graphical representation of data consisting of a circle divided into sectors whose angular sizes are proportional to the relative sizes of the quantities represented (see example in figure 36). Also known as a *circle chart*.

piezoelectric crystal A crystal that generates an electric field when distorted and undergoes a change of dimensions when an electric field is applied across it. Such crystals are used in a wide variety of *transducers*, eg in inexpensive record player *cartridges*.

pilot study A small-scale research study carried out prior to a larger study in order to test the logistics, etc. Such a study generally resembles the larger study in all important respects apart from the number of subjects. See also *pilot testing*.

pilot testing Carrying out small-scale trials of an exercise, program(me), etc (or part thereof) during its development; a type of *formative evaluation*.

pinboard 1. Another name for a *bulletin board*. 2. Another name for a *register board*.

pincushion distortion Distortion of a projected *image* whereby straight lines parallel to the edges of the field curve outwards at their ends (see figure 37); cf *barrel distortion*.

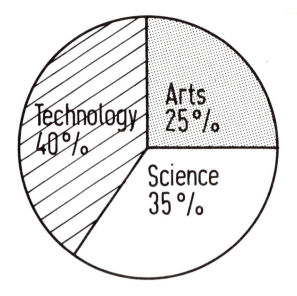

percentages of students
in different faculties
of College X in 1986

Figure 36 A typical pie chart

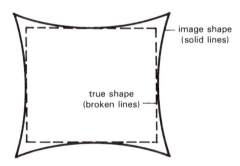

image shape
(solid lines)

true shape
(broken lines)

Figure 37 Pincushion distortion

pitch 1. The distance between successive regularly-occurring points or features, eg film *perforations*, or *video tracks* on *videotape*. 2. The frequency of an audible sound as perceived by a hearer.

pitch control A control on *audio* reproduction equipment enabling the drive speed to be accurately adjusted so as to produce the correct *pitch*.

pixel A picture element on a television or *visual display unit* screen. When an *image* is reproduced on such a screen, it is represented by a pattern of such pixels, with the size of the latter effectively determining the definition that can be obtained (see figure 38). See also *aliasing*.

planned learning experience Direction of an employee to undertake work that is relevant to the complementary training that he or she is currently undertaking or to his or her personal development program(me).

planographic A term used to describe a printing process (such as *lithographic printing*) where the surface of the printing *master* or *plate* is flat, with the *image* areas neither raised above nor etched into it.

original shape of
letter 'G'

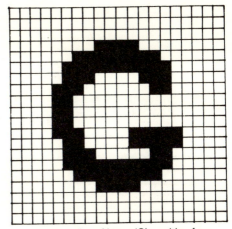

representation of letter 'G' resulting from
superposition
of pixel pattern on original shape.

Figure 38 How the shape of a letter is modified by the pixel pattern of a video screen

plate 1. In printing and *reprography*, a printing *master* made of metal, plastic, paper, etc. 2. See *photographic plate*. 3. A *print* made from an engraving. 3. A *page* in a book or other document (usually an illustration) that does not form part of the main text.

plate camera A large-format still camera that uses glass *photographic plates* or single sheets of cut film.

platen 1. The flat glass surface or platform in an *overhead projector* or *opaque projector* (*episcope*) on which the material to be projected is placed. 2. The heated metal plate against which the copy material and pigmented foil are pressed in a *hotpress printing machine*.

playback Reproduction of a signal that has previously been recorded, particularly an *audio signal* or *video signal*.

playback head A *head* in a *tape recorder* or *audiotape player* that is used during *playback*. In *audiotape recorders*, such heads are generally used only for playback purposes, but, in *videotape recorders*, the video playback heads are generally also used as *record heads*.

playing time The length of time that an *audio recording, videorecording, motion picture*, etc requires for it to be played or shown from start to finish.

plenary session A session involving all the participants in an exercise, program(me),

course, etc. Such a session is often used for *briefing* or *debriefing* purposes.

plotter A visual display or *computer* output device where the values of one variable quantity are automatically plotted against those of another. See also *calligraphic plotter, graphical plotter, x-y plotter*.

point See *point system*.

point system A system used in English-speaking countries to measure type height, one *point* being equivalent to 1/72 of an inch (0.351 mm); thus, type 1 inch high would be described as 72 point type.

pola filter A small sheet of *polaroid*, sometimes mounted in glass, designed for fitting in front of a camera lens as a polarizing *filter*.

polar diagram, response curve A schematic representation of the sensitivity or output in different horizontal directions of an *aerial, microphone, loudspeaker*, light source, projection screen, etc (see, for example, figure 9 on page 22 and figure 12 on page 28, which show the polar response curves of two different types of microphone).

polarized animation Production of an illusion of movement in still transparent displays such as *OHP transparencies* by using variably-polarized light (produced using a *polarizing spinner*) transmitted through polarizing materials incorporated in the display.

129

polarizing spinner A rotating disc of *polaroid* material used in *polarized animation*.

Polaroid 1. Transparent plastic sheeting capable of polarizing light transmitted through it (the name is derived from the brand name used by the US company that first developed such material). 2. The name of the first commercial photographic system based on a *photostabilization process*; a term applied to the special cameras and films used in the system.

polar response See *polar diagram, response curve*.

popping A sudden change in the position of the *transparency* of a non-glass-mounted photographic *slide* due to thermal expansion produced by the projection lamp. It generally results in the slide going *out of focus*.

population 1. A term used in statistics, research, etc to define a finite or infinite number of similar or like units. 2. See *target population*.

port A point at which access can be gained to the *central processing unit* of a *computer*.

portability A term used to give an indication of the ease (or otherwise) with which an item of *hardware* can be moved around and its resistance (or susceptibility) to damage while being so transported.

portapack A portable television camera and *videorecorder* system operated by rechargeable batteries.

portrait (format) A term used to describe the *format* of a page, book, document, photograph, drawing, etc with an *aspect ratio* less than 1 : 1, ie one whose vertical length is greater than its horizontal length. The term originates from photographic and artistic portraits, which are normally produced in such a format; cf *landscape (format)*. Also known as *vertical (format)*.

portrayal evaluation A quickly-produced *evaluation*, involving the reporting of personal impressions relating to the situation under scrutiny.

positive A photographic *image* in which the *tones* (or colo(u)rs, in the case of a colo(u)red image) reproduce those of the subject depicted. The term is used both as a noun and as an adjective; cf *negative*.

positive correlation A type of *correlation* between two *variables* which indicates that an increase in one is associated with an increase in the other, ie one where the *correlation coefficient* is between 0 and +1.0; cf *negative correlation*.

positive feedback 1. A type of *feedback* in which an increase in the output of a system causes the rate or level at which the system operates to increase even further; cf *negative feedback*. 2. A psychological term for behavio(u)r likely to increase motivation.

positive reinforcement A type of *reinforcement* in which it is the occurrence of the reinforcing event that increases the probability of a desired *response* being brought about by a particular *stimulus*; cf *negative reinforcement*.

positive skew See *skewness*.

positive transfer An increase in the efficiency of *learning* because of earlier or related learning carried out in a different situation; cf *negative transfer*.

post-compulsory education Education undertaken after reaching the minimum school leaving age (16 in the UK).

post-entry education A US term for in-service education which an employer provides outside normal working hours, particularly education given to prepare employees for promotion or greater responsibility.

poster A large pictorial or graphic illustration, generally conveying a single simple message, designed for display purposes; cf *wallchart*.

posterization Reproducing a photographic or video *image* using only a few specific *tones* or flat colo(u)rs, with most of the tonal gradation and detail suppressed.

poster paint Bright water-based paint used for preparing *posters* and other graphic materials.

post-sync In film and television production, recording synchronous dialog(ue) for a *scene* after it has been shot on *film* or *videotape*.

post-test A test administered after the completion of a course or program(me) of instruction in order to determine the extent to which the learner has achieved the specified *objectives*; cf *pre-test*. See also *retention test*.

postural discrimination An individual's ability to respond to postural or physical (as opposed to visual) *cues* in adjusting his or her working position. A type of *psychomotor skill*.

potted book A book which is intended to summarize and put into perspective the essential points, arguments, etc in a subject or topic. See also *handbook*.

pounce paper transfer A method of transferring the outline of an illustration from one medium to another, eg from paper to a chalkboard, by making small holes along the lines of the original, holding it against the surface to which the illustration is to be transferred, and dusting along the lines with a chalk duster or something similar. The resulting dots can then be joined to produce the required outline.

power amplifier The part of an *amplifier* system that increases the actual power of the signal, as opposed to the *pre-amplifier*. It may or may not be a separate unit from the pre-amplifier.

power test A test in which the *score* or level of *performance* attained is more important than the time taken to achieve the score or level; cf *speed test*.

practice frame In *programmed instruction*, a *frame* that provides practice in the material just presented; cf *teaching frame, test frame*.

practice items Trial *items* that are included in an examination, test or *questionnaire* in order to familiarize the subject with its form, and which are not taken into account when the examination, test or questionnaire is being marked or analyzed.

pre-amplifier The part of an *amplifier* system that prepares the signal for passing on to the *power amplifier*, usually incorporating volume controls, *tone controls* and other facilities by which the characteristics of the signal can be modified. It may or may not be a separate unit from the power amplifier.

precision teaching (PT) A method of *individualized instruction* in which the progress of each learner is continuously monitored by comparing it with his/her previous *performance* rather than with a fixed standard. For the purpose of such teaching, student behavio(u)r is broken down into small units that enable it to be recorded on standard behavio(u)r charts.

pre-coded question A question in which the answer has to be chosen from a number of alternatives supplied, usually by ticking or otherwise marking one of them. Such questions are widely used in surveys and *questionnaires*, particularly when the results are to be processed automatically. See also *fixed-response item, multiple-choice item, question*.

predictive assessment, appraisal *Assessment* or *appraisal* of an individual which enables the assessor to predict future *performance*, eg performance in a particular task or job, or performance in education.

predictive evaluation The term used in the US for *predictive assessment*.

predictive simulation A *simulation* (typically a *computer simulation*) whose main purpose is to predict future behavio(u)r, performance, trends, etc; cf *participative simulation*.

predictive validity The degree to which predictions made by a test (or inferred from test results) are confirmed by the subsequent *performance* or *achievement* of the subject(s) tested.

pre-echo Unwanted appearance of a signal before it should have manifested itself, eg from an adjacent groove of an *audio disc* or an adjacent turn of a *videotape* reel.

pre-employment course A course that is designed to prepare pupils about to leave school (and others) for specific types of employment.

preferential learning model A learning model that is designed in such a way as to build on the existing abilities and strengths of the learner.

pre-knowledge Relevant *knowledge* which a learner or participant should have before undertaking a course, instructional program(me), etc, or taking part in an exercise.

preliminaries A publishing term for any material that precedes the main *text* of a book or other document, eg title pages, contents lists, acknowledgements; cf *subsidiaries*.

pre-recorded materials Recorded materials (such as *audio discs, audiotapes* and *videotapes*) where the recorded signal was present at the time of purchase or acquisition.

prerequisite objectives A set of *objectives* that a learner is required to achieve before embarking on a particular course, program(me) or learning task. See also *entry level performance*.

pre-roll time The time that elapses between starting up a *videoplayer* or similar device and stabilization of the signal.

presence Boosting the *frequency response* of an *audio* system in the upper frequency range (3–8 kHz) in order to create the illusion that the source is near.

presentation programmer An electronic system which controls the synchronization of sound reproduction and/or projection devices in *multi-media* and multi-device presentations such as *cross-fade* tape-slide program(me)s.

presentation session A teaching session (such as a lecture or taught lesson) which is primarily intended for the presentation of information by the teacher/instructor to the learners, with little or no active participation on the part of the latter.

pre-service training, education Training or education that is undertaken prior to embarking on a specific career such as teaching; cf *in-service training*.

pressure pad A component of the *head* mechanism of a *tape recorder* or similar device that ensures good contact between the tape and the head surface.

pressure plate A component of a *motion picture camera*, film projector, film printer, etc that holds the film flat at the time of exposure, projection or viewing.

pressure roller A rubber-tyred wheel in a *tape recorder* or similar device that holds the tape firmly against the drive *capstan*, thus ensuring constant tape speed and preventing slipping.

pre-test A test administered prior to a course or program(me) of instruction in order to determine the *entry behavio(u)r* of the learner(s); cf *post-test*.

preview 1. In *video* work, the facility to see a picture before transmission or recording. 2. In film production, a special pre-release screening of a completed film.

primary colo(u)rs The three colo(u)rs from which all other colo(u)rs can be produced by mixing in the correct proportions. Where colo(u)rs are produced by *colo(u)r addition* (ie

by mixing light as in a colo(u)r television picture) the three primary colo(u)rs are red, blue and green. Where colo(u)rs are produced by *colo(u)r subtraction* (ie by mixing pigments as in colo(u)r printing) the three primary colo(u)rs are the *complementary colo(u)rs* of these colo(u)rs (ie cyan, yellow and magenta).

primary education The basic education given to children from the age at which they start formal schooling up to the age of about 11 to 12 years old, ie the education that they receive in UK primary schools and US elementary (grade) schools; cf *secondary education, tertiary education*.

primary mental ability A theory of structure of intellect proposed by Thurstone as an alternative to conventional theories of *general intelligence*. According to Thurstone, primary mental abilities include *verbal comprehension (V), numerical ability (N), word fluency (W)* and *rote learning*.

primary typewriter Another name for a *bulletin typewriter*.

print 1. To produce a *hard copy* textual or graphic *image* on an opaque medium such as paper from type, a *plate*, etc. 2. To produce a (usually *positive*) photographic *image* on an opaque medium such as *photographic paper* from a (usually *negative*) transparent original, or a (usually *positive*) copy of a *motion picture* film. 3. The *image* or copy produced in '1.' or '2.'

printed materials A generic term for textual and other paper-based materials produced by printing or reprographic methods as opposed to *audiovisual materials* such as *audiotapes, slides, videos* and *films*.

printer 1. A generic term for a *peripheral* to a *computer, word processor*, etc that gives *hard copy* output, either in *alphanumerical* or graphical form. 2. A system for producing photographic *prints* (usually *positive*) from original *film* (usually *negative*).

printout *Hard copy* output that a *computer* or *word processor* provides via a *printer*; cf *readout*.

print through The transfer of magnetization from one layer of *magnetic tape* to another while the tape *reel* or *cassette* is in storage.

proactive inhibition A form of *inhibition* in which material that has already been learned interferes with the *learning* of new material; cf *retroactive inhibition*. See also *negative transfer*.

problem method A method of instruction in which *learning* is stimulated by confronting the student with a series of challenging situations that require solution. See also *discovery learning, inductive method*.

problem-solving The process of inventing a complex rule or *algorithm* for the purpose of solving one particular problem and then using the method to solve problems of a similar nature. This is one of the types of intellectual skill identified by Gagné and Briggs. See also *problem-solving model*.

problem-solving model A model of *innovation* which is based on the assumption that innovation is part of a *problem-solving* process which goes on inside the user or client system; cf *research, development and diffusion model, social interaction model*.

process camera A special camera used for the production of photographic *intermediates* during the preparation of printing *masters*.

process-centred (centered) A term applied to a *game, simulation* or other participative exercise in which the activities the participants engage in are more important than the actual content; cf *content-centred (centered)*.

process colo(u)r work In printing and allied fields, the use of combinations of red, yellow, blue and black to reproduce the full colo(u)r range.

process evaluation *Evaluation* which studies the process as it takes place rather than the end point or outcomes; cf *product evaluation*.

processing Subjecting materials, data, etc to a manipulative procedure eg the processing of photographic materials (*developing*, printing, etc), the processing of data using a *computer*, or the processing of text using a *word processor*.

process shot 1. In film production, a general term for a trick shot created by *special effects* photography or optical processing. 2. A *studio* shot in which the background is a still or moving projected picture.

proctor See *Keller Plan*.

product evaluation *Evaluation* that focuses on

the end point or outcome of a process, system, etc rather than on the process or system itself; cf *process evaluation*. See also *summative evaluation*.

profile A set of measures of different characteristics of an individual or group that are presented in standard form in order to give an overall picture of the ability, performance, achievement or potential of the individual or group.

prognostic test A diagnostic test that is used to predict the future performance of an individual in a specific area, course, task, etc; cf *achievement test*.

program See *computer program*.

programmable calculator An electronic calculator with a limited amount of *memory* that can store short *programs*; some can 'remember' material even after they have been switched off, and others are effectively small *microcomputers*, complete with *external memory*.

program(me) An ordered set of activities, presentations, etc, eg a structured sequence of related learning activities, a radio, television or tape-slide sequence designed to be broadcast or viewed as a single unit, or a planned schedule for the implementation of a project or policy of some sort.

programmed instruction, learning A general term for instruction or *learning* that takes place in a systematic, highly-structured manner, generally in a step-by-step fashion with *feedback* taking place between steps.

programmed text A set of *programmed instruction* materials produced in the form of a printed text.

programming language A special language used to give instructions to *computers*. There are many different types and styles (see, for example, *high-level (programming) language, low-level (programming) language, machine code, author(ing) language*.

progress chart A graphic chart (usually some form of *bar chart*) that shows the completion of the various stages of a project, course, program(me), etc.

progressive matrices test A type of *non-verbal intelligence test* in which the subject has to complete a series of matrix-type designs of progressively increasing difficulty by selecting,

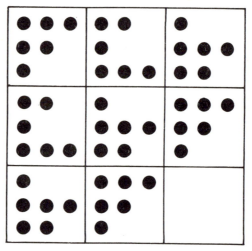

matrix to be completed

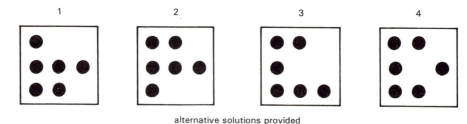

alternative solutions provided

Figure 39 A typical item from a progressive matrices test

in each case, one of a number of suggested solutions. A typical item from such a test is shown in figure 39.

progressive teaching A general term for teaching methods that are flexible, pupil-centred (centered) and stress *discovery learning* and related techniques, as opposed to the traditional authoritarian, teacher-centred (centered) approach.

project 1. A significant unit of practical or scholarly activity, generally involving the detailed investigation of a problem of some sort or the detailed study of a particular topic, issue or area; see also *project method*. 2. A US term for a (large) government-funded educational research activity. 3. To throw an *image* on to a screen by optical or optico-electronic methods; see also *projector*.

projected display materials, visual aids Display materials (*visual aids*) that require the use of a *projector* of some sort for their

display or study; cf *non-projected display materials, visual aids*.

projected, projection television A television display system that produces a large projected picture on an external screen by optical or optico-electronic means.

projection booth A soundproof enclosure in a classroom, lecture theatre, etc from which *motion pictures, slides*, etc can be projected without the noise from the *projector* being heard by the audience.

projective test A test (used in personality study and allied fields) that involves the subject responding to ambiguous or open-ended questions or *stimuli*, eg by completing pictures or sentences, or interpreting shapes or drawings.

project method A method of instruction in which learners (working individually or in cooperative groups) carry out *projects*, largely free of detailed supervision or control.

projector A device designed to throw an *image* on to an external or built-in *screen*, usually by optical means.

PROM Programmable read-only memory. A *read-only memory (ROM)* which can be programmed by the user provided that he/she has access to the necessary specialized equipment and possesses the necessary skills. See also *EPROM*.

prompt In *behavio(u)ral psychology, programmed instruction*, etc, a *stimulus* (eg a verbal or pictorial hint of some sort) that is added to another stimulus (eg a question) in order to make it more likely that a learner will give a correct *response*; also known as a *cue*. See also *formal prompt, thematic prompt*.

proportional spacing In typesetting, *lettering*, etc, spacing *characters* in proportion to their width; cf *constant spacing*.

protocol materials A US term for recordings (on *film, videotape* or *audiotape*) of the performance of teachers and pupils in real-life classroom and other educational settings that are used as *case study* materials in teacher training.

PSI See *personalized system of instruction*.

psychodrama The dramatic presentation of a personal conflict or crisis for diagnostic or therapeutic purposes, eg via *role play*. See also *sociodrama*.

psychological inventory A type of diagnostic instrument used in psychological *assessment* and investigation. A psychological inventory measures or records what the subject says he/she feels, and thus differs from a *psychological test*, which measures what he/she knows or can do.

psychological test A test devised by psychologists to measure some aspect of ability, performance or potential for research, *assessment*, personnel selection or some other purpose; cf *psychological inventory*. See also *psychometric test*.

psychometric test A *psychological test* that is designed to measure one or more specific *factors* and produce quantified results.

psychomotor Relating to the coordination of mind and body in carrying out some physical (motor) action or set of actions. See also *psychomotor domain*.

psychomotor domain One of the three broad sets into which *educational objectives* are conventionally divided as a result of the work of Bloom and his co-workers, containing all those associated with the coordination of mind and body in carrying out *psychomotor* activities. The definitive *taxonomy* of the psychomotor domain of educational objectives was published by Harrow in 1972.

psychomotor skill A skill that involves the execution of *psychomotor* activities.

PT See *precision teaching*.

pull-back A backward movement of a film or television camera away from the subject being shot.

pull-down 1. The act of moving a *motion picture* film onward by one *frame* through a camera or projector; it is produced by a retractable claw which engages the *sprocket holes* in the film at the appropriate times. 2. See *pull-down menu*.

pull-down menu A type of computer menu where the facilities or items available are shown at the top of the display. The user can obtain further information about any particular facility or item by placing the cursor alongside the facility or item and 'pulling down' the material required on to the main part of the screen.

pulse code modulation (PCM) A method of converting an *analog* signal into *digital* pulses which can be transmitted through a communications system at high speed. It involves sampling the wave form of the analog signal at fixed time intervals and expressing the magnitude that is observed as a pulse of corresponding size. Loss of information is minimized by keeping the sampling interval short.

punched card A rectangular card on which data can be stored in the form of a pattern of rectangular holes. Also known as a *memory card*.

punched tape See *paper tape*.

punishment In *behavio(u)ral psychology* and *programmed instruction*, presentation of an aversive *stimulus* in order to discourage and/or decrease the rate of an unwanted *response*. Should not be confused with *negative reinforcement*.

pup A small *spotlight*.

pupil-centred (centered) approach, learning, teaching See *student-centred (centered) approach, learning, teaching*.

pupil-paced learning aids, materials See *student-paced learning aids, materials*.

push-off In television production, a *wipe* effect that involves moving the entire picture sideways off the screen to reveal a different *image* or a blank screen.

Pygmalion effect Where an instructor's expectation of a learner's achievement becomes a self-fulfilling prophecy in that the learner performs in such a way as to match the instructor's preconceptions of him or her. Also known as the *Rosenthal effect*. See also *'halo' effect*.

Q

quadding In typesetting, fitting a blank space into a line of type in order to increase its length, eg for *justification* purposes.

quadraphonic A term applied to a sound recording or sound reproduction system that makes use of four discrete but related sound *tracks* or channels, employing two *loudspeaker* units placed in front of the listener (as in *stereophonic* systems) plus two behind, to increase the realism of the sound.

quadruplex A broadcast-quality *videotape recorder* system that makes use of four *heads* mounted at 90° intervals round a rotating *head*

drum to scan a tape 2 inches wide. Such a system differs from the more common *helical scanning* videotape systems in that the tracks run across the tape rather than along it, a process known as *transverse scanning* (see figure 40).

quality control Monitoring of a system so that adjustments can be made to correct any difference between actual performance and planned performance.

quality (rating) scale A standard *scale* used to help ensure consistency in the marking of essays, compositions, etc. It consists of a

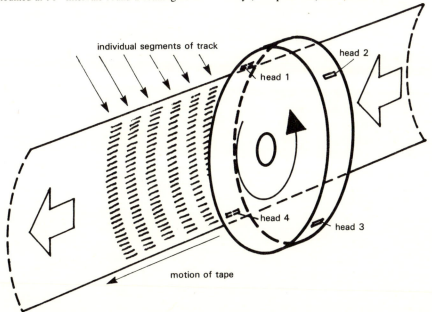

As the tape moves past the four revolving heads, each produces a short sequence of track across its width, so that four such segments are produced for each revolution of the head drum; when the tape is re-played, these separate segments are joined together electronically to produce a continuous signal.

Figure 40 The quadruplex videotape system

number of standard samples, graded and arranged in order of merit, against which comparisons can be made.

quarter track A term applied to *audiotapes* with four separate recording *tracks* and to *tape recorders* and *audiotape players* that employ such a track configuration. Also known as *four track*.

quasi-experimental design A technique used when social constraints preclude full control of experimental stimuli in a research study. It enables 'quasi-experimental' effects to be achieved by appropriate scheduling of data collection procedures.

question-and-answer method A method both of instruction and of oral *assessment* based on the use of a series of questions that have to be answered by the learner or testee.

questionnaire A diagnostic instrument in which members of a *population* being studied or surveyed are asked to answer a series of questions, usually presented on a form.

quiz mode A *programmed instruction* technique that involves providing the learner with the correct *response* immediately after he/she has made his/her own response to each item.

qwerty keyboard A *keyboard* in which the *alphanumerical* and standard control keys are laid out in the same way as on a standard typewriter (see figure 41). The name is derived from the top left row of letters.

Figure 41 The layout of the main part of a typical qwerty keyboard

R

ra See *reading age*.

radio frequency (RF) A term used to describe signals or electromagnetic waves having frequencies in the range used to carry radio or television signals, ie between 10^5 and 10^{12}HZ; cf *audio frequency*. See also *ultra-high frequency, very high frequency*.

radio listening group A group of people who meet in order to listen to and discuss radio broadcasts, often with the help of related *study guides* or other *printed materials*.

radio microphone A *microphone* connected to a small radio *transmitter* that can relay its signal back to the audio system with which it is being used without the need for connecting wires. Also known as a *wireless microphone*.

radiovision An audiovisual instruction system that uses special *filmstrips*, booklets and other visual materials linked with educational radio broadcasts.

ragged right A term applied to *text* that is not aligned on the right-hand side, ie is *unjustified*. Also known as *ranged left*.

RAM See *random-access memory*.

random access A term applied to any system from which items or material can be selected at random, without running through from the start of the system in order to reach the item or material required; cf *sequential access*. See also *random-access memory*.

random-access memory (RAM) A computing term for a *store* where any location can be read from or written to in a *random access* manner. The *working memories* in the *central processing units* of *digital computers* are all of this type.

random learning *Learning* acquired incidentally through everyday experience, casual

reading, etc as opposed to learning acquired deliberately in a course or through study.

range A measure of the *variability* of a statistical distribution, set of *scores* etc, being equal to the difference between the highest and lowest scores or measures in the distribution.

range of attention The extent to which an individual can attend to several different things at once. See also *span of apprehension*.

ranged left A term applied to *text* that is aligned on the left side only, ie is a synonym for *ragged right*. Also known as *unjustified*.

range finder An attachment to, or system incorporated in, a camera that indicates the distance from camera to subject and/or automatically adjusts the *focus* according to this distance.

ranking 1. Arranging *scores*, measures, items, individuals etc in order of merit or magnitude. 2. Determination of the position of an individual in such an order of merit. 3. The actual order of merit so obtained.

rank order See *ranking*.

rapid reading A technique for absorbing the essential information in textual material without actually reading every word, eg by using some form of *scanning* procedure.

raster scan A type of *scanning* that involves crossing the area being covered in a series of close, parallel lines, one below (or above) the other. This is the process by which a television picture is built up (see *interlaced scanning*).

rating scale 1. A *scale* by means of which an individual can give an indication of his/her attitude to or *evaluation* of an issue, topic, system, etc; see also *attitude scale, cumulative rating scale, summated rating scale*. 2. Any *scale* used in assessing attainment, performance, personality, etc.

ratio scale The highest of the four types of *scale* used in educational measurement, having all the properties of an *interval scale* and also a fixed anchor point. Height, for example, is a ratio scale since we can say that A (height 1.87 metres (meters)) is 1.1. times as tall as B (height 1.7 metres (meters)), whereas *intelligence* is not, since we cannot say that A (IQ = 110) is 1.1 times as intelligent as B (IQ = 100). See also *nominal scale, ordinal scale*.

rationale The underlying philosophy of a course, *curriculum*, etc.

raw data Original statistical or other data which has not so far been modified by mathematical operations. See also *scaling, standardization*.

raw score A *score* which has not so far been modified by mathematical operations such as *scaling* or *standardization*; cf *standardized score*. Also known as an *observed score*.

raw stock *Photographic film* that has still to be exposed and processed, ie is available for use.

RD and D model See *research, development and diffusion model*.

read To scan the information held in a particular location or set of locations in a *store* (read out or *readout*) or feed information into a particular location or set of locations from another source (read in).

readability A description of the ease with which a reader is able to read and obtain information from *printed materials*. See also *Cloze test, Flesch formula, fog index, reading age*.

reader 1. A device that produces an eye-legible *image* of a *microcopy* or *microimage* by projecting an enlarged image of the original on to a built-in *screen*. 2. A device that can recognize visual or coded messages held on *punched cards, punched tape*, or some other medium.

reader-printer A microcopy *reader* with built-in facilities for producing an eye-legible *hard copy* of any *page* or section required.

readiness test A test designed to determine whether a would-be learner has the characteristics that he or she will need to cope

satisfactorily with a particular course, program(me) of instruction, etc.

reading age 1. A measure of the reading ability of an individual in terms of the *chronological age* of the average *population* to which he or she is equivalent in reading ability; thus, an exceptionally bright child of chronological age seven years might have a reading age of eleven years, while a backward child of the same age might have a reading age of only four or five years. 2. A measure of the *readability* of a text in terms of the average minimum age at which it can be comprehended without difficulty.

read-only memory (ROM) A computing term for a *store* from which information can be read as often as required, but, once entered, cannot normally be changed; cf *read/write memory*. See also *firmware, PROM, EPROM*.

readout 1. The display of output from a *computer* or *word processor* in *soft copy* form, normally on the screen of a *visual display unit*; cf *printout*. 2. See *read*. See also *destructive readout, non-destructive readout*.

read/write head A *head* in a *computer terminal* or similar device that can be used both to *read* data out of, and to *write* data into, the system.

read/write memory A computing term for a *store* from which information can be read as often as required and can also be altered as and when necessary; cf *read-only memory*.

realia Real objects, as opposed to *models*, representations, etc.

real learning time In industrial training, the time taken for a trainee to become capable of working at the same speed and to the same standard as the average experienced worker.

real time A term applied to a process or data processing system that keeps exact pace with events in the real world, as they are actually happening, or to an exercise, *simulation*, etc that operates on the same timescale as the real world, as opposed to one that operates on an artificial (generally shortened) timescale.

rear projection Another name for *back projection*.

rearrangement test A test that involves arranging disordered items in the correct order or pattern.

recall test A type of *objective test* in which the subject is required to supply missing items of information (usually words, numbers or phrases) to complete statements relating to material previously encountered or learned.

receiver A device which receives data, particularly one that receives modulated radio or television signals off-air and produces a demodulated output; cf *transmitter*. See also *receiver/monitor*.

receiver/monitor A television *receiver* that can also be used as a *television monitor*, ie can handle both modulated *RF* signals received off-air and *composite video* line signals fed in by cable.

receiving An *affective* process that involves showing awareness of, and willingness to receive, certain *stimuli* such as the aesthetic properties of an object, system, etc. This is the lowest level (Level 1) of Krathwohl's *affective domain*.

recognition test A form of *recall test* in which the subject has to recognise objects, symbols, patterns, words, etc previously encountered or learned.

record 1. The common name for an *audio disc*. 2. A collection of related items of data. 3. To produce an *audiorecording* or *videorecording*, or *read* data into a *store*. 4. To write down data, eg on a *record card*.

record card A card on which is recorded data showing a learner's progress, attainment record, etc.

record(ing) head The *head* in an *audiotape* or *videotape* recorder or player or data storage device which is used to transfer an incoming signal on to the storage medium.

record player A device used to play back the material recorded on an *audio disc*. Some record players are free-standing units, containing built-in *amplifier* and *loudspeaker* systems, while others require separate amplifiers and loudspeakers. See also *compact disc player, transcription unit*.

recurrent education Education that continues throughout an individual's life rather than terminating at the end of the formal education that precedes entry into employment. See also *lifelong education*.

reducing glass The opposite of a magnifying glass — a special glass lens used to see how *artwork*, etc will look when reduced to the size in which it will eventually appear in printed form.

reduction printing Optical printing of a *motion picture* film carried out in order to produce a smaller *image* than the original, usually on a film of narrower *gauge* (eg 35 mm to 16 mm).

reduction ratio An expression of the factor by which a copy or *image* is smaller in terms of its linear dimensions than the original from which it was made.

redundancy 1. A term used in instructional design, communications theory, computing, etc to denote the incorporation in a signal, message, program(me), etc of more information or material than is actually needed to make it fulfil its intended function satisfactorily. 2. In computing, etc, provision of a back-up system which can be brought into use (often automatically) if the primary system fails.

reel 1. A flanged hub designed to hold *film, magnetic tape, paper tape*, typewriter ribbon, etc; also known as a *spool*. 2. A roll of *motion picture* film forming part of a *film* consisting of a number of such rolls.

reel-to-reel A term describing a process or machine in which tape or film moves from one *open reel* to a separate open take-up reel during processing, recording, playback, projection, etc.

re-establishing shot In film or television production, a *shot* (usually a *long shot* taken from a new angle) that is incorporated in the middle or at the end of a linked sequence in order to remind the audience of the context of the sequence. See also *establishing shot*.

reflex cabinet A type of *loudspeaker* enclosure designed to match the acoustic properties of the cabinet to the *frequency response* of the speaker unit(s) at low frequencies, and thus produce a *flat response*.

reflex camera A camera in which the *image* in the *viewfinder* is obtained through the main objective lens (*single-lens reflex*) or through a secondary lens immediately above it (*twin-lens reflex*), thus eliminating or reducing *parallax* effects, ie making sure that what is seen in the viewfinder (which is viewed from above the camera) is what will actually appear on the exposed film.

refresh To reactivate a system (such as a display on a *visual display unit*) which would otherwise fade.

refresher course A course that is designed to reinforce previously-learned skills, knowledge, etc which may have deteriorated through disuse or due to the passage of a long period of time since the material was originally learned. Such courses are widely used in industry and commerce, and are also provided for trained professionals of all types.

register 1. To place in exact position or alignment, eg when placing an *overlay* on an *OHP transparency* or drawing, or when locating successive *images* during film *animation* work; the corresponding noun is *registration*. 2. A *computer store* which holds information, addresses or instructions on a temporary basis, eg during a multi-stage calculation.

register board A surface with two or more vertical guides for holding *overlays* in the correct position during the shooting of cartoon films, etc. Also called a *pinboard*.

register marks A pattern of fine line crosses or other suitable marks designed to provide reference points for *registration* during the printing or photographing of *artwork*, *image* location with *reader-printers*, etc.

registration 1. Locating a *slide, frame* of a film, etc in exactly the right position in the *gate* of a *projector* or camera. 2. See *register* (1.).

regular 8 An alternative name for *standard 8* motion picture film, as opposed to *super 8*.

reinforcement 1. In *behavio(u)ral psychology* and *programmed instruction*, a process in which a *stimulus* presented immediately following a correct *response* increases the likelihood of the response being repeated when the same situation recurs; see also *negative reinforcement, positive reinforcement*. 2. In general educational parlance, the process of helping a learner to master new facts, principles, etc by repetition, rehearsal, demonstrating applications, etc.

reinforcer In *behavio(u)ral psychology* and *programmed instruction*, a *stimulus* that is used to produce *reinforcement*.

release A term used in the design of *mathetics*-type learning materials. It denotes a situation where the learner is required to carry out a particular *step* without the aid of *prompts*. See also *demonstrate*.

release form A form used to obtain written permission for the use of *copyright* material.

release print A *positive* copy *print* of a completed *motion picture* made available for public viewing, sale, use in education or training, etc.

reliability 1. A measure of the extent to which a test performs consistently each time it is used. 2. The capability of a device or system to function properly over an extended period of time.

reliability coefficient A statistical measure used to quantify the *reliability* of a test or between two forms of a test.

remedial branch, loop, sequence In *programmed instruction*, a *branch*, loop or sequence in a *branching program(me)* that causes the learner to be exposed to *remedial material* (see figure 18 on page 67 for a typical example).

remedial class A class organized for pupils or students who need special help to catch up with their peers in a particular subject or subject area.

remedial frame A *frame* in a *programmed instruction* sequence that forms part of a *remedial branch, remedial loop* or *remedial sequence*.

remedial instruction A specific unit (or system of units) of instruction designed to overcome a particular learning deficiency (or set of deficiencies) in a learner or group of learners. See also *remedial class; remedial branch, loop, sequence; remedial frame; remedial material*.

remedial material Instructional material designed to help a learner master subject matter, skills, etc with which difficulty has been experienced.

remediation 1. Provision during a course or program(me) of instruction *of feedback* that enables the learner to correct his/her performance. 2. Provision of *feedback* that enables a teacher or instructor to adjust or modify his/her methods, content or presentation in order to overcome some weakness that has become manifest.

remote control A mechanical or electronic facility that enables an operator to control a device such as a camera, *projector, videoplayer* or television set from a distance, or from another room or building.

remote terminal A *computer terminal* that is physically or geographically separated from the *central processing unit* to which it is (or is capable of being) connected. It may be anywhere from the next room to the other side of the world.

repertoire assessment *Assessment* of the nature and degrees of skill possessed by a learner prior to beginning a program(me) or course of instruction, ie determination of his/her *entry behavio(u)r*.

replication The repetition of a research study, *evaluation* program(me), etc under similar or slightly altered conditions in order to determine whether similar results are obtained.

reprography A term embracing all duplicating and office printing processes, all copying and microcopying processes using any form of radiation (including heat), and all ancillary operations associated with such processes.

research, development and diffusion (R, D, and D) model A model of *dissemination* and *innovation* that is used by a wide range of industries (eg the space, defence (defense) and agricultural industries) and is also regularly used in *curriculum* development. It has the following five phases: (i) basic research, (ii) applied research, (iii) development and testing of prototypes, (iv) mass production and packaging, (v) planned mass dissemination activities aimed at the *target population* of potential users; cf *social interaction model (of diffusion/innovation)*.

reserve collection 1. In academic libraries, a collection of materials in heavy demand which is kept separate from other stock and from which items may be borrowed only for short periods. 2. Library material which, although available for loan in the usual way, is kept apart from the normal shelf stock, usually in a part of the library to which only library staff have access; such collections often contain old books which have been superseded by more recent works.

reservoir pen A pen designed for indian ink drawing, *lettering* etc which incorporates a container for the ink.

resolution, resolving power A measure of the sharpness or clarity of the *images* that can be produced by a given system, eg in photography or *reprography* (where it is usually measured in line pairs per mm) or *computer graphics* (where it is ultimately determined by the size of the *pixels* on the display screen — see figure 38 on page 129). Also known as *definition*.

resource-based learning An individualized, *student-centred (centered) learning* system that relies mainly on *self-study materials* of various types, often made available through a *resources centre (center)* or *discovery area* of some sort; cf *direct teaching*.

resource(s) centre (center) A place — which can be anything from part of a room to a complex of buildings — that is set up specially for the purpose of housing, and making available for use, a collection of learning materials in different media, or for providing facilities for the production of same. The term is mainly used in the UK, the equivalent US term being *media centre (center)*. Also known as a *learning centre (center)*, *learning resources centre (center)* and a *self-study centre (center)*. See also *resource(s) island, peninsula; teachers' resource(s) centre (center)*.

resource(s) island, peninsula A discrete central or side area in a classroom where self-study and other learning materials are made available for use by pupils. See also *discovery area, resource(s) centre (center)*.

resource materials 1. The materials required for or used in a particular exercise, instructional program(me), course, etc. 2. A general term for materials used by learners or teachers.

respondent conditioning *Conditioning* that causes an organism to emit a desired *response* as a result of a *stimulus* which would not normally produce that response, as in the classical experiments of Pavlov in which a dog was conditioned to salivate on hearing a bell rung; cf *operant conditioning*. Also known as *classical conditioning, Pavlovian conditioning*.

responding 1. In general, replying to a question or *item*, completing a test, etc. An *affective* process that involves showing an interest in an object, system, etc as opposed to merely being aware of it. This is Level 2 of Krathwohl's *affective domain*.

response 1. In *behavio(u)ral psychology*, any implicit or overt change in an organism's behavio(u)r brought about by the application of a *stimulus*; see also *stimulus-response bond, connection*. 2. In educational parlance, the behavio(u)r that a learner carries out following an instructional *stimulus*, eg a question, or a request to perform some activity. 3. The performance of a system such as an *amplifier, microphone, aerial, loudspeaker*, etc over a given frequency range (see *frequency response*) or range of directions (see *polar response*).

response card, sheet A printed card or sheet used in an *objective test* as the vehicle for the person being tested to record his or her *responses*.

response-contingent test A form of individualized test in which the *items* that each subject is confronted with depend to a greater or lesser extent on his or her performance in earlier items, the process being designed to ensure that, so far as is possible, each person works just below or at the limits of his/her ability. Also known as an *adaptive test*.

response frame 1. A *frame* in a *computer-based learning* or *interactive videotex* sequence that requires a *response* from the user. 2. In *programmed instruction*, a *frame* which follows on from a *test frame* in a *branching program(me)*, providing either *reinforcement* or appropriate *remedial material* depending on whether the learner's *response* was correct or incorrect.

response orientation A type of *psychomotor skill*, being an individual's ability to select and make a correct or appropriate *response* from among several alternatives in a real or simulated work situation.

response time The time that elapses between a *stimulus* or input signal and the resulting *response* of the organism or system, eg the time that a learner takes to respond to an *item* in a *programmed instruction* sequence or the time that a *computer* takes to perform a given task. See also *latency*.

response wheel A classroom *feedback* device comprising a cardboard disc divided into several segments, each identified by a colo(u)r or symbol. The wheel is rotated in a holder, the desired response being indicated by means of a marker.

restricted response In instructional design, *assessment*, etc a *response* which is constrained in some way, eg having to choose a word from a number of given words or having to supply a word of x letters in response to a question.

restricted test Another name for a *closed test*.

retake Re-recording of a *scene*, sequence, etc, generally because the first recording was unsatisfactory for some reason, eg in television or film production or *audio recording*.

retention test A test administered some time after the completion of a course or program(me) of instruction in order to determine the extent to which acquired knowledge, skills, etc have been retained by the learner. See also *post-test*.

retroactive inhibition In *behavio(u)ral psychology* and *programmed instruction*, a form of *inhibition* where *learning* of a new skill, item of *knowledge*, etc interferes with the performance or recall of a previously-learned skill or item.

reverberation Multiple reflections of sound off the walls and other objects in a room; cf *echo*. See also *reverberation time*.

reverberation time The time take for sound to die away in a particular acoustic environment once the source of the sound is removed or terminated. Specifically, it is defined as the time taken for the sound intensity to fall by 60 *decibels*.

reversal film Normally, a *photographic film* produces a final *image* with opposite tonal or colo(u)r values to the scene or image to which it has been exposed once it has been processed, eg a *negative* image in the case of a photograph taken of an actual object or scene and a *positive* image in the case of a *print* made from a negative film. A reversal film is one in which the processing can be taken one stage further than normal, thus producing a final image with the same tonal or colo(u)r values as the original. Such film is used for a wide range of purposes, eg in producing photographic *slides*, in cine photography and in making copies of *motion picture* films. See also *reversal process*.

reversal process A process used with a *reversal film* to produce a final *image* of the required form, eg processing a photographic *transparency* that is to be used as a *slide* through the *negative* stage that would normally result from developing the exposed film in order to produce a *positive* image. Such image reversal can be achieved in a variety of ways, depending on the nature of the film being used and the purpose for which it is intended.

reverse angle shot In film or television production, a new *shot* of the same scene taken from the opposite direction.

review frame, item A *frame* or *item* in an instructional program(me) that causes the learner to repeat or review material already covered, usually for *reinforcement* purposes.

reward A satisfaction-yielding *stimulus* or

stimulus-object that is provided or experienced upon the successful performance of a task. Such a reward may be built into an instructional program(me) by the designers (eg display of a phrase such as 'Well done!' when the learner gets an answer right in a *computer-assisted learning* sequence) or may be purely internal (eg a feeling of satisfaction or achievement experienced by a learner); cf *punishment*.

rewind To wind a film or tape in the opposite direction to that in which it was shot, recorded, shown or replayed, back on to its original hub or spool, usually at high speed.

RF See *radio frequency*.

R factor The logical reasoning *factor* in *intelligence*.

RGB monitor A red-green-blue *television monitor* where the three *primary colo(u)rs* are treated as separate signals. Such a monitor gives a much better display of colo(u)red graphics than a colo(u)r television receiver.

RIAA curve The standard *equalization* characteristic for *audio* reproduction of the Recording Industries Association of America; this characteristic is now used in virtually all *audio recording* work.

ribbon microphone A type of *dynamic microphone* whose *transducer* is a metal ribbon that moves in a magnetic field, thus causing an electric current corresponding to the incident sound to be induced in the ribbon.

rifle microphone Another name for a *gun microphone*.

rigging Setting up lights, cameras, *projectors* or other equipment on a stage or *set*, in a presentation room, etc.

right-reading A term used to describe an *image* which is directly readable, as opposed to one that is *laterally reversed*.

river An un-planned alignment of spaces in a typeset or printed *text*.

role-play A technique (used in *games* and *simulations*) in which participants act out the parts of other persons or categories of persons, ie act out roles.

roll To start a *motion picture camera*, television camera, *tape recorder*, etc in order to shoot or record a given sequence or *scene*.

roll feed A system that enables a continuous supply of *software* to be fed across or through a device such as an *overhead projector*.

rolling plan, program(me) A long-term plan or *program(me)* that is revised at regular intervals, and which, at each successive revision, is projected forward for the same period as the original plan or program(me).

ROM See *read-only memory*.

roman 1. In printing, *lettering* etc the standard form of *typeface*, having vertical strokes as opposed to the inclined strokes of the *italic* form. 2. Numerals represented by symbols of the type used in classical Rome (eg IV, LX) as opposed to arabic symbols (eg 4, 60).

room darkening Reducing the light level in a room for projection or other purposes by either shutting out the external light or dimming the internal artificial lighting.

Rosenthal effect Another name for the *Pygmalion effect*.

rostrum 1. A raised platform in a *set, studio* etc. 2. A camera stand designed to hold in position and illuminate *captions, artwork*, etc so that they can be photographed or shot. See also *rostrum camera*.

rostrum camera A fixed film or television camera mounted vertically so that it can shoot graphical or animation material placed directly beneath it on a *rostrum*.

rotary gang An industrial training term for a group of trainees that is kept at more-or-less constant size, with members who leave after completing their training being replaced by new members.

rotary magazine A circular holder for photographic *slides* designed for use with an automatic slide *projector*. It can be of either the horizontal *carousel* type or of the vertical 'big wheel' type.

rotary stencil duplication See *stencil duplication*.

rote learning A type of *drill* in which material is learned by simple repetition, often recited out loud by a class. This is one of the *primary mental abilities* thought by Thurstone to constitute *intelligence*.

rough cut In film or television *editing*, the first assembly of *shots* in their intended order.

rounding (off) In computing, data processing, etc, removal of digits at the least significant end of a decimal number, with possible modification of the least significant retained digit. 26.152754, for example, would become 26.15 if rounded to four significant figures (or two decimal places) or 26.153 if rounded to five significant figures (or three decimal places); cf *truncation*.

round table discussion A discussion or conference in which, in principle, all participants have equal rank, standing or importance, an equality that is often signified by seating them at a round (as opposed to the conventional rectangular) table.

routine In computing, a sequence of instructions designed to make a *computer* carry out a single process or set of related processes.

routing page A *viewdata* term for a *page* whose function is to indicate a choice of other pages. See also *menu*.

rpm Revolutions per minute. This is the standard unit used to measure the playing speed of *audio discs*.

rubric 1. Instructions on an examination or test paper. 2. An introduction to a printed syllabus, course description or similar document.

ruleg A didactic technique that involves first giving a general principle, formula, classification, etc, (the 'ru' or 'rule') and then giving illustrative examples, instances, etc (the 'eg's'); cf *egrul(e)*.

rule learning A *cognitive* process that involves being able to learn relationships between concepts and apply these relationships in different situations, including situations not previously encountered. This is one of the types of intellectual skill identified by Gagné and Briggs.

rule-of-thumb learning See *trial-and-error learning*.

rumble Very low frequency *noise*, originating from the *turntable* system, sometimes heard during the playing of conventional *audio discs*.

rumber filter A low-frequency electronic *filter* designed to reduce the *noise* level when *audio discs* are being played using a *turntable* that produces a significant amount of *rumble*.

running costs The total on-going expenditure of funds needed to maintain and operate a system once the initial purchase, acquisition or construction costs have been met; cf *maintenance costs*. Also known as *operating costs*.

running heading, title A heading that is printed at the top of each *page* (or facing pair of pages) in a book or other document, typically giving the overall title on the left-hand page and the chapter or section title (or a shortened version thereof) on the right-hand page.

running shot In film or television production, a *shot* in which the camera moves at the same pace as a moving subject as the shot proceeds.

running time The total time needed to show a *motion picture*, play an *audiorecording* or *videorecording*, etc.

run out A length of blank film at the end of a *reel* of *motion picture* film used for *lacing* during rewinding.

run up The length of film or tape that has to be run through a camera, projector, recorder or player before it is operating smoothly at normal speed.

rushes In film production, *prints* of recently-taken *shots* that are produced from the *master* film in order to enable the production team to assess their acceptability, often at a special screening held at the end of the day's shooting.

S

safelight A source of visible light in a photographic *darkroom* whose colo(u)r and intensity allow unexposed, unprocessed exposed and other light-sensitive materials to be handled safely without unwanted *exposure*.

sample A group which is selected from a larger group or *population* for the purpose of detailed study, experimentation, testing, etc with a view to making generalizations about the nature or behavio(u)r of the population as a whole.

sampling error An error in a research study, experiment, etc that arises as a result of random variations between different *samples* drawn from the same *population* in respect of one or more of the *variables* being considered.

sandwich course A course in which a learner or trainee alternates between periods of full-time study at a *tertiary education* establishment such as a college or university and periods of training and/or work experience in industry, commerce, teaching or some other area of employment.

sandwiching Mounting two or more photographic *transparencies* in a single *slide* in order to create a desired effect (eg superposition of a *title* or *caption* on a *photograph*).

sanserif, sans serif In printing and *lettering*, a *typeface* without cross lines finishing off the ascending and descending strokes of letters, as in sanserif; cf *serif*.

SAT See *scholastic aptitude test*.

satisfier Any experience, situation or *stimulus* which meets an individual's needs or satisfies his/her innate drives.

scale An ordered series of symbols or numbers by means of which a measure of some aspect(s) of a person's or group's behavio(u)r or some aspect(s) or attribute(s) of a system can be given; see, for example, the four basic types of scale used in educational measurement (the *nominal scale, ordinal scale, interval scale* and *ratio scale*) and more specialized examples such as the *Likert scale* and *semantic differential scale*.

scaling Adjustment of test, examination or other marks or *scores* so that they conform to a standard distribution, agreed set of criteria, etc thus allowing meaningful comparisons or inferences to be made (see, for example, *grading on the curve*).

scanning Systematic inspection of all parts of an area, text, sequence of items, collection of data, etc by visual, optical, optico-electronic or electronic means. Such scanning may be carried out for a variety of purposes, eg to identify items of a given type, to gain an overview of the contents of a document, to build up a television picture, etc.

scattergram Graphical representation of data as isolated plots of the *dependent variable* as a function of the *independent variable* (see figure 43).

scenario Background information relating to the setting of a *game, simulation* or other exercise.

scene The basic unit of continuity sequence in a film or television production, planned for shooting as continuous, uninterrupted *action*.

schematic diagram A graphic representation of the main features or components of a device, system, etc generally omitting all unimportant details.

scholastic aptitude test (SAT) The US term for a test used by a university, college or similar establishment to assess the potential of prospective students.

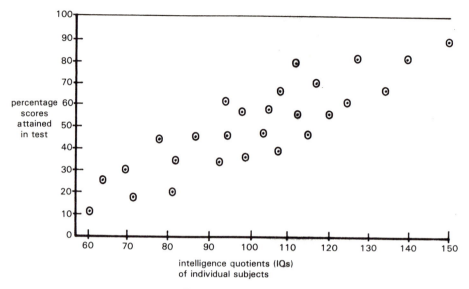

Figure 43 A scattergram

school edition A comparatively cheap version of a book intended primarily for school use. Such books are frequently produced in paperback form.

schools without walls An experimental type of school developed in some US towns in an attempt to serve deprived children in urban areas. Such schools have no formal campus, using public institutions, business premises, etc, and are organized on informal, progressive lines.

scientific notation Another name for *floating point notation*.

scoop A type of *flood(light)* used in photographic, film or television work to illuminate large areas at close range.

score 1. A number or credit assigned to an educational, research or other datum indicating its position on a *scale* of some sort. 2. To gain or assign such a number or credit.

scoring formula A standard formula by which a test, particularly an *objective test*, is *scored*.

scrambled text, book A text or book in which the sequence of *pages* does not follow logically and whose order of use is determined by the *responses* made by the reader to questions. It is a type of *branching program(me)*. See also *horizontal panel book, vertical panel book, zig-zag book*.

scraper board, scratchboard White-coated paper board covered with dark material such as Indian ink which can be scraped away to produce a high-contrast, white-on-black drawing.

screen 1. A specially-prepared surface used for the exhibition of a projected *image*. In *front projection*, such screens are usually opaque (see, for example, *matt(e) screen, silvered screen*) while in *back projection* they are translucent (see *translucent screen*). 2. The display surface of a television set, *visual display unit*, etc. 3. See *acoustic screen*. 4. See *silk screen printing*. 5. See *screening device, test*.

screen brightness The *luminance* of a projection *screen* when there is no *film, filmstrip, slide, transparency*, etc in or on the projector, and the projector is switched on.

screening device, test A *psychological test* or other instrument designed to identify individuals that satisfy some specific criterion or group of criteria, eg for the purpose of selecting *experimental groups* and *control groups* for a research study.

screenload The maximum number of *characters* that can appear on the *screen* of a *visual display unit* at any one time.

screenplay See *shooting script*.

script 1. The detailed scene-by-scene or frame-by-frame instructions for the production of a *film*, television program(me), *tape-slide program(me)*, *audio* program(me) etc. 2. The written answers produced by a person sitting an examination or test.

scroll A continuous roll of transparent film designed for use with an overhead projector *roll feed* system.

scrolling Adding a new *line* of information to an *overhead projector* display, *visual display unit* display, etc and accommodating it by moving the existing display upwards or downwards so that part of it disappears from the field of view.

S curve A curve that describes the development of a system where a *variable* of interest at first changes very slowly, then changes increasingly rapidly, and finally levels off at some constant value (the limiting or saturation value for the variable in question (see figure 42); see, for example, the *social interaction model (of diffusion/innovation)*, where the cumulative extent of *diffusion* generally follows such a curve.

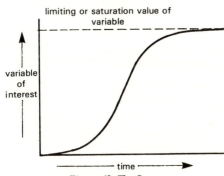

Figure 42 The S curve

search 1. See *fast (picture) search*. 2. *Scanning* the contents of or interrogating a *data base* in order to determine whether certain information is in storage, retrieve a particular set of data, etc.

SECAM Séquential Couleur à Mémoire. The system of encoding colo(u)r television signals used in France, the Soviet Bloc, and some African and Middle Eastern countries. See also *NTSC, PAL*.

secondary education The stage to which children normally progress when they have completed their *primary education*, generally by moving to a different school. In England and Wales, for example, secondary education starts at age 11 years old and continues to age 16–18 years. See also *tertiary education*.

secondary publication 1. The publication in another form of an already-published document for the purpose of wider dissemination, eg to a different target population from that for which the original document was intended. 2. A document which is produced for this purpose, eg an abstract, digest or popularized version of an original document, or a cheaper version such as a *school edition*.

second-chance institution An institution that provides educational opportunity (particularly at post-school level) for people who did not receive such education at the normal age because of personal or other factors (see, for example, *open university, Open Tech*).

second-generation computer A *computer* (of the type built during the 1960s) based on the technology of the discrete *transistor*. See also *first-generation computer, third-generation computer, fourth-generation computer, fifth-generation computer*.

selected response The *response* chosen by a learner in a multiple-choice situation such as a *multiple-choice item*.

self-appraisal, -assessment *Appraisal* or *assessment* by a learner or teacher of his/her own progress or performance, either against set criteria or by comparison with previous performance. One common method by which this is done is by self-administration of a progressive series of diagnostic tests.

self-coding questionnaire A *questionnaire* that is designed in such a way that the required information can be extracted directly from the *responses* made without the need for subjective interpretation, eg one that consists of a series of questions of the multiple-choice or 'yes-no' type, or of a series of objective *scales* such as *Likert scales*.

self-completion questionnaire A *questionnaire* that is designed to be completed by the actual respondee rather than completed on his/her behalf by an interviewer or researcher.

self-contained classroom A 'traditional' classroom of the type used in most primary and elementary schools in which one teacher is responsible for all aspects of the work of a class except for certain specialist activities (eg physical education and music).

self-display materials See *non-projected display materials*.

self-help group A group of students (eg students in a given area who are undertaking the same *distance-learning* course) who get together in order to share ideas, problems and experiences and generally help one another with the work of their course.

self-help materials Instructional materials that are designed to help individual learners working without ready access to supervision or assistance to master particular tasks, subject matter, etc. Also known as *support materials*. See also *self-instructional materials*.

self-instructional materials Instructional materials that are designed for study by individual learners, and which require no (or minimal) intervention or help from a teacher or instructor during their use. These are the sort of materials that are used in *distance learning* courses. Also known as *self-study materials*.

self-pacing A situation where the individual learner controls the rate or speed at which he/she carries out a given task, program(me) of work, etc as, for example, in the *Keller Plan*.

self-referenced assessment See *self-appraisal, -assessment*.

self-study centre (center) Another name for a *resource(s) centre (center)*.

self-study materials Another name for *self-instructional materials*.

semantic differential scale An *attitude scale* that takes the form of a series of pairs of antonyms joined by *interval scales* generally containing between 3 and 7 points, the respondee having to indicate the point on each of the latter that most closely represents his/her attitude, opinion or position regarding the topic or issue being dealt with (see figure 44); cf *Likert scale*.

semantic prompt (cue) In *behavio(u)ral psychology* and instructional design, a *thematic prompt* that is based on the meaning of language, eg 'The class of trees known as "conifers" get their name from the _____-shaped seed cases that such trees produce'; cf *syntactic prompt*.

semester See *semester system*.

semester system Division of the academic year into two equal *semesters*, each of roughly 15–18 weeks duration, rather than into three terms. This is an organizational system common in the USA, particularly in *tertiary education*.

seminar 1. A small class organized in order to discuss a specific topic, particularly one that is based on papers prepared and presented by the class members. 2. A short, intensive course on a particular subject or topic. 3. A conference of specialists in a particular field.

sensory stimulus A *stimulus* that is received via one of the five senses of an organism (sight, hearing, taste, smell or touch) rather than generated internally.

sentence completion item A type of completion item in which the learner has to complete a sentence by adding a missing word or words, eg 'The behavio(u)r emitted by an organism as a result of a _____ is known as a *response*'.

separation negatives In *photolithography* and similar photo-mechanical printing systems, *negative* copies made of a full-colo(u)r original through special red, green and blue filters in order to prepare the three separate *plates* used to print a colo(u)red *image*.

SEPMAG Separate magnetic — a term applied to a *double system sound* motion picture in which the sound is recorded on a separate *magnetic tape* or *magnetic film*; cf *COMMAG*.

I consider the course to be: (mark appropriate box on each row of scale)

easy							difficult
inflexible							flexible
too theoretical							too applied
poorly structured							well structured

Figure 44 Part of a semantic differential scale used in a course evaluation questionnaire

SEPOPT Separate optical — a term applied to a *double system sound* motion picture that has an *optical sound track* on a separate film from the picture film; cf *COMOPT*.

sequence prompt Another name for a *temporal prompt*.

sequential access A term applied to any system in which a specific item or section can only be reached by running through the entire system up to the item or section required; cf *random access*. Also known as *serial access*.

serial access Another term for *sequential access*.

serial file A *file* in which items are entered in logical sequence, so that they must also be searched for sequentially; cf *inverted file*.

serial(ist) learning Learning to make a series of *responses* in the correct order, in the manner of a *serialist*. See also *atomistic learning*.

serialist According to Pask, a person who learns, remembers and recapitulates a body of information in terms of string-like *cognitive* structures where items are related by simple data links; cf *holist*.

serif A *typeface* with cross lines finishing off with ascending and descending strokes of letters, as in serif; cf *sanserif*.

set 1. In television production, film production, photographic work, etc, an area that is specially furbished for shooting a particular *scene* or sequence of scenes. 2. A defined group of items. 3. A group of pupils constituted according to ability or achievement in a given subject; see *setting*. 4. A *psychomotor* process that involves making preparatory adjustments for carrying out a particular psychomotor activity; Level 2 of Harrow's *psychomotor domain*.

setting *Streaming* of pupils in different subjects according to their ability in each subject. See also *set* (3.).

S factor The spatial ability *factor* in *intelligence*.

shadow area A geographical area not reached by broadcast radio or television signals because of natural barriers such as hills.

shaping In *behavio(u)ral psychology*, the modification or alteration of behavio(u)r using *reinforcement* techniques.

sharpness The degree to which a television or other picture shows fine detail. Also known as *definition, resolution*.

shelf life The period of time from manufacture during which a material such as *photographic film* can be used with acceptable results if it has been properly stored.

shooting script A detailed *script* used during the shooting of a *motion picture*. Also known as the *screenplay* for the film.

shoot To operate a camera. See also *shooting script, shot*.

short-answer question, item An examination or test question requiring only a short answer (which can vary from a single word or number to a few sentences) rather than an extended essay, discussion, proof, etc.

short-term memory That part of the human *memory* in which material is stored on a short-term, temporary basis before either being forgotten or transferred to the *long-term memory*, eg the short-term memory is used when looking up a telephone number and then dialling it.

shot 1. In film or television production, a *scene* or sequence that is photographed or recorded as one continuous *action*. 2. A particular *photograph* taken with a *still camera*.

shotgun microphone See *gun microphone*.

shredding 1. Submitting possible *multiple-choice items* to a *battery* of diagnostic procedures in order to determine whether they are suitable for inclusion in a multiple-choice test or examination, ie a combination of *item editing* and *item trial testing*; see also *validation*. 2. Disposing of unwanted documents by passing them through a device which reduces them to unreadable shreds.

shutter A device that can be opened in order to allow light to enter or pass through an optical system such as a camera for a predetermined period, as and when required, eg during the taking of a *photograph* or the projection of a *frame* of a *motion picture* film. See also *shutter speed*.

shutter speed The interval (measured in fractions of a second) for which the *shutter* of a camera remains open during an *exposure*. The standard shutter speeds are 1, $\frac{1}{2}$, $\frac{1}{4}$, $\frac{1}{8}$, $\frac{1}{15}$, $\frac{1}{30}$, $\frac{1}{60}$, $\frac{1}{125}$, $\frac{1}{250}$, $\frac{1}{500}$ and $\frac{1}{1000}$ seconds.

signal learning A type of *learning* in which an individual learns to make a general diffuse *response* to a *stimulus* as a result of *respondent conditioning*; the lowest level (Level 1) of Gagné's eight types of learning.

signal-to-noise ratio The ratio of the strength of the wanted signal to that of the unwanted *background noise*, usually expressed in *decibels*.

silent film A *motion picture* with no associated sound recording, as opposed to a *sound film*.

silk screen printing A printing process that uses silk or a closely-woven, synthetic fabric stretched on a frame. A *stencil* is produced on the silk by the application of chemicals, and paint or ink is then squeezed through this on to the surface being printed. This technique is widely used in graphic design work.

silvered screen A metal projection *screen* with a silvered surface that produces a very high reflectivity close to the axis of projection. It is often used as a *daylight screen*. See also *lenticular screen*.

silver halide process The standard photographic process, where a *latent image* is formed by the action of light or other radiation on silver halide-sensitized materials, the image being made visible and stable by subsequent chemical processing.

simulated case study A *case study* that is based on a *simulation* as opposed to a real-life situation (see figure 49 on page 178).

simulation 1. In general, any operating (ie ongoing) representation of a real system or process or part thereof). 2. An educational, training or research exercise that incorporates such features. See also *participative simulation, predictive simulation* and figure 49 on page 178.

simulation game An exercise that includes all the essential characteristics of both a *game* and a *simulation*. See also figure 49 on page 178.

simulator An electronic, electro-mechanical or mechanical system designed to provide a realistic *simulation* of an actual machine, system, etc eg for training people to use or operate the latter.

single concept loop film (film loop) A *loop film* that presents, demonstrates or illustrates a single concept, idea, process, etc.

single frame Another term for *half-frame*, as applied to a *filmstrip*.

single-frame exposure Exposing one frame of a *motion picture* film at a time, eg during *time-lapse photography*.

single-lens reflex (camera) A *reflex camera* with a moveable mirror that enables the same lens to be used both for viewing and for photographing, thus completely eliminating unwanted *parallax* effects; cf *twin-lens reflex (camera)*.

single system sound In *sound film* production, a system whereby the sound is recorded on the same film as the pictures, as either an *optical sound track* or a *magnetic sound track*; cf *double system sound*.

single-track A term used to describe: 1. A recording tape that carries only one recording *track*, 2. A set of *programmed instruction* materials with only one possible *track* or route through them, ie a *linear program(me)*.

sitting next to (by) Nellie A UK term for the process whereby a new employee picks up the techniques associated with a particular job by working next to, and watching how they are executed by, an experienced worker. See also *buddy system*.

sixteen millimetre (16 mm) film A standard size of *motion picture* film 16 mm wide. This is the most common *gauge* used for making instructional films.

skewness (sk) A measure of the deviation of a statistical distribution from symmetry. If such a distribution is perfectly symmetrical (curve B in figure 44), it is said to have *zero skew*; if, on the other hand, it has more (fewer) scores at the low end than at the high end, it is said to have *positive (negative) skew* (curves A and C respectively in figure 45); cf *kurtosis*.

skill(s) analysis Further, more detailed *analysis* of the major tasks identified in a particular job during *job analysis* in order to identify the skills that each requires.

skill model An example for imitation, eg the recorded speech of a native speaker presented as an example to imitate during foreign language instruction.

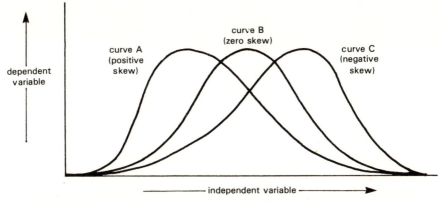

Figure 45 Frequency distributions possessing positive skew, zero skew and negative skew

skill testing Testing the level of attainment of a particular skill or group of skills, usually with the object of determining the amount of training that would be required to achieve satisfactory performance or the level attained after training.

Skinnerian program(me) A term sometimes applied to a *linear program(me)*.

skip branching In *programmed instruction*, a type of *forward branching* in which not all the *frames* are necessarily worked on, depending on the progress of the learner.

skip frame 1. A technique for speeding up the action of a *motion picture* by printing only selected *frames* from the original film. 2. A *frame* in a *programmed instruction* sequence which is missed out by faster learners.

slant track recording Another name for *helical scanning*.

slave unit 1. A device or part of a system that is controlled by another device or part (the *master*). 2. A *tape drive* on which blank tapes are run for the purpose of simultaneously duplicating two or more copies of a *master* tape.

sleep teaching Another name for *hypnopaedia*.

sleeve A protective envelope of card, paper or plastic for an *audio disc, floppy disk*, etc.

slide 1. A single *positive* photographic or other *image* on transparent material (a *slide transparency*) held in a *mount* and designed for projection; see also *compact slide, jumbo slide, lantern slide, superslide*. 2. A glass-mounted specimen prepared for viewing through a microscope.

slide binder, cover, mount A metal, plastic or cardboard *frame* (with or without glass windows) in which a *slide transparency* is mounted for projection.

slide duplicator A *copystand* fitted with all the equipment used in the photographic duplication of *slides*.

slide sequence A series of *slides* that are assembled or produced for consecutive showing or viewing in order to present a connected visual theme, with or without a live or recorded spoken commentary.

slide spot A spot, dot, mark etc placed on one corner of a *slide* to indicate whether the slide is correctly oriented when placed in a *projector* or projector *magazine*. The spot is generally placed on the bottom left-hand corner of the front of the slide, so that it appears on the top right-hand corner when the slide is correctly loaded for normal projection. Also known as a *thumb mark*.

slide-tape program(me) Another name for a *tape-slide program(me)*.

slide transparency A photographic or other *transparency* produced for use as a *slide*.

slide viewer A device fitted with a built-in magnifier or *back projection* screen designed for viewing individual *slides*.

slip binder A plastic grip that is slid over the left-hand edge of a loose bundle of sheets in order to bind them into a document such as a report.

slip case An open-fronted box used to contain and protect a book or set of books.

slot loading A facility whereby tape or film can be loaded laterally into a player, recorder, projector, etc without the need for *lacing* (*threading*). Also known as *channel loading*.

slotted cards Rectangular cards incorporating coded patterns of open-ended and closed slot-shaped holes round their edges, patterns which can be used to indicate particular characteristics of the information that the cards carry. For retrieval of information of a certain type, rods are inserted through the pack so that the ones required will drop out when the pack is lifted by the rods.

slow motion A technique for slowing down *motion picture* action by running the camera faster than normal (*overcranking*) and then showing the resulting film at normal speed; cf *slow play*.

slow play A technique for slowing down the action of a *film* or *video* sequence by operating the *projector* or *playback* machine slower than normal; cf *slow motion*.

small assembly session A session in an instructional program(me) or exercise in which the learners gather in small groups in order to discuss a particular problem, aspect of the work, etc, for example, a *buzz session*.

small caps In printing and *lettering*, capital letters with the same height as the *x-height* of the same *typeface*, as in SMALL CAPS.

smart terminal A *computer terminal* that has a certain amount of built-in data processing ability, but not as much as an *intelligent terminal*; cf *dumb terminal*.

snap change A very rapid *slide* change between two *projectors* of a dual or multi-projector system made possible by the use of *shutters*.

Snellen chart A printed chart showing rows of letters or other symbols of graded size that is used in testing eyesight.

snoot A conical hood designed to reduce the width of the beam emerging from a light source.

snow A continuously-changing random pattern of white dots in a television picture indicating a low *signal-to-noise ratio* or, if it is the only thing appearing on the screen, the complete absence of a signal.

snowball group A discussion group which moves or is guided through successive phases of idea sharing, with one idea leading on to another. See also *one-two-four snowball technique*.

social/anthropological approach (to evaluation) A subjective approach to educational *evaluation* that is more concerned with studying the on-going process of education than with trying to measure specific outputs; cf *agricultural/botanical approach (to evaluation)*. Also known as *illuminative evaluation*. See also *subjective evaluation*.

social interaction model (of diffusion/innovation) A model of *diffusion* of innovation which places emphasis on the patterns by which innovations diffuse naturally through a social system, with the adoption behavio(u)r of a particular user depending both on the network of social relations in which he/she is involved and on his/her particular place within this network; the diffusion mechanism is crucially dependent on informal contacts, with the cumulative extent of adoption generally following an S curve; cf *research, development and diffusion model*.

social stimulus A *stimulus* that is social rather than physical, physiological or psychological in origin.

sociodrama The use of *role play* as a means of providing experience or of seeking a solution to a social problem of some sort. See also *psychodrama*.

sociogram A diagram used in sociometry and *group dynamics* to record and show the pattern of social choices and rejections among the members of a group, and hence show the group structure (see figure 46).

soft copy (readout) *Computer* output that is displayed on to *screen* of a *visual display unit* or similar device, or read directly into a storage medium such as a *floppy disk*; cf *hard copy*.

soft focus Deliberately producing, for effect, an *image* with less than the maximum *sharpness* of which a system is capable, eg in photography or film production.

soft keyboard A representation of a *keyboard* on the *screen* of a *visual display unit* that can be used to input data into a *computer* by pointing a *light pen* at, or touching, each required *character* in turn.

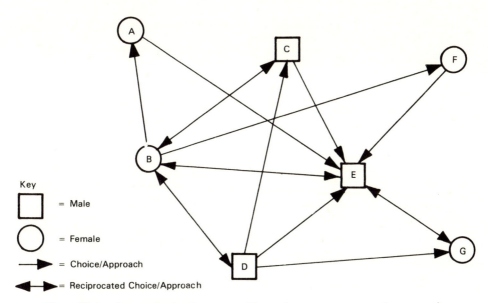

Figure 46 A sociogram showing the pattern of interactions among a group of seven people

soft skills A term applied to skills that are particularly susceptible to influence or manipulation, particularly those that do not involve the use of equipment (eg interpersonal skills of various types).

software 1. A general term for *audiovisual materials* that are used in conjunction with *hardware* (eg *videotapes, audiotapes, slides, films* and *CBL* materials). 2. A general term for the programs and supportive documentation that are used in conjunction with *computers* and other data processing systems; cf *courseware*. See also *system software, software package*.

software package See *package* (2.).

solander case A box in the form of a book used for the storage of documents.

sound disc Another name for an *audio disc*.

sound drum See *drum* (2.).

sound effects In a *film*, television program(me), *audio* program(me), etc any sound from any source other than dialog(ue), *narration* or music which is introduced in order to produce or enhance a desired effect or illusion (eg a crack of thunder or the sound of footsteps).

sound film A *motion picture* with an associated sound recording; cf *silent film*. See also *single*

system sound, double system sound.

sound filmstrip A *filmstrip* with an associated sound recording, usually on a *compact cassette*.

sound gate A separate *gate* used instead of a *sound drum* in some *optical film projectors* to keep the *sound track* properly aligned with the scanning beam.

sound head 1. The mechanism in *sound film* equipment for recording or playing back the optical or magnetic sound record associated with a film. 2. The mechanism in *audio* or *video* equipment for recording or playing back the sound signal.

sound mixer A device for combining *audio signals* from different sources into a single composite signal. It generally incorporates facilities that allow the relative strengths and characteristics of the various sounds to be controlled and modified before mixing occurs.

sound-on-slide Another name for an *audioslide*.

sound-on-sound A process in which a new *audio signal* is added to a previously-recorded one as the latter is being played, and the combined signal is re-recorded on another machine.

sound page, sheet Other names for an *audiopage*.

sound synchronizer A device which can be used to link an ordinary *audiotape recorder* to an ordinary automatic slide projector so that the latter can be made to advance automatically by any *synchronizing signals* recorded on the tape. It is used during the presentation of *tape-slide program(me)s*; cf *presentation programmer*. Also known as a *synchronizing unit*.

sound tape Another name for an *audiotape*.

sound track 1. The optical or magnetic strip on a *single system sound* motion picture film that carries the sound signal; see also *magnetic sound track, optical sound track*. 2. A *track* on a *magnetic tape* that carries a discrete sound signal. 3. The actual sound recording in '1.' and '2.'.

spacing loss A loss of high frequencies in *magnetic tape* recording or playback due to imperfect contact between the *head* and the tape.

span of apprehension The maximum number of objects, items, etc which can be correctly apprehended simultaneously by an individual.

spatial ability The ability to recognize and understand differences and relationships between objects in three-dimensional space, to perceive the spatial properties of objects, to manipulate solid objects of different shapes and sizes, etc.

speaker Another term for a *loudspeaker*.

Spearman-Brown formula A standard formula that enables the overall *reliability* of a test or measure to be related to the *split-half reliability*.

special effects 1. In film and television production, *scenes* in which an illusion of the *action* required is created by the use of special equipment and processes, eg the use of *models* to depict space craft in films such as 'Star Wars'. 2. In television production, visual effects such as *split screens, wipes, inlays* and *superimpositions* that are produced using a *special effects generator*.

special effects generator An electronic device which can combine and/or modify *video signals* in order to produce *special effects*. Also known as an *effects box, generator*.

specification A concise statement of a set of requirements to be satisfied by a product, material, program(me), etc.

speech compression See *compressed speech*.

speech synthesis The production of speech by artificial means, eg by using a *computer* to generate the component sounds.

speech track A *sound track* on an *audiotape* or other recording that carries only speech, as opposed to general sound, music or sound effects.

speed-of-arm movement A type of *psychomotor skill*, being the speed with which an individual can make different arm movements.

speed test A test in which the total number of *items* or questions answered in the allowed time is an important factor; cf *power test*.

spherical aberration A form of *aberration* in which rays well away from the *optical axis* of a spherical lens or mirror are brought to a *focus* at different points from rays close to the axis.

spineless publication A general term for pamphlets, booklets, etc that lack a stiff spine of the type that is present in a conventional book.

spiral binding A form of *mechanical binding* in which the sheets of a document are held together by a helical wire passed through holes along their edges; cf *comb binding*.

spiral curriculum A *curriculum* in which ideas are first introduced in simple form, then covered in greater depth later in the year or in the following year, continuing similarly.

spirit duplication Another name for *hectograph(ic) duplication*.

spirit master Another name for a *hectograph master*.

splice 1. To make a physical join between the ends of two sections of tape or film using cement or adhesive tape. 2. The resulting cemented or taped join.

split brain theory The theory that the left hemisphere of the brain is used mainly for auditory, manual and visual tasks and is the place where 'logical thinking' occurs, while the right hemisphere is used mainly for handling qualitative (eg spatial, non-verbal and sensory) symbols and is the place where 'intuition' and 'creative thinking' occur.

split-half reliability A statistical term for the value of the *reliability* of a test or other measure that is obtained by splitting it into two similar halves and then comparing them. See also *Spearman-Brown formula*.

split program(me) An instructional program(me) in which formal education alternates with industrial, professional or other training, as in a *sandwich course*.

split screen Projection or showing of two or more different *images* on different parts of the same *screen*; cf *multi-screen*.

spoilers Guide pins in a *tape recorder* or *audiotape player* that prevent tape-to-head contact during *fast forward* or *rewind*.

spool Another term for a *reel*.

spot, spotlight A *luminaire* that gives a narrow beam of light.

spot question A test or examination question requiring a short, usually factual answer rather than a more discursive essay-type answer, a lengthy derivation or proof, etc. See also *short-answer question, item*.

spotting 1. Marking *slides* with *slide spots*. 2. Attempting to predict the questions that will be set in an examination on the basis of previous papers, the coverage of material in *lectures*, etc.

sprite A small *computer graphics* element (such as a face) which can be controlled and moved as a unit. Sprites are used in many computer games, and are also used in systems that use the LOGO *high-level programming language*.

sprocket A toothed drum or wheel in a camera, *projector*, etc that engages holes along one or both edges of a *film, filmstrip* or tape (*sprocket holes*) for transport and *registration* purposes.

sprocket holes See *sprocket*.

sprocketted full-coat *Magnetic tape* of either 16 mm or super 8 *film gauge* fitted with *sprocket holes*. Such tape is used for recording the sound component of *SEPMAG* motion picture films.

squawker Another name for a *mid-range speaker*.

squeal *Noise* produced during the *playback* of an *audiotape* caused by worn or dirty *pressure pads* or by the use of tape that lacks the special lubrication treatment that is normally used to prevent such noise.

squeezezoom A device that enables the geometry of a *video* image to be manipulated for artistic or other effects.

S-R bond, connection See *stimulus-response bond, connection*.

staff development The various mechanisms (both systematic and incidental) whereby teaching staff develop their skills and expand their knowledge, eg through attending courses, *seminars* and conferences, carrying out research and consultancy, engaging in professional activities, etc. Also known as *faculty development*.

stage left, right On an actor's left (right) when looking at the audience.

stamping in A *behavio(u)ral psychology* term for the process of impressing effective *stimulus-response bonds* on the mind of an individual during *learning*.

stand alone (capability) The capability of an item of *courseware* or *hardware* to function independently of other items of equipment.

standard deviation (σ) A measure of the *variability* of a statistical distribution, being equal to the square root of the *variance*. See also *standard error*.

standard 8 Standard *eight millimetre (8 mm) film*, as opposed to *super 8*.

standard error A statistical index that gives a quantitative measure of the accuracy of a conclusion reached by statistical analysis. It is equal to the *standard deviation* that would be produced if the analysis were carried out an infinite number of times.

standardization Transformation of a set of *raw scores* so that they have a given *mean* and *standard deviation*, thus enabling them to be meaningfully compared with other scores that have been similarly treated. See also *standardized score*.

standardized score A *score* that has been subjected to a process of *standardization*; cf *raw score*.

standard performance A *work study* term for the average rate of output that a fully-trained, experienced worker will achieve naturally without over-exertion.

start-up costs The total costs involved in launching a project, program(me), etc over and above any *operating costs* subsequently incurred.

station See *work station* (2.).

statistical significance A result or conclusion obtained as a result of statistical analysis is said to have statistical significance if the analysis shows that it is highly unlikely to have occurred by chance, ie by the normal random variations that occur naturally within most statistical *populations*.

stem The introductory part of a *multiple-choice item* containing the information on the basis of which the respondee makes his/her own choice from the various options that follow.

stencil 1. A sheet of material in which an *image* is cut by mechanical or other means, and through which ink, paint, etc can be fed or forced in order to create a representation of same on a receiving sheet. See also *stencil duplication* 2. A similar system that can be used as a guide for the drawing of such a representation using a suitable pen or scriber. See also *mechanical lettering device*.

stencil duplication A reprographic process in which a paper *stencil* master is attached to the outer surface of a rotary drum made of porous material through which ink is forced, thus producing a printed *image* on sheets of copy paper when the stencil is pressed against them. Also known as *rotary stencil duplication*.

step In *programmed instruction*, another term for a *frame*.

step-and-repeat camera 1. A camera that can be used to produce a matrix of *microimages* on a single sheet of *photographic film* (eg during the production of a *microfiche*) or a row of such images on a section of roll film (eg during the production of a *microfilm*). 2. In printing, a camera that is used to produce multiple *images* of the same original material in different positions on a given film, plate, etc.

step printing *Motion picture* printing in which the film is exposed *frame* by frame.

stereo An abbreviation for *stereophonic* or *stereoscopic*.

stereo camera A camera with two separate lenses, arranged side by side, that is used for taking *stereographs*.

stereograph A pair of *slides* or *transparencies* designed to produce a three-dimensional effect when viewed using a suitable *viewer* or *projector*. Also known as a *stereoscopic slide*. See also *anaglyph*.

stereophonic A term used to describe a sound recording or sound reproduction system that employs two discrete but related *sound tracks*, channels or sources, thus creating a 'three dimensional' effect that is absent if only one channel is used; cf *monophonic, quadraphonic*. Also called *binaural recording, reproduction*.

stereoscope An optical device for viewing *stereographs*.

stereoscopic A term used to describe a *photograph, motion picture*, etc that produces an illusion of three dimensions by use of double *images*. See also *anaglyph, stereograph*.

stereoscopic slide Another name for a *stereograph*.

stethoset Set of *headphones* of similar form to a doctor's stethoscope, with small *transducers* or sound tubes that fit into the users' ears.

still camera A camera designed for taking single *photographs*, as opposed to a *motion picture camera* or television camera.

still frame Continuous display of a single *frame* from a moving sequence such as a *film* or *video* for a period that is considerably longer than the normal frame display time. See also *freeze frame*.

Stilling Tests Standard tests of colo(u)r vision similar to the *Ishihara Test*.

Stillitron A learner-response device consisting of a printed circuit board that is slipped under a page of a specially-printed book. The learner responds to *items* or questions by pressing appropriate areas with a *stylus*, and receives a visual display indicating whether the response is right or wrong.

still motion slide A stationary *slide* or *transparency* in which an illusion of movement is produced by the use of *animation*, eg by the use of polarized light or *moirée fringes*.

stimuli Plural of *stimulus*.

stimulus 1. In *behavio(u)ral psychology*, an external force, pulse of energy or other signal that is applied to an organism in an attempt to activate sensory receptors and internal data processing systems, and hence elicit a *response*, or an internal process that produces a similar effect. 2. In learning, a signal, message, question, etc that is given to a learner in an attempt to elicit a desired *response*. See also *covert stimulus, overt stimulus, stimulus-response (S-R) bond, connection*.

stimulus-response (S-R) bond, connection In *behavio(u)ral psychology, programmed instruction*, etc the link between a *stimulus* and the *response* that it elicits.

stimulus-response learning A behavio(u)rist view of the *learning* process which regards it as consisting essentially of the establishment of *stimulus-respond bonds*. This is one of Gagné's eight types of learning (Level 2).

stop In photography, the relationship between the effective *aperture* of a lens and its *focal length*, expressed in terms of its *f-number*. In most cameras, the effective aperture can generally be varied through a range of fixed 'stops', each of which lets through half as much light as the one before.

stop frame Another term for *freeze frame*.

stop motion Operation of a *motion picture camera*, motion picture *printer* or film *projector* one *frame* at a time, as in *time-lapse photography* or *animation work*.

stop motion projector Another name for an *analyzing projector*.

storage capacity In computing, this term is used to denote the quantity of data (ie the number of *bits, bytes, characters* or *words*) that a *computer store* can hold, usually expressed in *k*'s (multiples of 1024).

store See *computer store*.

storyboard A series of sketches or pictures and any corresponding *text* or production instructions used in the planning of a *film*, television program(me), *tape-slide program(me)*, etc.

storyboarding The activity of preparing a *storyboard* during the planning of a *film*, television program(me), *tape-slide program(me)*, etc.

streaming Dividing children of the same *chronological age* into separate groups or classes on the basis of overall ability, or ability in a particular subject. See also *ability grouping, setting*.

string In computing, data processing, etc a linear sequence of *bits, characters* or *words* recording a particular set of connected data.

stringout The first stage in *editing* a *motion picture*, involving arranging the original *shots* in the required sequence and splicing them together.

striped film *Motion picture* film that carries down one edge a narrow strip of magnetic oxide on which a *magnetic sound track* may be recorded.

strobing A disturbing effect in a *motion picture* or television display when periodic motion (especially rotary motion) is distorted by stroboscopic effects associated with the framing frequency (the effect that sometimes makes carriage wheels in films look as if they are rotating backwards). See also *stroboscope*.

stroboscope 1. A variable-frequency flashing light used to measure the frequency or freeze the motion of rotating or vibrating systems. 2. A disc with equally-spaced marks round its edge (or similar marks round the circumference of a *turntable*) used to monitor rotation speed under a mains-frequency light source; if the speed is correct, the marks appear to be stationary.

structural communication A form of *learning* that involves the use of a detailed set of *objectives*, an extended presentation of material which the learner has to study and investigate, and a grid on which *responses* have to be made, these being used to provide information about the learning in the form of a written discussion. See also *structural communication item, test*.

structural communication item, test An *item* or test in which the subject is presented with a grid containing a number of (correct) statements relating to a particular topic and has to select and arrange pieces of information in response to questions on the topic. See also *structural communication*.

structured essay, essay-type question, item An essay question in which some guidance is given as to the structure and content of the required response, often by dividing the question into parts. One common form involves the use of a first part in which nearly all learners will perform well, a longer middle part which most learners will attempt and a final part which only a few learners will attempt; cf *unstructured essay*.

structured interview A pre-planned interview in which the discussion is limited to those specific areas that are of interest to the interviewer(s); cf *unstructured interview*.

structured programming A systematic way of designing, building, validating and documenting *computer programs* (including *CBL* programs) which, if carried out correctly, leads to the production of error-free, efficient and reliable *software*.

structured teaching Putting together a lesson or series of lessons in a systematic, highly-organized way in which all activities are pre-planned; cf *opportunistic teaching*. Also known as *systematic teaching*.

student-centred (-centered) approach, learning, teaching An approach to instruction that concentrates on the needs of the individual student, and in which the teacher/instructor and the host institution play supportive rather than central roles; cf *teacher/institution-centred (-centered) approach, subject-centred (-centered) approach*.

student development The on-going process by which a learner is conditioned and educated to become a 'sophisticated consumer' of education. See also *study skills, self-appraisal, -assessment*.

student-paced learning aids, materials Instructional materials (generally of a self-study nature) that are designed so as to allow each student to work at his/her own natural pace.

studio A specially-designed or adapted area used for artistic, graphic or photographic work, or for the production of *audio* program(me)s, television program(me)s, *films*, etc.

study circle A group of people who meet in order to discuss and study a subject of common interest. See also *self-help group*.

study guide A document that provides learners with instructions and/or guidance designed to help them cope with the work of a particular course, learning program(me), etc, particularly if it is of the self-instructional type.

study pack A folder or container that holds papers, documents, *audiotapes*, etc on a particular topic. Such a study pack may be used in conjunction with a *worksheet*.

study skills The set of skills that a learner needs to develop in order to study efficiently and effectively.

style of learning See *learning style*.

stylus 1. A 'needle' used to read the *audio signal* from the groove of a conventional *audio disc*, usually made of diamond or sapphire. 2. A pen-like device used to input data into a *data tablet*, select material from a computer *menu*, etc. 3. A pointed scriber used in *stencil* preparation, graphics work, etc.

subject-centred (-centered) approach An approach to instruction which emphasizes the content of a *syllabus* or *curriculum* rather than the particular needs of individual learners; cf *student-centred (-centered) approach*.

subject-centred (-centered) curriculum A *curriculum* that is based on a specific academic subject or discipline or a group of separate subjects or disciplines, as opposed to one that employs an integrated, cross-disciplinary approach.

subject index An *index* in the form of an alphabetical list of the subjects, topics or areas dealt with in a document together with reference to the place(s) where each occurs; cf *author index*.

subjective evaluation *Evaluation* based on the accumulation of qualitative data which is subsequently analyzed and interpreted; cf *objective evaluation*. See also *illuminative evaluation, social/anthropological approach (to evaluation)*.

subliminal Literally, 'below the threshold'; a term applied to: 1. A *stimulus* that is too weak to be specifically noticed and reported but is sufficiently strong to exert an influence on conscious processes or behavio(u)r. 2. The effect produced by such a stimulus.

subroutine In computing, a minor sequence of instructions that is often repeated, and which is held in a *store* so that it can be called up as and when required rather than repeated in full every time it is used in a *program*.

subscript A small figure, letter or *character* printed below the normal level of a line of type, as in H_2O; cf *superscript*.

subsidiaries A publishing term for any material following the main *text* of a book or other document, eg notes, appendices and indices; cf *preliminaries*.

substitution drill A type of *drill* in which one word or item is substituted on each successive repetition.

sub-system A discrete, orderly whole forming part of a larger *system*.

subtitle Any explanatory and/or subordinate part of the title of a book, document, program(me), etc that follows the *main title*.

success ratio The number of people who satisfactorily complete a course or program(me) of instruction, expressed as a percentage or fraction of the total number entering or attempting the course or program(me).

suite 1. A set of inter-related *computer programs* which can be run consecutively as a single job. 2. A related set of *learning packages*, instructional exercises, etc. 3. A set of rooms or equipment set aside for a particular purpose (eg an *editing* suite in a film or television studio).

summated rating scale Any *attitude scale*, *inventory test*, etc which has the following basic characteristics: (i) a set of *items* which are of equal value; (ii) a method of indicating intensity of agreement/disagreement with each item; (iii) a set of *responses* which are standard throughout the scale, and which can therefore be totalled to give an overall measure of the factor or parameter being investigated, eg a measure of an individual's overall political attitude or degree of extroversion/introversion.

summative evaluation *Evaluation* that is carried out at the conclusion or completion of a project, activity, etc in order to provide data for *product evaluation* or to determine the overall effectiveness of a course or other activity.

summer school 1. An extended group instruction session incorporated into an individualized *distance learning* or *open learning* course; usually held during the summer. 2. A short course run by a *tertiary education* establishment during the summer vacation for people other than its normal students.

super 8 A type of *eight millimetre (8 mm) film* with a larger *image* size than *standard 8*, thus producing better-quality pictures.

superposition, superimposition In television production, graphics work, etc, adding one *image* on top of another so that they are both visible, eg addition of an *overlay* to an *OHP transparency* or a *caption* to a projected or television image. Also known as *incrust*.

superscript A small figure, letter or *character* which is printed above the normal level of a line of type, as in x^2; cf *subscript*.

superslide A *slide* with the same size of *mount* as a standard *compact slide* but a much larger *image* area (generally 40 mm × 40 mm). Also known as a *jumbo slide*.

supply reel, spool Other names for a *feed reel, spool*.

supported self study A UK scheme that enables learners to study in groups that would normally be considered too small to warrant teacher support. It involves the learners carrying out the bulk of their work without teacher support (ie by self-study) and the remainder with a teacher.

support materials Another name for *self-help materials*.

surface chart Another name for a *band curve graph*.

surface processing A type of study method in which a learner scans material in order to acquire straightforward factual knowledge or an overview of the content, rather than an in-depth understanding of the latter; cf *deep processing*.

switched-star system A high-capacity *cable television* distribution system in which users are connected via *fibreoptic (fiberoptic) cables* to local distribution centres (centers) which are, in turn, linked to the main distribution centre (center). Some systems of this type enable two-way communication to take place between the users and the distribution centres (centers); cf *tree-and-branch system*.

switcher A US term for a *vision mixer*.

syllabus An outline or brief description of the main points or areas covered by a *text*, lecture or course.

sync An abbreviation for synchronized, as in *synchronized sound*.

sync generator In television production, an electronic generator that supplies *sync pulses* for controlling the synchronization of signals. See also *time base corrector*.

sync pulses 1. The part of a *composite video* signal that controls the repetition of the *scanning* system (see figure 22 on page 76). 2. The component of the sound record of a *COMMAG* or *SEPMAG* film that synchronizes the sound with the pictures.

synchronized (sync) sound In a *motion picture* or television sequence, sound which matches and occurs simultaneously with the pictures; cf *wild sound*. See also *lip sync*.

synchronizer 1. Two or more *sprockets* on a common shaft system designed to enable a corresponding number of *films* (or films and sprocketted tapes) to be driven through in lockstep. 2. See *frame synchronizer*.

synchronizing signal, pulse 1. An audible or inaudible signal or pulse that is incorporated in an *audio recording* (often on a separate *track*) in order to cause a *frame* of an accompanying *slide sequence* or *filmstrip* to be advanced manually or automatically at the appropriate time. Also called an *advance cue, signal*. 2. A pulse that is incorporated in a recorded *video signal* in order to ensure proper synchronization of the various parts of the signal when it is played back (see figure 22 on page 76, which shows the field sync pulses on a typical videotape).

synchronizing unit Another term for a *sound synchronizer*.

syndetic A term that is used to describe an *index*, catalog(ue), glossary etc that shows relationships between entries, eg in the form of 'cf', 'see' and 'see also' entries.

syndicate A small group of participants in a course, program(me) or exercise who are separated from the rest of the participants (who may themselves be divided into other syndicates) in order to undertake a specific task or investigation related to the work being carried out.

syndicate method An instructional method that is based on the use of *syndicates*. It is widely used in business schools and similar establishments.

syntactic prompt (cue) In instructional design, a *formal prompt* that is based on the nature of

grammar or the structure of language, eg in the *completion item*: 'The home of an eskimo is called an ____', where the use of 'an' preceding the required word indicates that it begins with a vowel; cf *semantic prompt*.

synthesis A *cognitive* process that involves rearranging elements, parts, items, etc into a new and integrated whole; Level 5 of Bloom's *cognitive domain*.

synthesizer An electronic system used to generate *sound effects*; electronic music, etc.

system The structure or organisation of an orderly whole, clearly showing the interrelationship between the different parts (or *sub-systems*) and between the parts and the whole. See also *systems approach (to instruction)*.

systematic classroom observation A type of *classroom observation* that involves observing, encoding and decoding classroom interactions, using pre-specified categories to describe the observed events, without actually taking part in the activities being observed; cf *participant classroom observation*.

systematic teaching Another name for *structured teaching*.

systems approach (to instruction) A term used to denote the systematic application of *instructional technology* to an educational or training problem, starting by identifying the input (the *entry behavio(u)r* of the learners) and output (the desired *terminal behavio(u)r* of the learners) and then determining how best to convert the former into the latter by employing an appropriate instructional *system*. The latter is often represented as a *Black box*, as shown in figure 47 (the simplest possible representation of the systems approach).

system software *Computer programs* (usually prepared and supplied by the manufacturer of a *computer*) that provide the link between user programs and the computer *hardware*, eg the programs that control the operation of the computer itself and *compilers* for the *high-level programming languages* that can be used with it.

System X A computerized telephone switching system developed by British Telecom. It has a much higher capacity than traditional systems, and also operates at much higher speed.

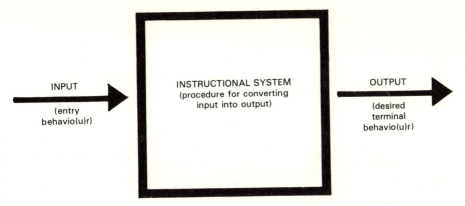

Figure 47 A schematic representation of the systems approach to instruction

T

tablet arm A writing surface that is attached to (or built into) the arm of a chair in order to facilitate note taking and similar activities.

tachistoscope A device similar to the *shutter* of a camera that enables momentary exposure of *slides* (or portions of slides) to be made during a presentation or an instructional program(me).

tactile keyboard A *keyboard* that is laid out on a flat surface and activated by touch rather than by physical movement of *keys*. See also *soft keyboard*.

tag In a machine-readable *record*, a *character* (or group of characters) that is added to a set of data for identification purposes, usually either at the beginning or the end.

tailored test Another name for a *response-contingent test*.

take In film or television production, a *scene* or sequence that is recorded as continuous *action*.

take-up reel, spool The *reel* (*spool*) which receives film or tape that has just passed through a camera, projector, player, recorder, etc; cf *feed reel, spool*.

talking book A spoken text recorded on either an *audiotape* or an *audio disc*, eg for use with young children or the visually handicapped. Should not be confused with a *talking page*.

talking page Another name for an *audiopage*. Should not be confused with a *talking book*.

tape 1. See *magnetic tape, audiotape, videotape*. 2. See *punched tape*.

tape deck An *audiotape recorder* that requires ancillary equipment (usually separate *amplifier* and *loudspeaker* systems) to reproduce an *audio signal*.

tape drive 1. The mechanism in an *audiotape recorder, videotape recorder*, etc which moves the tape past the *heads*, usually a *capstan* of some sort. 2. A *computer peripheral* which can be used to read data into or off *magnetic tape*.

tape recorder A term that covers both *audiotape recorders* and *videotape recorders*, but is often used as a synonym for the former.

tape-slide program(me), presentation An instructional program(me) or presentation in the form of a *slide sequence* accompanied by an *audiotape*, the two being synchronized by means of audible or inaudible *synchronizing signals* recorded on the tape. See also *audible advance, inaudible advance*. Also known as a *slide-tape program(me)*.

tape store A data storage system in which data is held on *magnetic tape*.

tape typewriter An electric typewriter which, in addition to producing a normal eye-legible *hard copy* of what is being typed, encodes it on a *punched tape* for feeding it into a *computer* or similar device.

target population That portion of the total *population* for which a particular course, product, etc is designed.

task analysis A detailed *analysis* of a task or operation that is carried out in order to identify sub-elements or components thereof. See also *job analysis, skill(s) analysis*.

taught course A course in which students learn by being taught prescribed course material, as opposed to a course based on *project* or research work.

taxonomy A classification system organised in terms of a *hierarchy* of relationships, eg the taxonomy of the *cognitive domain* produced by Bloom.

teacher/institution-centred (-centered) approach The 'traditional' approach to education in which virtually all aspects of the instructional process are under the control of the institution mounting the course and the teaching staff; cf *student-centred (-centered) approach*.

teacher's guide An explanatory *handbook* for the teacher produced to accompany an educational *package*. See also *organizer's guide*.

teachers' resource(s) centre (center) A comprehensive *resource(s) centre (center)* operated for the benefit of the teachers in a town or region. Such centres (centers) generally provide advice and back-up services for teachers carrying out innovative work or producing resource materials, as well as providing a loan service of educational resources.

teaching aid Any *audio aid, visual aid* or *audiovisual aid* that is used in the teaching process. Should not be confused with *teaching aide*.

teaching aide, assistant, auxiliary An unqualified or partly-qualified person who is employed in a school, college, etc to help teachers in the actual classroom.

teaching frame In *programmed instruction* a *frame* that provides the user with new knowledge or helps him/her to re-structure knowledge already possessed; cf *practice frame, test frame*.

teaching/learning unit (TLU) A *package* of instructional materials that incorporates both a *teacher's guide* and a set (or sets) of *resource materials* for use by learners.

teaching machine A term applied to the various mechanical and electro-mechanical devices that were developed during the 1960s and early 1970s as *delivery systems* for the *programmed learning* materials that were being developed at the time. Such machines are now virtually obsolete, having been replaced by *computer*-based delivery systems, and the term is now seldom used.

teaching point The smallest level of detail in a *lesson plan* or other outline of material to be presented in an instructional program(me).

teaching practice A period (generally of several weeks duration) spent by a student or trainee teacher in a classroom situation in order to observe teaching being carried out by an experienced teacher (or teachers) and to obtain some personal experience of real-life teaching.

team project Another name for a *group project*.

team teaching A situation where two or more teachers share the responsibility for running a lesson, exercise, instructional program(me), *module*, course, etc with the same group of learners, generally being present at the same time. Should not be confused with *group instruction* or *group teaching*.

team training 1. Training that is carried out by a team of trainers, working together as in *team teaching*. 2. Another name for *group training*.

tear sheet A sheet designed to be torn out of (or off) a document, leaflet, etc for some specific purpose, eg replying to a *questionnaire* or enrolling for a course, conference, etc.

teazle board, teazlegraph Alternative names for a *hook-and-loop board*.

technology in education The use of *hardware* and *software* within the context of educational situations; cf *technology of education*.

technology of education The application of the principles of *instructional technology* to the design of courses, learning systems, etc; cf *technology in education*.

telebeam projector Another name for a *television projector*.

telecine chain A facility for feeding *motion picture* sequences into a *television signal* using a linked film projector and camera. Also called a *film chain*.

teleclass Another name for *telephone instruction*.

teleconference A conference arranged by connecting geographically-separated delegates through the public telephone system; such a conference may use *audio* links only (an *audioconference*) or may use both audio links and slow-scan television links (a *television conference*).

telecopier A device used in *facsimile transmission* for producing copies of documents at a distance.

telecourse Another name for a *distance learning* course.

telegraph A system for transmitting information along hard-wire communication links, using codes based on simple on-off conventions. See also *telex*.

telelecture An arrangement which enables a speaker or lecturer to communicate with several classes in different locations simultaneously, using public telephone links.

telemotion A sophisticated audiovisual presentation technique involving the use of multiple *projectors* of various types behind a large *back projection* screen, together with associated *audio* equipment.

telephone instruction Instruction in which practically all direct communication between the instructor and the learner is carried out via the public telephone system. Also known as a *teleclass*.

telephone seminar A *seminar* in which participants are connected via the public telephone system.

telephone tutoring A technique whereby a *distance learning* student communicates with his/her tutor by telephone.

telephoto lens A special lens that is attached to a camera for shooting distant objects. Such a lens consists of a combination of separate converging and diverging lens systems, thus producing the same effective *focal length* (and hence *image* size) as a simple *long-focus lens* with a very much longer *back focus* and a considerably longer *lens barrel* (see figure 48).

teleprinter A typewriter-like device that can be used to feed data into a data transmission circuit and print out information received via the circuit in *hard copy* form. Also known as a *tele-type terminal*.

teleprompter A device that was originally developed to feed *cues* and other information to television presenters, newsreaders, etc. It reveals text in front of a speaker at the same rate at which he/she is speaking. Also known as an *autocue*.

telerecording The process of recording television pictures on *motion picture* film. It is usually carried out by filming the *image* produced on an extra-high-definition cathode ray tube using a special *motion picture camera*. See *kinescope*.

teletex An internationally-agreed standard for handling messages using a variety of *microcomputer* and word processing equipment.

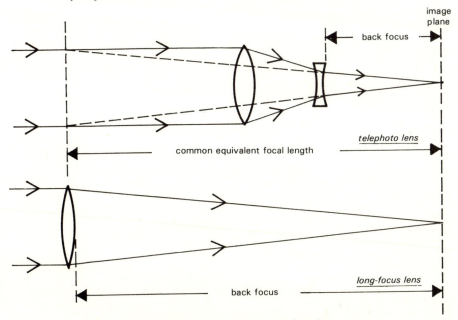

Figure 48 Comparison of telephoto and long-focus lens systems

The name has become the generic term for a world-wide network set up in order to link *word processors* via the public telephone network. Should not be confused with *teletext*. See also *telex*.

teletext A free magazine information service available from UK broadcasting authorities where a teletext decoder is fitted to the receiver. The user can select pages available, but cannot interact with the system. Also known as *broadcast videotex(t)*. Should not be confused with *teletex*.

tele-type terminal Another name for a *teleprinter*.

television beam projector Another name for a *television projector*.

television conference A conference or meeting between geographically-separated individuals or groups that is made possible by setting up two-way television links between the locations involved. For practical reasons, such conferences are usually restricted to two or three venues. Also known as a *videoconference*.

television monitor A television display system similar to an ordinary television *receiver* except that the signal is generally fed in by cable rather than picked up by an *aerial* and the picture quality is higher; television monitors are used in television production, in closed-circuit television systems and as *visual display units*. It is often referred to simply as a *monitor*.

television projector An optico-electronic device which projects television *images* on to a large external *screen*, usually for viewing in large rooms or spaces by comparatively large groups of people (eg a class of students in a lecture theatre). Also known as *telebeam projector*, *television beam projector*, *video projector*.

television signal An electronic or electromagnetic signal carrying both television pictures and any associated sound; cf *video signal*.

telewriter A device that enables hand-written or hand-drawn material to be fed directly into a transmission system so that it can be displayed or viewed elsewhere, usually on a *visual display unit* screen.

telex A world-wide communication system that uses *teleprinters* linked by a dedicated hard-wire *telegraph* network.

telop An *opaque projector* that is used to feed pictures into a television camera.

temporal prompt In *programmed instruction*, a *thematic prompt* that is based on information contained in an earlier part of the program(me), usually in the preceding *frame*. Also known as a *sequence prompt*.

terminal 1. A device for sending and/or receiving information over a communications channel, eg a *teleprinter* or *visual display unit*. 2. See *computer terminal*. 3. Relating to the end of a course or program(me), as in *terminal assessment, terminal behavio(u)r*, etc.

terminal assessment *Assessment* that is carried out at the end of a course, program(me) of instruction, etc; cf *continuous assessment*.

terminal behavio(u)r The set of knowledge, skills, behavio(u)rs, etc that a learner is expected to have acquired by the end of a course or program(me) of instruction. Also known as *terminal performance*.

terminal course A course in a subject that is not likely to be taught again during a student's subsequent studies. See also *terminal education*.

terminal education Education undertaken as an end in itself rather than as a preparation for continued study at a higher level.

terminal frames *Frames* that form the final section of a *programmed instruction* sequence. Such frames are often used to revise, review or summarize earlier material.

terminal objectives *Terminal behavio(u)r* expressed in terms of *objectives*, generally *behavio(u)ral objectives*.

terminal performance Another name for *terminal behavio(u)r*.

tertiary education Advanced education that a person normally enters on completion of formal *secondary education*, usually at a university, college or similar institution.

test battery See *battery*.

test chart, pattern A special chart containing geometrical figures, graded sets of parallel lines, standard colo(u)rs or *tones*, etc that is used to test the quality of the picture displayed on a television *receiver, television monitor* or *visual display unit*, eg during manufacture or repair, or when the system is being adjusted for optimum performance.

test frame In *programmed instruction*, a *frame* (usually at the end of a sequence of *teaching frames* and *practice frames*) that tests the user's mastery of the material covered therein. Such frames may also serve as *gate frames*. Also known as a *criterion frame*.

testing machine A machine that is designed to test rather than teach a learner; cf *teaching machine*.

test item 1. An *item* in a test. 2. An *item* in a *programmed instruction* sequence that is designed to test the learner in some way.

test tape A pre-recorded *magnetic tape* used for the *alignment* and testing of tape equipment.

text 1. Information that is presented in *alphanumerical* rather than graphical form. 2. The main body of a book or other document, excluding *preliminaries, subsidiaries*, etc.

textbook An instructional book that covers the principles of a subject or branch thereof in a systematic, progressive and comprehensive way, and is therefore suitable for use as the basic source of information on that subject or branch during the teaching or study of same. See also *handbook*.

text processing Composing, *editing* and subsequent printing and/or storing of *text* using a *word processor* or similar system.

T-group A group in which members study their own social interactions and try to improve their interpersonal and social skills. See also *T-group training*.

T-group training Use of *T-groups* to help individuals to develop interpersonal and social skills in a training situation.

thematic prompt (cue) In *behavio(u)ral psychology* or instructional design, a *prompt* (*cue*) which takes the form of the presentation or implying of meaningful associations that are likely to help the subject or learner to give the desired *response*; cf *formal prompt*. See also *semantic prompt, temporal prompt*.

therblig A standard code system used to describe and record bodily movements during *time-and-motion study*. The word is an anagram of 'Gilbreth', the inventor of the system.

thermal copier A reprographic device that makes use of some form of *thermographic process* to produce a copy of original material.

thermionic valve See *valve*.

thermographic process A reprographic process that makes use of heat for the formation of an *image* on special heat-sensitive *film* or paper. See also *thermal copier*.

thesaurus A structured collection of lists of terms which are related in some way, typically lists of synonyms and antonyms related to different ideas or concepts.

thesis A formal write-up of the results of a research study, investigation, etc prepared by the author as part of the work of a course or for *assessment* in connection with the award of a higher degree or other qualification. Also known as a *dissertation*.

think-tank A group of people, usually of an inter-disciplinary nature, that is assembled in order to make long-term predictions, suggest solutions to complex problems, devise novel systems or policies, etc. See also *brainstorming, Delphi approach*.

third-generation computer A *computer* that uses microcircuits (complete electronic circuits, including networks of transistors and switches, contained in thin silicon chips) as its main components. Such computers started to be built during the early 1970s. See also *first-generation computer, second-generation computer, fourth-generation computer, fifth-generation computer*.

thirty five millimetre (35 mm) film A standard *gauge* of still *photographic film* and *motion picture* film. *Compact slides* and *filmstrips*, for example, are made using film of this gauge.

threading The US term for *lacing*.

threshold In *behavio(u)ral psychology*, the minimum level or intensity at which a *stimulus* is perceived, or the minimum difference between stimuli that can be detected.

throat microphone Another name for a *Lavalier microphone* or *clip-on microphone*.

throw The distance from the projection lens of a *projector* to the centre (center) of the projection *screen*. See also *long-throw lens* and figure 27 on page 99.

thumb mark Another term for a *slide spot*.

tie microphone Another name for a *clip-on microphone*.

tilt To rotate a camera in the vertical plane in which its *optical axis* lies; cf *pan*.

time-and-motion study A technique used in *work study* and *task analysis* involving the measurement of the time needed to perform specific jobs, tasks or parts thereof. See also *therblig*.

time base corrector An electronic device for synchronising the *frame* speed of a *video signal* (eg from a *videotape*) with that of the system into which it is being fed.

time chart A type of chronological *wallchart* used in the teaching of history, geology, etc, divisions of time being represented by spaces of corresponding width and events being depicted in these spaces.

time-compressed speech See *compressed speech*.

time-division multiplexing A form of *multiplexing* in which several different signals are transmitted down the same communication channel by encoding them in *digital* form and transmitting the pulses representing the different signals at different times; cf *frequency-division multiplexing*.

time-expanded speech Recorded speech that is slowed down by electronic means without altering the *pitch* or introducing distortion. See also *compressed speech, variable speech*.

time-lapse photography A technique for visualizing normally invisibly slow processes by shooting one *frame* of a *video* or *motion picture* sequence at a time at suitable intervals and then showing the resulting sequence at normal speed.

time sharing A system whereby several users can, through *remote terminals*, each use the facilities of the same large *computer* at the same time so that each appears to have exclusive use of his/her own computer. See also *multi-access, virtual machine*.

titles In a film or television presentation, textual information which does not form part of the *scene* being depicted (eg a *caption* that is superimposed on a sequence of pictures).

TLU See *teaching/learning unit*.

tone 1. A constant *audio frequency* sound or sound signal. 2. A variable characteristic of a colo(u)r or *monochrome* image.

tone arm The pivoted arm on a *record player* or *transcription unit* which carries the *cartridge* and *stylus*.

tone control A facility for modifying an *audio signal* by boosting or suppressing certain frequencies, eg the *bass (tone) control* and *treble (tone) control* that are incorporated in most *audio amplifiers, tape recorders*, etc; cf *equalizer*.

toner The black powder that is used to produce the dark *image* in *electrostatic copying*.

tooling Use of heated hand tools to produce a design on or add *lettering* to the casing or binding of a book, often using *gold transfer foil*.

tool subject A subject (such as mathematics) through which key skills needed for use in studying other subjects are acquired. See also *core subject*.

topping up 1. Obtaining passes in additional subjects or papers in an examination in which some passes have already been achieved. 2. Adding more advanced qualifications to qualifications already obtained, eg taking a master's degree in a subject in which one has already obtained a batchelor's degree.

touch screen terminal A *terminal* with a *screen* via which information can be fed into a *computer* or similar device by touch, eg using a *soft keyboard*.

tracing method See *kinesthetic method*.

track 1. A discrete strip or groove on a *film, videotape, videodisc, audiotape, audio disc, disk store*, etc on which a particular signal (or section thereof) is recorded (see, for example, figure 22 on page 76). 2. A particular path through a course, *programmed instruction* sequence, etc. See also *single track, multiple track*.

tracking 1. Physical movement of a camera and its mount towards or away from the subject, or to follow a moving subject; see also *dolly*. 2. Moving a *head, stylus*, etc along a *track* in order to read in or read out a signal. 3. Following an individual learner through a learning sequence, eg through a day at school.

tractor-feed printer A *printer* that uses continuous stationery, the paper being pulled through the system by sprocket wheels which engage perforations on the edges of the paper. Such printers generally have *dot matrix printer* systems, and produce output of sub-letter-quality.

trade test See *job knowledge test*.

trailer A length of *leader* film at the end of a *motion picture* film.

trainability test A test designed to assess a person's potential for learning a new skill or set of skills, particularly those associated with a specific job.

training bay An area within an organization that is set aside and equipped for training purposes, although it is not a completely separate *training centre (center)*.

training centre (center) An establishment, or a self-contained unit within a firm or organization, that is specially equipped and staffed to carry out industrial or other training; cf *training bay*.

transaction In computing, data processing, etc, any event which requires that a *record* be processed.

transactional analysis A method of analyzing conversations, negotiations, etc that involves identifying each initiation, response, etc in terms of a particular role (eg parent, child, adult).

transceiver A *terminal* (such as a *teleprinter*) which can be used both to transmit and to receive information.

transcoder An electronic system for transforming a *television signal* from one colo(u)r standard to another, eg from *NTSC* to *PAL* or vice versa.

transcribe To copy a recording or a set of data from one storage system or medium to another, eg to transfer an *audiorecording* from an *audio disc* to an *audiotape* or to read a *computer program* from one *disk* on to another.

transcript 1. A written record (generally verbatim) of what has been said in a speech, at a meeting, in a broadcast, etc. 2. An official copy of a student's educational record, showing courses taken, qualifications obtained, etc.

transcription 1. An extra-large *audio disc* (roughly 16 inches in diameter) used in broadcasting work. 2. In data processing, an exact copy of a set of data, *records*, etc. 3. The act of making a *transcript* of spoken material.

transcription unit Originally, a high-fidelity *turntable* and *pick-up* system designed for playing *transcriptions*. It is now applied to any high-quality turntable/pick-up system for playing conventional *long-playing records*.

transducer 1. A device for converting electrical signals into mechanical vibrations or vice versa — the key component of a *microphone, loudspeaker* or record player *cartridge*. 2. An *information technology* term for any device designed to convert signals from one medium to another.

transfer 1. In general, any movement of people, equipment, material, information, data, etc from one place, system or medium to another (see, for example, *peripheral transfer, transfer film, transfer lettering*). 2. A technical term used in *behavio(u)ral psychology* and *learning* theory to denote the effects of previous experience or learning on later learning. See also *horizontal transfer, vertical transfer, positive transfer, negative transfer*.

transfer film 1. Transparent, translucent or shaded *film* with a pressure-sensitive adhesive backing that can be used to add colo(u)r, shading, etc to *OHP transparencies* and *artwork*. 2. Clear, transparent *film* with a pressure-sensitive adhesive backing that can be used to transfer *images* produced on special clay-coated paper to *OHP transparencies*.

transfer lettering, letters, type A term for sheets of letters, numbers and other *characters* which can be transferred to another material by application of pressure during the preparation of *artwork*, etc. Also known as *instant lettering*.

transfer of learning, training See *transfer* (2.).

transfer test A test designed to assess the extent to which *learning* acquired in one situation can be applied to other situations, eg to assess the adaptability of learning. See also *transfer* (2.).

transistor A solid-state electric component that can be used to switch or amplify signals — the basic component of all solid-state electronic systems such as *computers*. Transistors (whose name derives from 'transfer of electricity across a resistor') were originally discrete components, but are now generally incorporated in integrated circuits produced in silicon chips.

translucent screen A projection *screen* with a translucent rather than an opaque surface. It is used in *back projection*.

transmitter A device which transmits data, particularly one that broadcasts modulated radio or television signals; cf *receiver*.

transparency An *image* on a transparent medium such as *photographic film* or acetate sheet designed for copying, viewing or projection by transmitted light. See also *OHP transparency, slide transparency*.

transverse scanning A *scanning* system used in *videotape recorders* in which the video *heads* move across the tape rather than along it as in *helical scanning*. The *quadruplex* system is a well-known example (see figure 40 on page 137).

travel(l)ing A UK term for *tracking* (of a film or television camera).

tray A US term for a slide *magazine*, particularly one of the horizontal *carousel* type.

treble A term used to denote the highest frequencies of the *audio spectrum*; cf *bass*.

treble (tone) control A *tone control* for enhancing or suppressing the upper frequencies of an *audio signal*; cf *bass (tone) control*.

tree-and-branch system A *cable television* distribution system in which users are connected to the distribution system by a branching system of coaxial cables; cf *switched-star system*.

trial-and-error learning A method of *learning* that involves making largely random attempts to solve a problem until one of them succeeds. Also known as *rule-of-thumb learning*.

tripod A support system (for a camera, light, etc) with three legs of adjustable length.

truck Another term for *crab*, especially in the US.

true-false test An *objective test* in which the subject has to mark each *item* 'true' or 'false', eg by ticking the appropriate box.

true score 1. The (hypothetical) *mean* of an infinite number of observations, applications of a test, etc. 2. A *score* that has been corrected for errors, subjected to *standardization*, etc; cf *raw score*.

Trump Plan A system of instruction or curricular organization (developed in the USA by J. Lloyd Trump) whereby methods of teaching, student groupings, scheduling, and teacher and pupil activities are adjusted to fit the purposes and content of the instruction. It utilizes three basic learning structures: large-group instruction, small-group instruction and individualized instruction.

truncation In computing, data processing, etc, removal of digits at the least significant end of a decimal number without modifying the least significant digit retained; cf *rounding (off)*.

T-test A statistical test used in analyzing data, eg for determining whether the *mean* of a *sample* differs significantly from the *mean* for the *population* as a whole, or whether the means of two samples differ significantly from one another.

tuner An electronic system which receives radio or television signals, usually from an *aerial* (*antenna*), and converts them into *audio signals* and/or *video signals* suitable for passing on to an *amplifier*. Tuners may be built into radio or television *receivers*, or may be separate units.

tuning 1. Carrying out fine adjustments to a system in order to optimize its operation, eg when finalizing the design of an exercise, instructional program(me), etc. 2. Adjusting a *tuner* in order to receive a particular program(me) or signal.

turntable The rotating platform in a *record player* or *transcription unit* on which the record is carried during play.

turret See *lens turret*.

turtle A small robot, shaped like a turtle, that is controlled via a *microcomputer*. The robot has a pen which can be dropped or retracted, enabling the controller to program its movements. Turtles are used in systems that use the LOGO *high-level programming language*.

tutor 1. A person (who can be either a member of the instructional staff of a college etc or a fellow learner) who provides a learner with individual assistance, guidance, etc. 2. The member of staff responsible for running a group *tutorial*.

tutorial 1. A one-to-one instruction session involving a learner and his/her *tutor*. 2. A small-group instructional session in which a member of staff discusses problems raised by students; cf *seminar*.

tutorial mode A type of *computer-assisted learning* in which the computer interacts with the learner in a similar way to a live *tutor*, engaging in a dialog(ue) whose course depends on the *responses* made by the learner.

TV reader *See overhead camera.*

tweeter A *loudspeaker* unit designed to handle only the top part of the audible spectrum (above about 3 kHz).

twinkle A rapid *image* intensity fluctuation effect used in *slide* projection.

twin-lens reflex (camera) A *reflex camera* that uses separate (coupled) lenses for viewing and taking; cf *single-lens reflex (camera)*.

twinning stand A stand for mounting two automatic *slide* projectors one above the other for use in *double projection* displays.

two-by-two (slide) A photographic *slide* whose outer dimensions are 2″ × 2″. This is the standard size used in most modern slide projectors.

two-track Another name for *half-track*.

typeface A set of *characters*, available in a *printer*, *word processor*, typewriter, etc, that are of the same general design (eg *roman*, *italic*, *sanserif*) and are generally available in a range of sizes. See also *character set*.

U

U-format A *U-wrap* videocassette recording system that uses ¾ inch tape. See also *U-matic*.

UHF See *ultra-high frequency*.

ultrafiche, ultramicroform A *microfiche* (*microform*) with a *reduction ratio* greater than 1:90.

ultra-high frequency (UHF) A term applied to electromagnetic waves or signals in the frequency range 300–3000 MHz. This range is used for television *carrier waves* in the UK and many other countries.

ultrasonic A term applied to sound or mechanical vibrations with a frequency above the upper limit of the audible range, ie above 20 kHz.

U-matic The commercial name of the most widely used *U-format* videocassette recording system. It is available in two standards, namely *high-band U-matic* (which is of broadcast standard) and *low-band U-matic* (which is of semi-professional standard).

unblooped A splice in a *COMOPT* motion picture film which has not been subjected to *blooping* and which may therefore give rise to unwanted sound on projection.

unconditioned reflex A natural or normal *response* to a psychological *stimulus*; cf *conditioned reflex*. Also known as an *unconditioned response*.

unconditioned response Another name for an *unconditioned reflex*.

undercranking Exposing *motion picture* film at a lower speed than the intended projection speed in order to speed up the action; cf *overcranking*.

underexposure In photography or *reprography*, *exposure* of sensitive material to light or heat at too low an intensity or for too short a time to produce a properly-formed *image*; cf *overexposure*.

underware A term sometimes applied to those aspects of *instructional technology* which underlie the use of *hardware* and *software*, but which cannot be placed in either category, ie the principles and methodologies of the field.

unidirectional microphone Another name for a *cardioid microphone*.

unique answer question A question in a test, instructional program(me), etc that has a single correct answer or solution; cf *open-ended* question.

unit-perfection requirement Where it is laid down that a learner must demonstrate mastery of particular unit, stage or area of a course or program(me) of instruction before being allowed to proceed to the next unit, stage or area. Also known as *mastery requirement*.

unit plan A type of *curriculum* that outlines relatively large units of instruction rather than detailing individual lessons or sessions, leaving the organization of the latter to the individual teacher or instructor.

university of the air An *open university* that relies heavily on television and radio broadcasts to deliver instruction to its students.

university without walls A university (such as an *open university*) that provides a considerable part of its teaching outside its actual buildings or campus.

unjustified A term applied to *text* which has an irregular right-hand edge, ie text to which the process of *justification* has not been applied. Also known as *ragged right, ranged left*; cf *justified*.

unobtrusive assessment *Assessment* based on

observation that is carried out without the knowledge of the individual or group being assessed.

unstructured essay An essay or essay question in which little or no guidance is given to the writer as to the required structure and detailed content; cf *structured essay, essay-type question.*

unstructured interview An interview in which there is no predetermined plan or structure, the interviewer asking such questions as he/she deems appropriate in the light of the development of the discussion; cf *structured interview.* Also known as a *non-directive interview.*

up A term applied to a *computer* or other system which is operational at the time in question; cf *down.*

updating course, training A course or program(me) of training that is undertaken by an individual in order to bring him/her up to date with the latest technological or other developments in his/her field of work; cf *upgrading course, training.*

upgrading course, training A course or program(me) of training that is undertaken to prepare for taking on a more demanding job, position, etc.

upper case In printing, *lettering*, etc, a term applied to normal-sized capital letters like A, B, C, D, . . .; cf *lower case, small caps.*

up-stage The performing area on a stage or *set* furthest from the camera or audience; cf *down stage.*

up-time The period (absolute or fractional) for which a *computer*, device or system is fully operational and available for use; cf *down-time.*

use life The maximum amount of time (or number of times) for which a system can be used under normal conditions without deteriorating past the point of usefulness.

user-friendly A term applied to a machine or system which is specifically designed so as to be as simple to operate or use as possible, eg to a *computer-based learning* package that requires no specialist knowledge of computers or computer programming on the part of the user — simply the ability to switch on the machine, insert or call up the *program*, and follow the instructions contained therein.

user-oriented language A computer *programming language* that is designed for use by ordinary computer users rather than by specialist computer staff. See also *high-level (programming) language.*

U-wrap A tape path in a *helical scanning* videotape system shaped like the letter 'U', thus giving only 180° contact between the tape and the *head drum* (see figure 22 on page 76).

V

V See *verbal comprehension*.

vacation training Training related to a student's course of study that is undertaken during vacation time, usually in the summer.

vacuum tube The US term for a *valve*.

validation 1. *Assessment* of the effectiveness of instructional materials, etc by the use of appropriate *summative evaluation* or other techniques. 2. Critical scrutiny of a proposed course by a committee within the organizing institution (internal validation) or outside body (external validation) with a view to determining whether it is up to the required standard. 3. A procedure for checking the *validity* of *items* or questions for tests.

validity 1. The extent to which a test or other measuring instrument fulfils the purpose for which it is designed, ie assesses or measures what it purports to assess or measure; see also *content validity, construct validity, predictive validity*. 2. See *external validity, internal validity*.

valuing An *affective* process that involves accepting that an object, system, etc has worth or value. This is Level 3 of Krathwohl's *affective domain*.

valve A vacuum tube device that can be incorporated in an electronic circuit for amplification, rectification or switching purposes. Such valves formed the basis of the electronics industry until the invention of the *transistor* in the late 1950s; they are now only used for a few specialized purposes, having been almost completely replaced by solid-state components.

vanishing In *behavio(u)ral pscyhology*, the progressive removal of more and more of the components of a specific chain of *responses* as a *learning* process proceeds. Should not be confused with *fading*.

variability A statistical term for the way in which individual *scores* or sets of scores within a distribution are scattered or dispersed. See also *variance, standard deviation, analysis of variance*.

variable A quantity which varies, or is capable of varying or being varied. See also *continuous variable, discrete variable, dependent variable, independent variable*.

variable area sound track An *optical sound track* in which the width of a track of constant optical density is modulated to correspond to the *audio signal*; cf *variable density sound track*.

variable density sound track An *optical sound track* in which the optical density of a track of constant width is modulated to correspond to the *audio signal*; cf *variable area sound track*.

variable speech A technique used in *audio* instruction in which the listener can vary the rate at which spoken information is presented without varying the *pitch* or introducing distortion. See also *compressed speech, time-expanded speech*.

variance A statistical measure of the *variability* of a set (or series of sets) of *scores*. It is obtained by adding the squares of the deviations of the individual values being considered from the *mean* of these values and dividing by the total number of values. See also *standard deviation, analysis of variance*.

variate A random *variable*, ie a quantity which make take any of the values within a specified set or within a given range with a specified relative frequency or probability.

varispeed A continuously-variable speed control on an *audiotape recorder*, etc, eg for *pitch* control.

VCR See *videocassette recorder*.

VDU See *visual display unit*.

velcro board A type of *hook-and-loop board*.

velour paper Paper with a velvet-like backing used in preparing *feltboard* display materials.

Venn diagram A series of intersecting circles or other closed geometrical figures drawn to indicate the relationship between a number of *sets* (see, for example, figure 49, which shows how the sets of *games, simulations* and *case studies* overlap to form various types of 'hybrid' exercise such as *simulation games* and *stimulated case studies*).

verbal ability Ability to understand and use language in speech and writing. See also *verbal comprehension (V)*.

verbal association The process of learning chains of items where the links between them are verbal in nature. This is Level 4 of Gagné's eight types of learning.

verbal comprehension (V) Another name for *verbal ability*. This is one of the *primary mental abilities* thought by Thurstone to constitute *intelligence*.

verbal intelligence test An *intelligence test* that involves the use of written or spoken language; cf *non-verbal intelligence test*.

vertical file materials Items such as pamphlets, newspaper or magazine clippings, pictures, etc which, because of their form, are stored in vertical files in drawers or filing cabinets for ready retrieval and reference.

vertical (format) See *portrait (format)*.

vertical panel book A *programmed text* in the form of a book in which the pages are divided vertically into panels. These are not read in the normal logical sequence, the reader being directed to a particular panel on the basis of his or her previous performance in the work of the program(me).

vertical transfer (of learning) A form of *transfer of learning* in which a previously learned skill, item of knowledge, etc is put to use in a higher-order or more complex situation of which it is a component; cf *horizontal transfer (of learning)*.

very high frequency (VHF) A term applied to electromagnetic waves or signals in the frequency range 30–300 MHz. This range is used for both television and *FM* radio *carrier waves*.

vestibule course A course whose purpose is to prepare learners for another course or to

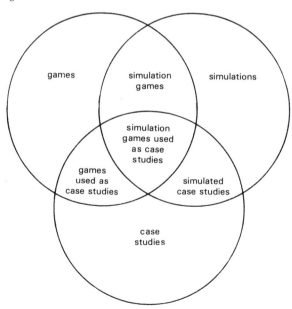

Figure 49 A Venn diagram showing the overlapping sets of games, simulations and case studies

introduce them to a particular subject, area or field.

vestibule theory An approach to education which considers the main function of each stage to be to prepare the learners for the next stage.

VHF See *very high frequency*.

VHS Video home system. This a widely-used domestic-quality *videocassette recorder* system that use ½ inch tape held in cassettes slightly large than those used in the *Betamax* system, to which it is otherwise similar.

video 1. A term applied to all visual aspects of television signals, equipment, etc, as in *video signal*, *video amplifier*. 2. A loose but widely-used term for a *videorecording* or for any machine that can be used to record and/or play back such recordings (*videocassette recorders*, *videotape recorders*, *videodisc players*, etc).

video amplifier An *amplifier* that is designed to handle a *video signal* (or the *video* component of a *television signal*). It therefore operates at very much higher frequencies than an *audio amplifier* (up to several MHz).

videocassette A *cassette* containing *videotape*.

videocassette recorder (VCR) A *videorecorder* that uses *videocassettes* as its storage medium.

videoconference Another term for a *television conference*.

videodisc A disc on which *video signals*, with or without sound, are electrically or optically recorded. Such discs have a variety of instructional applications, and are particularly important in the field of *interactive video*. See also *contact videodisc*, *optical videodisc*, *capacitance*, *capacitive videodisc*.

videodisc player A *videoplayer* that can be used to play back *videodiscs*.

video display unit (VDU) Another name for a *visual display unit*.

video frequency A term used to describe an electromagnetic signal with a frequency in the range used in *video signals*, ie up to several MHz; cf *audio frequency*.

videogram 1. A pre-recorded *videotape* or *videocassette*. 2. The program(me) content thereof. Should not be confused with a *videograph*.

videograph A quickly-reproduced permanent copy of a television picture, produced using a special television display tube. Should not be confused with a *videogram*.

videophone A telephone system that enables users to see as well as hear one another, with the pictures being displayed on a small television screen.

videoplayer A generic name for an electronic device which can play back pictures and sound from a *videorecording*.

video projector Another name for a *television projector*.

videorecorder A generic name for an electronic device which can both record and play back *video signals* and/or *television signals*.

videorecording 1. A generic term for a medium on which *video signals* or *television signals* are recorded. 2. A *video signal* or *television signal* so recorded. See also *videodisc*, *videotape*, *videogram*.

video signal An electronic signal, either in *analog* or in *digital* form, representing a visual scene and capable of being used to reproduce that scene; cf *audio signal*, *television signal*.

videotape Special *magnetic tape* on which *video signals* or *television signals* are (or can be) recorded.

videotape recorder (VTR) Strictly speaking, a term that covers all *videorecorders* that use *videotape*, whether in *open reel* or *videocassette* form. It is, however, generally confined to machines of the open reel type, machines that use videocassettes being referred to as *videocassette recorders* (*VCRs*).

videotex(t) The display and exchange of information using *computers* and television screens. One-way videotex(t) is called *teletext* and interactive two-way videotex(t) is called *viewdata*.

video track A *track* on a *videotape* or *videodisc* that carries a *video signal*.

Video 2000 A domestic-quality *videocassette recorder* system that uses ½ inch tape.

video typewriter Another name for a *caption generator*.

view angle See *angle of view*.

viewdata Two-way interactive *videotex(t)*.

viewer An optical device for individual inspection of a *slide, filmstrip, film*, etc.

viewfinder An optical or optico-electronic system incorporated in a *still camera, motion picture camera* or television camera in order to show the operator what is being 'seen' through the main camera lens.

viewing light box Another name for a *light box*.

vignetting Gradual shading of the edge areas surrounding an *image*.

virgin medium A data storage medium on which no data is recorded as yet.

virtual machine Any means whereby users feel themselves to have exclusive use of a *computer* (as in time sharing), or when a computer is able to emulate another, sometimes larger, computer.

virtual memory The extension of a computer's central *memory* by using peripheral stores such as *disks*, thus giving the computer a 'virtual memory' that is effectively larger than its central memory.

vision mixer An electronic control panel for combining separate *video signals* to form a synchronized composite signal; used in television production.

visual aids, materials, media Instructional materials which communicate primarily through sight, eg charts, *slides* and *OHP transparencies*; cf *audio aids, audiovisual aids*.

visual display unit (VDU) A *terminal* for a *computer* or similar system that incorporates a cathode ray tube screen similar to that found in a *television monitor*, a screen on which material generated by the computer and/or user can be displayed in *soft copy* form. Also known as a *video display unit*.

visualizer Another name for an *art-aid projector*.

visual learner A learner who, in a visual sense, views a system as a whole rather than analyzing it in terms of discrete elements; the visual version of a *holist*; cf *haptic (learner)*.

visual noun A term used to describe a basic element of *visual material* (eg a chart, *slide* or *loop film*) which can be used in a variety of instructional contexts.

viva, viva-voce (examination) Other names for an *oral examination*, especially in the UK.

vocabulary test A test of *verbal ability* designed to assess the range of a person's vocabulary, ie his/her store of understood words.

vocational test A *psychological test* designed to assess vocational interests, job aptitudes, etc.

vocational training Training designed to teach the skills and knowledge required for a particular field (or related set of fields) of employment, eg training in secretarial or workshop skills.

vocoder A device used in *speech synthesis*. It produces speech that is semantically clear, but does not resemble 'natural' speech in tone quality, etc.

voice activation Operation of a device or system by means of spoken signals that the device or system is programmed to recognize and respond to.

voice over A narrative accompaniment to a film or television program(me), heard without the speaker being seen.

voice response system (VRS) A system whereby a *computer* gives oral responses to messages, questions or commands fed in by the user, responses that are either pre-recorded or produced by *speech synthesis*.

voice switching Use of special electronic switching and differential amplification circuits during a *teleconference* to concentrate on the voice that is loudest at any given time.

volume 1. The intensity (actual or apparent) of a sound signal or sound. 2. One of a number of books forming a related set or series. 3. The set to which a particular issue of a journal or other periodical publication belongs.

VRS See *voice response system*.

VTR See *videotape recorder*.

vu-foil, vu-graph US names for an *OHP transparency*.

vu-meter Another name for a *level indicator*.

W

W See *word fluency*.

wallchart A relatively large opaque sheet, exhibiting information in graphic or tabular form, designed to be attached to a wall for display purposes. A wallchart differs from a *poster* in that it generally contains much more information.

wand A stick-shaped device which can be used to read optically-coded *labels* such as *bar code* labels.

washahead Another name for *forward branching*.

washback Another name for *backward branching*.

weave Periodic lateral unsteadiness in a projected *motion picture* image; cf *bounce*.

weighting The assignment of differential values to test *items*, *scores*, terms in an *index*, etc in order to give them the required degree of relative importance.

wet carrel A *carrel* that is fitted with one or more mains outlets, so that electrically-operated equipment can be used in it; cf *dry carrel*.

wet mounting *Mounting* a *photograph*, drawing, etc on a cardboard or other backing using wet adhesive material of some sort; cf *dry mounting*.

wet processing Photographic or reprographic *processing* that involves the use of liquid chemicals that are not incorporated in the actual materials being processed.

wetware A term used in *artificial intelligence* and similar fields to denote the biological equivalent of *hardware*, eg the human brain.

whip pan In film or television production, a *pan* made at such high speed that the resulting *image* becomes indistinct or blurred, usually in order to produce a special effect.

whiteboard A *marker board* with a white surface.

white ink Dense white ink used for writing, drawing or producing *lettering* on dark surfaces, eg for making television *captions*.

white noise Random *noise* covering the full range of the spectrum being handled by an electronic or other system.

whole-class approach A method of teaching in which all the members of a class carry out the same activity at any given time.

whole learning An analytical method of teaching a topic that involves starting by looking at the topic as a whole and then looking at its constituent elements.

whole method A term used in industrial training to describe the process of teaching an operation as a whole rather than breaking it down into parts; cf *cumulative-part method*, *part method*.

whole-part learning Another name for *global learning*.

wide-angle lens A lens with an extra-short *focal length*, thus giving it a wide *acceptance angle* (greater than 60°). See also *fisheye lens*.

wide screen A term applied to *motion pictures* presented using a screen of *aspect ratio* greater than 1.4:1, eg films made in the cinemascope format.

wild shooting Shooting pictures for a film or television production without simultaneously recording a synchronized sound signal. See also *wild sound*.

wild sound Sound recorded during the shooting

of a film or television sequence without synchronizing it with the pictures; cf *synchronized sound*. See also *wild shooting*.

wild subject Any subject in a course or program(me) of studies which bears little relationship to the main subject(s) of the course or program(me).

Winchester disk A widely-used type of *hard disk*.

window 1. In *computer graphics*, a specified area that is selected for enlargement, thus effectively defining a 'window' through which that particular part of the display can be viewed in more detail (see figure 50); such a window is usually rectangular, its area generally being selected by defining two opposite corners. 2. See *windowing*.

developed in Winnetka, Illinois in 1919. It involves a combination of self-paced individualized work in basic and essential subjects and group work in more social and creative activities. See also *Dalton Plan*.

wipe In television production, etc, replacement of one *image* by another image that progressively displaces the first from the screen area by movement of the boundary between the two (see, for example, *iris wipe, push off*).

wireless loop Another name for an *audio induction loop*.

wireless microphone Another name for a *radio microphone*.

wire recorder A device that records signals on a spool of steel wire by modulating the

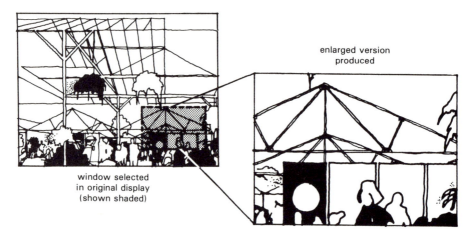

enlarged version produced

window selected in original display (shown shaded)

Figure 50 A window in a computer graphics display

windowing A facility available with some *microcomputer* systems whereby multiple *inlays* (*windows*) can be incorporated in existing screen displays, the user then being able to work on any chosen section of the display. In linked windowing systems, altering one section automatically brings about corresponding changes in other parts of the system. See also *icon, mouse, pull-down menu*.

windshield A shield fitted to a *microphone* to cut down wind *noise* when it is used out of doors.

Winnetka Plan An educational system first

magnetization of the wire in correspondence with the signals.

WOOD Write once optical disk. A type of *digital optical disk* on which a user can record data, but, once recorded, it cannot be erased or re-recorded. It comes in various sizes from 2 inch to 14 inch, and has data storage capacities in the *megabyte-gigabyte* range.

woofer A *loudspeaker* unit (usually large) designed to handle the lowest frequencies of the audible range; cf *squawker, tweeter*.

word In computing, data storage, etc, an

ordered set of *bits* representing a unit of data and occupying one storage location within the system. It is usually treated by the computer as a single unit, and transferred as such.

word fluency (W) One of the *primary mental abilities* thought by Thurstone to constitute *intelligence*.

word processor An integrated system incorporating a *keyboard, visual display unit, microcomputer, store* and *printer* that enables *text* to be composed, edited, stored and printed in *hard copy* form as and when required. This type of system is gradually replacing conventional typewriters in many areas.

workbook A text produced for use by an individual learner as a study guide cum exercise book. It usually incorporates exercises, problems, practice materials, etc.

work card A reusable card carrying instructions relating to a specific piece of work, and (usually) giving background information relating to same; cf *worksheet.*

worker characteristics The physical, intellectual and other qualities needed by a candidate for a particular job.

work experience Part of the *curriculum* in vocationally-oriented secondary schools designed to give pupils experience and understanding of working life and of the way skills learned at school will eventually be of use at work.

working memory That part of the *memory* in the *central processing unit (CPU)* of a *digital computer* that is actually available to the user at any given time. It is always less than the total memory capacity of the CPU, the exact amount available depending on how much of the memory is taken up by the operating *programs* that are being used at the time.

work print In film production, any *print* (usually *positive*) intended for use in the *editing* process. Also known as *cutting copy.*

work sample test An *aptitude test* designed to

assess a person's ability to learn a particular skill or job. It takes the form of a short instructional session on some aspect of the work followed by a practical test based on same.

worksheet A sheet carrying instructions, information, etc relating to part of an instructional program(me) or exercise. Such sheets often incorporate spaces for learner *responses*, thus making them non-reusable; cf *work card.*

workshop 1. A practical or enactive instructional session designed to illustrate the underlying principle, logistics or mechanics of an exercise, program(me), etc without necessarily working all the way through it. 2. A room, building etc that is designed and equipped for the teaching of practical subjects or the provision of technical back-up services.

work station 1. In general, a place in a workshop, factory, office, teaching *laboratory, language laboratory* etc where an individual works. 2. A *terminal* whereby an individual can gain access to the facilities of a *computer, word processor, data base, interactive video* system, etc or to a combination of systems of this type.

work study Carrying out detailed study and analysis of an area of work with a view to making it more efficient or more economic.

wow Periodic variations in the operating speed of a recording or playback system in the frequency range 1–10 Hz; cf *flutter*

wpm Words per minute. A measure of typing speed, shorthand speed, etc.

wrist-finger speed A *psychomotor skill* associated with a person's ability to make rapid rotary or other wrist movements.

write To feed data into a *computer store.*

write-on slide A *slide* with a translucent *matt* surface on which information can be written or drawn by hand.

X

x-axis Conventionally the horizontal axis of a *graph*, oscilloscope, *plotter*, etc. This is the axis along which the *independent variable* of a system is normally plotted; cf *y-axis*. See also *x-y plotter*.

xerography A widely-used term for *electrostatic copying*.

Xerox A term that is widely used to denote a device used for carrying out *electrostatic copying* or a copy made using such a machine.

It is derived from the name of one of the leading companies that manufacture such machines.

x-height The vertical size of the *lower case* letters of a particular *character set*, ie the height of the letter 'x'. It is usually measured in *points*.

x-y plotter A *plotter* in which the two *variables* are respectively plotted along a horizontal *x-axis* and a vertical *y-axis*.

Y

y-axis Conventionally the vertical axis of a *graph*, oscilloscope, *plotter*, etc. This is the axis along which the *dependent variable(s)* of a system is (are) normally plotted; cf *x-axis*. See also *x-y plotter*.

yearbook 1. A reference book or source book in a given field or area that is intended to be revised annually in order to keep it up to date. 2. A book that is published annually in order to report on the year's activities in a given field or area.

yoke In a *computer terminal* or similar device, a group of *read/write heads* that are fastened together.

yon plane In a three-dimensional *computer graphics* display, the (imaginary) plane behind the *screen* that defines the rearmost limit of the display; cf *hither plane*.

Z

zap To erase material from a *computer store*.

zero skew See *skewness*.

zero-sum game A type of *game* in which the sum of all the gains made by the winner(s) and the losses made by the loser(s) is always zero; cf *non-zero-sum game*.

zig-zag book A *scrambled text* in which pages are divided into cut sections which can be turned forwards or backwards independently of one another.

zimdex A cueing technique used in *audio* instruction. It involves numbers or pulses being recorded on one *track* of an *audiotape* in order to mark or index the contents of the other (main) track.

zoom 1. A visual effect in which it appears that a camera is moving rapidly towards or away from the subject; it is normally achieved by using a *zoom lens*, although, in *animation* work, the actual camera is sometimes moved.

2. A similar effect in *computer graphics*.

zoom lens A lens system with a *focal length* that can be continuously varied over a given range. Such lenses are used on film and television cameras to produce *zoom* effects and to accommodate different subject distances, and are also used on *projectors* to accommodate different *throws*.

zoom microphone A *microphone* whose directional properties can be continuously varied so as to create an illusion of moving towards or away from the source of sound.

zone curve See *zone curve graph*.

zone curve graph, chart A *graph* that shows maximum and minimum values for each reading rather than a single point, these maxima and minima being linked so as to define a broad curve which, when shaded in, is known as a *zone curve* (see figure 51); cf *band curve graph, chart*.

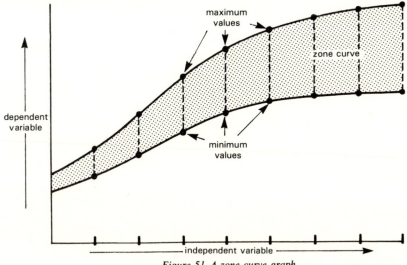

Figure 51 A zone curve graph